Tuskegee Airman Fighter Pilot:
A Story of An Original Tuskegee Pilot
Lt. Col. Hiram E. Mann

Dr. Patrick C. Coggins

Trafford
PUBLISHING

Order this book online at www.trafford.com/07-2231
or email orders@trafford.com

Most Trafford titles are also available at major online book retailers.

Note for Librarians: A cataloguing record for this book is available from Library
and Archives Canada at www.collectionscanada.ca/amicus/index-e.html

ISBN: 978-1-4251-4732-7

*We at Trafford believe that it is the responsibility of us all, as both individuals
and corporations, to make choices that are environmentally and socially sound.
You, in turn, are supporting this responsible conduct each time you purchase a
Trafford book, or make use of our publishing services. To find out how you are
helping, please visit www.trafford.com/responsiblepublishing.html*

*Our mission is to efficiently provide the world's finest, most comprehensive
book publishing service, enabling every author to experience success.
To find out how to publish your book, your way, and have it available
worldwide, visit us online at www.trafford.com/10510*

 www.trafford.com

North America & international
toll-free: 1 888 232 4444 (USA & Canada)
phone: 250 383 6864 ♦ fax: 250 383 6804 ♦ email: info@trafford.com

The United Kingdom & Europe
phone: +44 (0)1865 722 113 ♦ local rate: 0845 230 9601
facsimile: +44 (0)1865 722 868 ♦ email: info.uk@trafford.com

10 9 8 7 6 5 4 3 2

Dedication

NO REGRETS; WELL, MAYBE A FEW

"As I look back on an ended career and my waning years, I am able to ac-cess it from several levels: The Beginning, the Mid-way, and Winding-down."

"This book is dedicated to Kathadaza Marie (nee Henderson) Mann, my loving and devoted wife of three score plus years. Her steadfast insistence and belief in me assisted me to remain resolved to be tenacious."
-Lt. Col. Hiram E. Mann, USAF, Ret.

The salute to all of the Original Tuskegee Airmen, rendered by the Commander in Chief, "For salutes ignored and/or unreturned during World War II, on behalf of the United States of America, I proudly salute you!"
-Hiram

Acknowledgements

THE AUTHOR ACKNOWLEDGES Lt. Col. Hiram E. Mann for sharing the deepest and most precious regions of his life and memory of details that enabled me to complete this biography with a sense of accuracy and authenticity. Alpha Phi Alpha is proud of our most distinguished brother and Tuskegee Airman, fighter pilot, Hiram Mann.

The author acknowledges all of the Tuskegee Airmen that I met since 1997 to the present and whose experiences helped shape the ideas in this book.

I owe special thanks to the following people who assisted in the process of publishing this book:

I thank Connecticut Appellate Court Judge Lubbie Harper Jr. for his foreword which enhances the understanding of the important niche that the Tuskegee Airmen have in the annals of history.

Primrose Cameron Hall, for her editing and numerous interviews with Lt. Col. Hiram E. Mann, USAF, Ret

Melviona Thomson, Assistant Principal, for taking time to edit the final text.

Milagros Cruz Ruiz, Marialuisa Rodriguez de la Viuda and Alexis Hart for typing the final document.

Doug MacIsaac for editing and suggestions for the final manuscript.

Dilshod Saidov for his help with the art work on both of the covers and editing the text.

Foreword

DURING THE MARCH 29, 2007 ceremony in which the Tuskegee Airmen were awarded the Congressional Gold Medal, Ret. Gen. Colin Powell offered his thanks to the servicemen, declaring, "The only reason I'm able to stand proudly before you today is you stood proudly for America sixty years ago."[1] This sentiment, voiced by Ret. Gen. Powell but felt by many, is one of the reasons why this book honoring the life of Lt. Col. Hiram E. Mann is an important work that comes at a timely moment in our history.

As Dr. Patrick C. Coggins notes, we are engaged in an ongoing struggle to ensure that the Tuskegee Airmen are preserved fully --and accurately-- within our nation's collective memory. Many Americans have heard generally of the Tuskegee Airmen, and are aware of the significant contribution, which these brave individuals made toward the allied countries' victory during the Second World War. What largely remains to be told, however, are the unique stories of the people that comprised these special military units? This book serves the important function of bridging that historical gap between the abstract details of the Tuskegee Airmen's accomplishments and the personal stories of the airmen themselves. It adds dimension, depth and texture to the "experience" at Tuskegee during that important period in our nation's history.

Lt. Col. Mann's "experience" was one that was uniquely personal in that he had to overcome many challenges in order to receive his wings as a military pilot. Yet his experience was also, as he reminds us, one that encompassed the hopes, struggles and sacrifices of many others who helped him during his time at Tuskegee. In a humble tone, Lt. Col. Mann stresses repeatedly that the phrase "Tuskegee Airmen" is a misnomer because many of the people involved never flew as a part of their famed missions; they were neither pilots nor men.

---

1 Transcript of March 29, 2007 Ceremony awarding the Tuskegee Airmen the Congressional Gold Medal , located at
http://www.pbs.org/newshour/bb/military/jan-june07/airmen_03-29.html.

His words include the voices of the members of the ground crew personnel that maintained the aircrafts, those of the doctors and nurses and hospital staff, as well as the voices of wives and other family members. The sacrifices of these people were less documented but of no less importance to the overall success of the pilot training program. This theme of remembrance, not only of the Tuskegee Airmen themselves but also of the people who aided them in their achievements, is one of the two recurring threads that bind this work together.

The other thread, relating to the encouragement of future generations that may be interested in a similar career trajectory, is of particular interest to me as a judge that frequently encounters misguided youth. Too often, these young people are simply unaware of the alternative paths that were blazed for them by earlier generations. With any luck, a young person, perhaps in need of guidance, will hear the story retold in this book and be inspired to improve his or her life circumstance and assist others who are doing the same.

Finally, having had the honor of serving as a judge for over a decade, I am painfully aware that equality, justice and freedom, the principles for which the Tuskegee Airmen risked all, have yet to become fully actualized. If we are to keep progressing toward their achievement, we must follow the example set by these Americans and continually take collective action with these goals in mind. Lt. Col. Mann's fight for dignity, freedom and respect was hardly finished when he flew his last mission as a member of the 332nd Fighter Group. Upon being retired in 1972, Lt. Col. Mann dedicated himself to the broader struggle domestically for recognition as a full-fledged American, entitled to equality of treatment and opportunity in the military and elsewhere. It is my hope that in telling his story and through it, the story of other Tuskegee Airmen, we will all be reminded to renew our fight to advance these time-weathered goals which are enshrined in our Constitution. As Lt. Col. Mann's story demonstrates, it is only through courage, struggle and sacrifice that there will be any hope of their future attainment.

The Honorable Lubbie Harper, Jr.
Connecticut Appellate Court Judge

Table of Contents

CHAPTER VI
Ret. Lt. Col. Hiram E. Mann's Life Before and After the Military _ 59

CHAPTER VII
Military Experience of Lt. Col. Hiram E. Mann _____ 65

CHAPTER VIII
Timeline of the Tuskegee Airmen Experience _____ 108

CHAPTER IX
The Epistles According to Lt. Col. Hiram E. Mann _____ 122

CHAPTER X
The Reaction and Recognition _____ 187

"You are one of a kind; no one can really predict to
what heights you might soar. Even you will not know
until you spread your wings"
(Gil Atkinson)

CHAPTER I

A True Tuskegee Airman: More Than Just Flying

THE PRIMARY REASON for writing this book is to highlight the accomplishments of the Tuskegee Airmen and pilots especially Lt. Col. Hiram E. Mann, USAF, Retired who not only successfully completed the Tuskegee Airmen Experience, but was also one who completed the pilot training at Tuskegee Institute in Tuskegee Army Air Field, Tuskegee, Alabama. He went on to be a World War II combat pilot along with other African American pilots who helped shape the reputation and history of African American combat pilots as skillful and intellectual contributors in all phases of life including the complex task of flying an airplane.

As the author reflected on his other motivation for writing this book, it became clear that he was not inspired by any information that was learned from World History classes, nor, from any study of the experiences of World War II, or even, information gleaned from the college courses on race relations or on the history of African Americans. Three events sparked my interest in writing this book about the Tuskegee Airmen, these events were: 1) In 1979, I saw the ABC special entitled "Blacks in White America". This documentary, narrated by Ronald Reagan who later became President of the United States of America, portrayed the contributions of the Tuskegee Airmen. 2) In 1994, I talked extensively to the now deceased Retired Sergeant Elton Williams, a decorated WWII veteran, serial number 31464521, as he recounted and explained the prejudice, racial discrimination and other struggles that all African Americans

1

who were in the military had to endure each day of enlistment in the Armed Services. He was very convinced that the efforts of the Tuskegee Airmen and fighter pilots played an important role in the success of the ground soldiers who like the pilots, had the awesome responsibility of fighting the common enemy under the allied flags and the flag of the United States of America. 3) In 1997, the author served as the First Eminent Scholar in Residence for Multicultural Studies and African and African American Studies, Palm Beach County School District.

I participated as a consultant to the District's Program that hosted the retired officers of the Tuskegee Airmen Experience in 1997, 1998, and 1999. While serving as one of the hosts, I introduced over a dozen Tuskegee Airmen to large audiences and had the opportunity to get them engaged in conversations about their experiences during World War II.

RET. LT. COL. HIRAM E. MANN AND HIS ACCOMPLISHMENTS

The key day for me was during my keynote speech during the Founder's Day celebration of the Alpha Phi Alpha Fraternity, Inc. in Titusville, Florida. On December 4, 2000, the day I met Lt. Col. Hiram E. Mann, USAF,Ret.; one of the original Tuskegee Airmen who had gone through the now famous Tuskegee Airmen Training Experience in Tuskegee, Alabama. I was delighted to know that he was my Alpha Phi Alpha Fraternity brother. Furthermore, it was clear that I was indeed captivated by the military accomplishments and military record that included:

- Member of the Class of 44-F, Single Engine pilot training at Tuskegee Army Air Field (TAAF), Tuskegee Alabama.
- Combat Fighter with the 332nd Fighter Group.
- Combat missions with the 302nd and the 100th Fighter Squadrons during World War II.
- Graduate of the Command and Staff College of the Air University at Maxwell Air Force Base (MAFB), Alabama. In his class of 1957, of the 990 plus officers, there were only four African Americans, of which was the late General Daniel "Chappie" James Jr. was one with whom he studied.

Additionally, my professional affiliations were also germane to my interest in this important historical event. At that time, I was the Vice-Chair for the Florida Commissioner of Education African American History Task Force and Eminent Scholar in Residence at Palm Beach County School District.

As Scholar in Residence, I was responsible for leading a team of consultants and district staff in writing the Interdisciplinary African American History Curriculum. The Florida Legislature in 1994 passed Florida Statute 233:061(1) (f) as amended by Florida Statute 1003.42 (h) (2) (2002). It states that:

> *"The history of African Americans, including the history of African peoples, the political conflicts that led to the development of slavery, the passage to America, the enslavement experience, abolition, and the contributions of African Americans to society."*

This new law requires that *"members of the instructional staff of public schools shall teach efficiently and faithfully, using books and materials required, following the prescribed course of study, employing approved methods of instruction."*

It was in this context of the new law that the author felt strongly that it was important that all students be taught African American history. Contributions of the Tuskegee Airmen and the achievements of these combat pilots in the context of African American and World War II history were essential historical information. During that time, The Palm Beach County School District team planned for the arrival of the Tuskegee Airmen. They came to Palm Beach in 1997, 1998, 1999, 2000, and toured the elementary, middle and high schools. They visited churches, attended receptions, and community forums. The audiences were noticeably happy and interested in meeting the Tuskegee Airmen. It is noteworthy to mention that with the exception of those individuals who served in the military during World War II, most people reported that they were not aware of the Tuskegee Airmen. In addition, audiences were surprised to learn that information about the Tuskegee Airmen was absent from the records of World War II History and that the contributions of African American servicemen and the Tuskegee Airmen were not fully reported in the textbooks.

The author recalls that during a reception in 1998 hosted by the local city government of West Palm Beach, all of the guests, whether White or Black, were glad to meet the Tuskegee Airmen. At this reception, I remembered a moment of tension among the reception organizers and the Tuskegee Airmen when a White World War II veteran stunned the crowd when he cried out and said "I came here to thank you [Tuskegee Airmen] for saving my life. I was a bomber pilot in World War II and my plane was hit. The other White pilots took off leaving me to fend for myself when suddenly I saw the 'Red Tail' airplanes surrounding my aircraft and escorted me back to the base. Then they took off. I am here tonight to thank all of the Tuskegee Airmen." Thus, it was a moment of tears as the Tuskegee Airmen, Lt. Pompey Hawkins, Lt. Walter Palmer, Captain Charles Hill, Captain Mary Hill, Major Roland Brown and others converged on the White World War II veteran and in unison embraced each other. As time stood still in amazement while spouting into the air energy of healing, reclamation, forgiveness and an enormous sense of relief and joy for this mutual recognition of the contributions of the Tuskegee Airmen.

WHY WAS THE HISTORY OF THE TUSKEGEE AIRMEN KEPT SILENT?

I left the Palm Beach reception that evening in 1998 pondering why it has been so difficult for the military of the United States of America and the public to highlight the contributions of the Tuskegee Airmen and other World War II African American service members who were loyal to the military and to the United States of America. They honorably defended the flag and the freedom of a world that was discriminating against them in terms of equal education, equal accommodations, equal housing, equal pay, and equal justice. It was painful to see Sgt. Elton Williams, a retired World War II decorated war veteran, with tears in his eyes as he said, "We left our families and went to Europe and other parts of the world, and we risked our lives, and were shot at each day, yet, were determined to prove ourselves as soldiers and as worthy men." It is important to remind the reader that during World War II and the era of the 1940s the Tuskegee Airmen Pilot Training was conducted during a time in United States history when "Jim Crow" was alive and active; a time when the Supreme Court of the United States in Plessy v Ferguson (163 U.S. 537, 16 S. Ct. 1138, 1896) held that "separate but equal," and segregation of the races was legally right. The fact that the Tuskegee Airmen Experience occurred during this time was remarkable.

FOUR EVENTS THAT ARE LINKED TO THE TUSKEGEE AIRMEN EXPERIENCE

Another lingering question that remained unanswered in the author's mind was how the Tuskegee Airmen Experience stacks up with four critical events in American and African history. These events were: The Underground Railroad, Rosa Parks and the Bus Boycott, the Haitian Revolution for Independence, and Denmark Vesey's Rebellion in Charleston, South Carolina. I proceeded to research the Tuskegee Airmen Experience and concluded that the accomplishments and achievements of the Tuskegee Airmen must be recognized and discussed in the same breath as the fine contributions of the Underground Railroad experience, the Denmark Vesey Rebellion, The Rosa Parks Bus Boycott experience and the Haitian Revolution.

It is important to note that it is not my intention to argue that any of these events in African American history was more important than other events. Rather, it is my hope that the reader will glean from this discussion that these events demonstrate the strong will of African Americans and people of African descent during different time periods of American history to push for dignity and self-respect despite the harsh effects of racial and social discrimination. This period affected every aspect of life including education, economics and social interactions across the races and access to accommodations to name a few.

Let us explore the events that will provide a glimpse of the ways African descent people in the Americas sought to secure their liberation, freedom and justice, namely:

I. The Underground Railroad

The Underground Railroad was a story about trust among Blacks and Whites who risked their lives to secure freedom. The efforts of Harriet Tubman and others include Whites who sacrificed their safety to ensure that the freedom of the enslaved Africans was secured. Oboe Onomake, the author's brother said it best, "Harriett Tubman was able to go back and forth to the South where her life could have been taken at any moment during the 300 plus trips, but, she was safe because there was the spirit of God guiding her hands and her steps."

II. The Slave Rebellion of Charleston: Denmark Vesey

This was an organized attempt to free enslaved Africans from the grips of slavery, although Vesey's own enslaved brothers and sisters betrayed his attempts, the event had far reaching implications for the struggle for freedom. This event provided the essence for a moral, spiritual and physical resistance, which became one of the building blocks that led to the Emancipation Proclamation in 1865 and the 13rd Amendment to the United States Constitution, i.e., "The Abolition of Slavery."

III. Rosa Parks and the Bus Boycott

This experience was the demonstrative economic boycott that showed African Americans that if they band together and use money and economic resources, they could get positive civil rights results. This was not easy since for it was a protracted struggle that required trust, cooperation and long-suffering for success. This single event by the "mother of economic resistance" in civil rights taught a lesson that guns and bricks could not have done so effectively. The readers should understand the courage of Rosa Parks as an example of the determination of African Americans and women in particular to fight for Montgomery freedom from the shackles of racial discrimination in Alabama and in the United States of America.

IV. *Haitian Revolution*

This struggle was an ongoing push for freedom from the shackles of harsh slavery in Haiti. The result of this tireless struggle culminated in an event in 1841 that created the first freed African Nation in the Western Hemisphere. It provided a sense of pride and a belief that freedom from slavery was possible and could only be won by personal, spiritual, psychological, and physical struggles. It had all of the ingredients of determination, planning, against all odds (Napoleon's French Army), the treachery of victims' oppressed faith and a sense of loyalty.

WHAT IS THE PRIMARY REASON FOR THIS BOOK?

Now, I come to the deeper reason for this book. As I examined all of these events, I observed that they had common themes of trust, liberation, struggle, faith, oppression, resistance, and economic well-being. The Tuskegee Airmen Experience had a dangerous and explosive element that everyone has overlooked. The Tuskegee Airmen Experience or Experiment, as was often referred to in some publications, was not just about discrimination and segregation. This Experience was a deliberate attempt to destroy the essence of humanity, the mind and the intellect of African Americans. A close look at the purpose of the Tuskegee Experience, as expressed by so many in Congress at that time was, "to prove that Blacks do not have the intelligence and the mind set to fly a complex instrument such as an airplane". The Tuskegee Airmen Experience was about African Americans who beat the cruel racial odds and proved to the United States of America and the world that they had the intellectual muster to fly a complex instrument called the "airplane". The Tuskegee Airmen and all of the World War II African American veterans proved that the color of one's skin does not determine one's intelligence and capacity. "It is one's attitude that determines one's altitude" and ability to achieve difficult goals and objectives.

If the Tuskegee Airmen had flown without such an outstanding record, the results would have been devastating for all African Americans in the United States and African descent people living in the Diaspora. Their successes erased the prevailing thinking by some that Blacks "cannot think." Beyond the Tuskegee Airmen Experience's success, there is well-documented evidence of the intellectual success of African Americans in diverse areas. For example, such notables as George Washington Carver, Garrett T. Morgan, Nathaniel Hale Williams, Elijah McCoy, Lewis Howard Latimer, scholars such as Dr. Booker

T. Washington, Dr. William E. Dubois, Dr. Maya Angelou, Dr. Henry Louis Gates, Dr. Cornel West, Toni Morrison, Madame C.J. Walker, Rosa Parks, Dr. John Hope Franklin, Rev. Dr. Martin Luther King and others.

SIX THEMES THAT ANCHOR THE TUSKEGEE AIRMEN SUCCESS

Six themes that punctuate this story about African Americans who were Tuskegee Airmen and other World War II pilots and veterans, namely:

1. Intellectual Attainment

These Tuskegee Airmen were bright, trainable and had the ability to pass all tests. Passing these tests was the first step in breaking the color barrier in the military. As Lt. Col. Hiram Mann stated, "anyone who became a Tuskegee Airman and was accepted into the pilot training program was an African American who had some, at least two years of college or university education and single". Before World War II started and until sometime in 1942, all American military pilots had to have been college graduates. The requirements were changed in 1942 to indicate that all military pilots had to have completed a minimum of two years of college. Later the requirements was changed to no college but instead anyone who could pass the rugged mental and physical tests could get into the Flying Training Program. "The story in the HBO special is true for those enlisted men who were in the Tuskegee Experience who had to retake the written exam twice because one of the White officers felt either they cheated or that they were not smart enough to score that high on the test. In fact on the second retesting each of the African Americans scored nothing less than 97 out of 100 points."

2. Collective Responsibility

In all accounts about the African American World War II veterans and the viewing of the HBO video on the Tuskegee Airmen, it was clear that there was a strong sense of collective responsibility for the success and well being of each other. They worked together to dispel the myth that people of African descent will betray and undercut each other as was seen in the Denmark Vesey rebellion, which was betrayed by other enslaved Africans. The Tuskegee Airmen Experience was to determine whether African Americans could be supportive of each other. They worked together and supported each other in every way. As Lt. Col. Mann said, "I was unable to find one incident where a Tuskegee Airmen deliberately sabotaged or deceived other enlisted personnel. We were under siege and we really had no time to sabotage each other. Rather there was a strong spirit of cooperation and help for each other. There was a feeling of not only collective responsibility but also unless we take care of each other, then we would never reach our collective destiny, I mean of being pilots who were capable of flying any military aircraft."

3. Creativity

These Tuskegee Airmen went beyond the textbook and what their White/ Black instructors taught them. They flew formations unheard of with modified gas tanks. They reached into the depths of their minds and hearts and became one of the most feared fliers called the "Red Tails." The Germans reported that they were concerned and feared the Tuskegee Airmen's effectiveness as fliers. As Lt. Col. Hiram Mann and Lt. Walter Palmer said, "We were well trained and we were not about to lose any aircraft to the German enemy so we came up with some formations and combat strategies that went beyond what our basic training provided us."

4. Faith

One must be able to observe that in life it is hard to succeed in any task or activity unless one has an unwavering faith in one's self and one's abilities to succeed and overcome the blatant discrimination and the remnants of the harsh "Jim Crow" laws that existed in the United States of America. The Tuskegee pilots' belief in their own abilities came through as one saw the event of the Tuskegee Airmen as portrayed in the recent HBO film, can feel the pain of hearing, "You don't belong here," and "go home, you can't fly." Despite these hurtful things and the vicious taunts from their fellow White American pilots, they never lost faith in their abilities and in each other. As Lt. Col. Mann said, "We were on a mission to help the African American community and ourselves. If we had failed, then, they would have been disappointed in us and we would have been disappointed in ourselves."

5. Fear

In all of my previous discussions with the Tuskegee Airmen and World War II veterans, they recounted that they were not afraid of dying in combat. The greatest fear was whether they would ever be accepted as being effective and qualified combat pilots and soldiers. "The fear of failure and failure itself was not an option for us." We could not let the "Black Community" down they were depending on us. The success of the Tuskegee Airmen is an example of how African Americans, despite the fears experienced in a segregated society, were determined to succeed.

6. Determination

The determination of Harriet Tubman was etched on the minds of the

Tuskegee Airmen. They overcame the discriminatory treatment including separate sleeping quarters, separate and segregated fifty units and racial insults. Yet, they succeeded because they understood that the future of the African American community rested on their success. Any failure would have set the struggle for human and civil rights back. They were determined and they succeeded. "It is important to understand that this was one of the foundational tests for the Civil Rights movement in that we were trying to integrate the military, trying to receive the same equal treatment in lodging, training and combat involvement. Also we were trying to combat Jim Crow laws that were thriving in the military. This was a matter of intelligence …are we smart enough to fly a plane? If we failed then it would have been a reflection on all of the Black population in the United States and the world".

Therefore, as we reflect on the contributions of African American military personnel including the Tuskegee Pilots it is critical to remember that African Americans fought in the Civil War in the United States of America with a patriotic zeal that exemplified them as excellent and efficient soldiers. Yet, they were treated with disrespect and hatred because of their skin color and race. Nearly 180,000 Blacks were in the Union Army and an additional 30,000 were in the Union Navy. These numbers do not include the vast numbers who worked as laborers in the service units. Of these approximately 3,000 died in battle, and another 65,000 perished due to disease, accidents and other illnesses.[1]

In all of my classes on Cultural Diversity and Multicultural Education, I often encounter students who find it hard to believe that the United States military services were segregated. How there was no room for African Americans to become pilots during World War I and World War II because of the intricate layers of segregation in the military during that era.

A study conducted by the Army War College in 1925 sealed the fate of African Americans and supported the widespread stereotype and discrimination against Blacks. This 1925 study concluded that the "colored Americans lack the necessary qualities, i.e. physiological, psychological, and intellectual attributes to lead as officers and to fight in a combat. Furthermore, they lack aptness, agility, and dexterity, all of which are necessary to operate a machine as complicated as an aircraft."[2] As painful as history can be, this study demonstrates the government of the United States of America's thinking at that time and certainly until the passage of Public Law 18, in 1939, which provided for the expansion of the Army Air Corps and permitted the creation of training programs at Black colleges in various areas of flying and Air Corps support services.

The determination of African Americans to seek justice and equal opportunity in American society continued to be an ongoing struggle for African Americans. The example of the Tuskegee Airmen pilots in being efficient, effective and competent pilots, was the experience that assured the African American community that their children can and will succeed in every and any intellectual endeavor not limited to flying an airplane.

Thus, this book is written to reflect on the African American Tuskegee Airmen who were World War II pilots and veterans who broke the back of segregation in the military and influenced President Truman in 1948 to declare the military as an integrated institution.

CHAPTER II

The Four Events in African American History that are as important as the Tuskegee Airmen and Africans in the Military

I PONDERED FOR SOME time as to why the Tuskegee Airmen Experience and African Americans in the Military were overshadowed by these four events, which tend to dominate the discussions during "Black History month". These four events are, 1) The Montgomery Bus Boycott, 2) The Underground Railroad, 3) The Haitian Revolution and 4) The Slave Rebellion in Charleston, South Carolina. These four key events are of equal importance to the events surrounding African Americans in the military including the Tuskegee Airmen. Thus, we have an obligation to teach our children the history and contributions of all African Americans as part of the history of the United States of America.

FOUR CRITICAL EVENTS

Rosa Parks and the Montgomery Bus Boycott

Rosa Parks, a pioneer of Civil Rights is cited by many historians as dating the beginning of the Modern Civil Rights Movement in the United States to December 1, 1955.th On this day Rosa Parks, an unknown seamstress whose husband Raymond Parks volunteered and helped free the Scottsboro defendants, created history by her sincere and determined actions. She joined the

NAACP in 1943, after attending Alabama State College in 1932, but, her commitment to equal rights was not actualized until December of 1955.

On December 1, 1955 she was arrested for disregarding an order to surrender her bus seat to a White passenger in the front, rather than ride in the usual back seats set aside for Blacks. She elected to be fined for her act of defiance. However, this led to an organized Black effort to end legal segregation. The Montgomery Improvement Association that was organized at that time, selected a young pastor of the Dexter Avenue Baptist Church, Dr. Martin Luther King, Jr. to provide the leadership around the pending boycott. The association orchestrated a boycott of the city owned buses for 382 days. The boycott succeeded in ending the discrimination and outlawed racial segregation on public transportation in Montgomery. The organized determination of the Black protesters for 382 days bred new life into the liberation movement by affirming a new strategy of economic boycott coupled with focused negotiations. The result was the breaking of the back of segregation in Montgomery, Alabama with respect to bus transportation.

The author had the opportunity to meet Mrs. Rosa Parks during her visit to DeLand, Florida in 1993. Her words: "I do the best I can to look upon life with optimism, but, much is still left to be done for freedom". These words continue to haunt the author's mind, but they also provide the motivation to push for freedom, fair treatment, and the inclusion of African American history in the curriculum.

The Underground Railroad: Harriett Tubman's Triumph

Harris (1996)[3] argued that the beginning of the Underground Railroad dates back to the 1500's but it was perfected and a sophisticated system developed between 1830 and the 1860's. Ringgold puts it well in saying that this effort of Harriett Tubman "was a mystical underground railroad in the sky." Harriett Tubman, a freed slave who fled to North Ashburn, New York, joined this railroad. There in 1848, she joined and inspired the revival and expansion of the Underground Railroad, which went through the South to most Northern, states such as Delaware, Maryland, Kentucky, District of Columbia, Virginia, Indiana, New York, Rhode Island, Connecticut, Illinois, Canada, and other areas. In 1859, over 3000 people worked in the Underground Railroad (Harris, 1996). Harriett Tubman and others, including many Whites, inspired a vast network of activists who organized a system of secret codes to inform passengers (enslaved Africans) about the safe routes and safe houses and places of hiding until they reached their destination to freedom. This major event, which preceded the Civil War, was underscored by tension between the North and South. In the midst of this turmoil, Harriett Tubman made at least 15 return trips to the heart of the South to conduct over 300 fugitive slaves, including her own family members. Traveling the backcountry at night, Harris stated that Harriet Tubman signaled people with a song. They learned to use the stars in the "Big Dipper" to help guide them on their way. Though she could not read or write well, she knew her faith in God as she often said, "I ventured only where God sent me." Despite being considered a threat and over $46,000 reward for her recapture, she persevered.

The significance of the Underground Railroad is embodied in the sheer number of freed persons, which ranged from some estimates of 60,000 to more than 100,000 (Harris, 1996). The drive for freedom since 1840-50's is no longer underground. It is open and is expressed through protests and legal actions like in the state of Florida where Blacks were denied the right to cast their vote in the 2000 presidential elections. Blacks organized and protested the denial of their Constitutional right to vote. The struggle for freedom happening in this contemporary period of our history each day, each month, each year in the United States and the World alike.

The Haitian Revolution: A Source of Pride for all Liberated Africans[5]

In mid 1700's there were enslaved Africans in Saint Dominique also known as Hispaniola? Today these nations are known as one-half of Santa Domingo and the other half as Haiti. The enslaved African people began to rebel and there were increasing runaways (Civan p. 7). These runaway slaves were called Maroons who lived in safety in the mountains and forest while forming guerrilla bands, which attacked the European Colonists. In 1791, led by Boukman, a Maroon and voodoo priest and Georges Brasson and his aide Toussaint L' Overture. (See Walter Dean Myers, Toussaint L' Overture: New York Simon & Schuster Children's publishing Division (1996).[6] These attacks were responded to by brutal reprisals. Thus, the Mulattos entered the struggle against the French enslavement under the leadership of Alexander P'etion and others.

After the conflict, changing of sides among the Africans occurred. Some sided with the French and others with the British and still others with the Spanish. Toussaint L' Overture, well positioned, then made a crucial decision to support France and with strategic victories, he controlled much of Saint Dominique and Hispaniola. Soon he defeated the Spanish and took control, abolishing slavery in both parts of the island. Napoleon Bonaparte sent a fleet of ships and troops under General Charles Le Clerc to defeat Toussaint. Initially the French won victories, but hundreds of French soldiers died. Toussaint eventually agreed to a cease-fire on June 7, 1802 and was taken prisoner and exiled to France.

The enslaved Africans now had a choice to be re-enslaved or fight for their freedom. Under the leadership of Jean-Jacques Dessalines, a former slave, the mulattos and Africans continued to struggle for their freedom. In November 1803, Napoleon, sensing he was losing the battle on all fronts in 1803 agreed to the sale to the United States, the purchase of Louisiana. On January 1, 1804 Dessalines declared Haiti's independence, becoming the second nation (after the United States in 1776) in the West and the first freed African (Black) Republic in the world in the midst of a slave holding countries of the United States, Britain, France, Portugal and other nations.

As Civan et al. (1994, p. 9), said, "While France recognized Haiti as an independent nation in 1838. The United States did not recognize Haiti until 1862, after the slave holding South had seceded from the Union." This independence of the Haitian was an example for the liberation struggles and revolutions to be free of slavery by African descent people and other groups in the Caribbean, the United States and other parts of the World.

The Slave Rebellion of South Carolina: Denmark Vesey

Denmark Vesey (1767-1822) who led a slave rebellion in July 1822, like Nat Turner, was an avid reader of the Bible; saw the only way to freedom from slavery was through armed rebellion. Nat Turner's rebellion experienced some success and made the point that the struggle for freedom is possible, yet fought with setbacks including Turner being hanged with sixteen of his supporters. Nat Turner sailed with his master, Captain Vesey, to the Virgin Islands and Haiti for 20 years. He enjoyed a considerable degree of mobility in his homeport of South Carolina.

In 1817, Nat Turner purchased his freedom and immediately began to plan a slave revolt in Charleston, South Carolina. The revolt was scheduled to begin on July 14, 1822. With the help of several other African descent people, especially five of them, recruited as many as nine thousand slaves. Of course, word of the revolt leaked out. Vesey and his persons moved the date of the revolt to June 16, 1822. Again, word was leaked out to the slave owners and the State of South Carolina. The state militia was mustered and an intense investigation about the pending plot was revealed. The result was that 135 slaves were arrested. Ninety-seven were bound over for trial. Forty-five were transported out of the country to places in the Caribbean including the Bahamas. Vesey and 34 enslaved Africans were hanged.

Vesey's attempt led other states to be more vigilant and in particular, strengthened their slave codes. On the other hand, it gave rise to the idea that slavery can be resisted. The key to successful resistance of slavery was to have an organized effort based on trust, determination and efficient leadership. It is my opinion that the Underground Railroad, under Harriett Tubman, learned from the lessons of Vesey and created a system of individual leaders who operated as independent entity. Within the context of the overall plan, which was a way to safely move enslaved Africans from the shackles of the slavery system in the South to a new and free life in the Northern states of the United States and Canada.

In summary, it is important to identify what did the events of the Montgomery Bus Boycott, the Underground Railroad, the Haitian Revolution and the Slave Rebellions in Charleston, South Carolina have in common with the Tuskegee Airmen Experience and the African Americans in the Military. These common threads were three–fold: First, it was triumph against segregation and racial discrimination. Second, it was a demonstration of the benefits of collective and concerted actions directed towards one's liberation. These episodes, like the Tuskegee Airmen Experience, were grounded in the hearts and minds of the people who believed the words of President Dwight D. Eisenhower, who said, "We have heard much of the phrase 'peace and friendship.' This phrase, in expressing the aspiration of America, is not complete. We should say instead, 'peace and friendship, in freedom.' This, I think is America's real message to the rest of the world."[4] In addition, this author would add, to the rest of the United States of America, too. Third, these results that can be derived from the struggle for human and civil rights will require that the participants are clear about their goals and outcomes and that the energies be focused on the prize of freedom, equality and justice for all. The dreams and struggles of African Americans and others can best be summarized in the words of Reverend Doctor Martin Luther King, Jr. who said?

"I have a dream that one day this nation will rise up and live out the true meaning of this creed; we hold these truths to be self-evident that all men are created equal; that they are endowed by the Creator with certain unalienable rights; that among these are life, liberty, and the pursuit of happiness...."

THE VALUING OF HUMAN LIFE

Finally, the message that emanates from these struggles of African Americans is that "the care of human life and happiness, and not destruction, is the first and only legitimate object of good government."(Thomas Jefferson, p. 32). The challenge for African Americans and other disenfranchised groups has been to persuade Federal, State, and local governments who have the courage and will, to protect their rights and the rights of all citizens. As you will read later, it was the government that enforced a segregated military, which guaranteed that African Americans would live a daily life of torment, injustice and discrimination. The government was charged with the responsibility of protecting the rights of every citizen regardless of one's race or ethnicity. These rights are stated in the Constitution of the United States of America. It is the duty of every citizen to be vigilant and ensure that the rights and freedoms guaranteed by the Constitution and Bill of Rights of the United States are realized each day in every aspect of human life.

"We must build a new world, a far better world, and
one in which the eternal dignity of man is respected"
(President Harry Truman)

CHAPTER III

Why Tell the Tuskegee Airmen Story: An Episode about African Americans in the Military

I USED THE FOLLOWING approach to write this book. This approach included, 1) Utilization of data based on the research of printed materials 2) Speaking with Ret. Lt. Col. Hiram E. Mann, an Original Tuskegee Airmen and pilot who is still alive and was able to give first hand accounts of his and others' experiences in the military 3) Taping Tuskegee Airmen's presentations and comments to derive an accurate account of their experiences and 4) Attending over 25 lectures to hear the Tuskegee Airmen tell their stories. The information that follows represents a short summary of some of these Tuskegee Airmen and military personnel of World War II experiences that had a real impact on his life and the content in this book.

ACKNOWLEDGING AFRICAN AMERICANS' CONTRIBUTIONS

The contributions of the African descent men and women who served in the military are a portion of the United States history that every American and the people of the world should know and embrace. The Tuskegee Airmen and other African American soldiers are not alone. This legacy could be traced back to the revolutionary wars as Buffalo soldiers in the Indian wars. These men fought wars in the United States, Cuba, Puerto Rico, Philippines, Pacific Islands, North Africa, and Europe during World War I and World War II, in the Panama Canal, Haiti, Grenada, the Gulf War, Middle East, Afghanistan,

17

Iraq and other areas. Lest we forget the more than 100 families who fought in Fort Mose, St. Augustine, Florida. It is well document about that the bravery acts of these freed Africans who fought on behalf of Spain in protecting the Northern flank of St. Augustine from the assaults of the British and were significant in helping the Spanish to hold off the assault of the British on St. Augustine. The involvement of African Americans in these and other wars can be best expressed in their efforts as being "all in the name of protecting the interests of the United States of America and other Nations in the world," according to the decorated Ret. Sgt. Elton Williams, a World War II veteran.

"WHY TELL THIS STORY" BY RET. LT. COL. HIRAM MANN

Lt. Col. Hiram Mann said, "It is important about the difference in treatment of the Negroes as compared to the Whites or others. Many people had no idea that there was such a gap in the treatment of African Americans who were discriminated against and had to struggle to secure equal rights in the military and other parts of American life at time of World War II. Despite the constant obstacles that discrimination placed in our paths, we proved that we were capable of doing things involving the highest level of intellectual skills, other than menial jobs. It is important that for the most part before World War II, the military was segregated and the main jobs for Negroes were truck drivers, mess hall attendants and other low skill jobs. I know this for a fact since it was documented in the 1925 study of the Army War College in an expose entitled, "Utilization of the Negro Soldier of World War I." This publication by the Army described the Negro soldier as "being afraid, and not fighting with intensity". The truth of the matter is that "each of us who enrolled in the military was determined to fight and build our reputation as able bodied individuals." The proof of the matter was "that once we were trained and given the chance to fight on the front lines we turned out to be the 'red tails,' which was one of the most successful fighter pilots during World War II." So this book is devoted to sharing the life experience of Ret. Lt. Col. Hiram Mann and the achievements of the Tuskegee Airmen during World War II.

WHY WAS THE TUSKEGEE AIRMEN EXPERIENCE IMPORTANT TO THIS AUTHOR?

As historians discuss World War II, the focus is on dialogue of liberation of the Jewish people and others in Europe under Hitler's power and genocidal actions. It is the author's view that World War II had a very critical undercurrent event, which was going on in the United States. In 1939, an apprehensive United States Army Air Corps embarked on a program that would forever change the face of United States military aviation."[8] This program was conducted at the Division of Aeronautics of Tuskegee Institute, which was founded by Booker T. Washington in Tuskegee, Alabama in 1881. Tuskegee was located between the capital city of Montgomery and the Georgia border traveling along I-85 highway. Alabama was chosen for the military aviation program because it was already known for its engineering and other achievements. Tuskegee Institute was already conducting a Civilian Pilot Training Program, and it eventually became the primary military pilot training school in the United States for all Black pilots. The trained Black pilots became the Tuskegee Airmen, although the Germans called them "Black Birdmen." Once they began to fly the planes with "Red Tails", they were called "Red-Tailed Angels."[9] These were the planes, which flew alongside the bombers and protected them during World War II. Little did these men know that they were going to fight Nazi Germany over an issue called "racism," the same issue that their very own country was struggling with at that time?

In 1907, when the United States Army Air Corps began, African Americans were not admitted into the flying programs. Most people felt they were not as smart as Whites were and did not have the courage to fight in battle.[10] During 1907 to 1940, African Americans were used in non-flight positions in the Army Air Corps such as bus boys, kitchen help, construction workers, and truck drivers. The general view held by Army officials was that Blacks lacked the ability to operate machinery as complicated as an airplane. The truth of the matter, however, was that African Americans had been flying planes for years. Proven pilots such as Bessie Coleman, Willa Brown, Dr. A. Porter Davis, Albert E. Forsythe, and Charles Alfred Anderson are just a few of the African Americans who learned to fly prior to the start of the Tuskegee Airmen Experience in 1939.[11] The airplane below was owned by Dr. A. Porter Davis in 1929, one year after he received his license as a pilot in 1928.

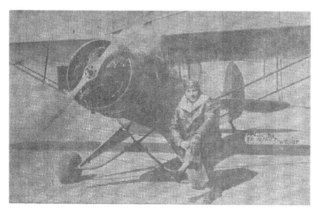

Dr. A. Porter Davis and His Porterfield Monoplane

AFRICAN AMERICANS IN THE MILITARY: FIGHTING TO PRESERVE OTHERS' FREEDOM

In thinking about African American men serving in our military forces, one must start at the beginning with the facts. In the Civil War between the states, "Black men compromised 12% (178,895) of the Union Army and 25% (30,000) of the Union Navy. Thousands more served as laborers in the various service units. There were approximately 2,751 soldiers were killed in battle and another 65,427 died from disease and other causes."[12]

African American men also fought in the Spanish American War, as they did in the Philippines War. They also were involved in the Mexican Punitive Expedition, and the nicknamed "Buffalo Soldiers".[13] During World War I, over 200,000 Black men served in the American Armed Forces. President Franklin D. Roosevelt wanted to build up the United States Military for protection in case of war. He came up with the idea of training African American civilians. The first such program was the Civilian Pilot Training Program established in April of 1939. This was only the beginning of how far our Black soldiers would take the United States not only in victories of wars, but also gave us a lesson in learning to accept all citizens of the United States Military as equal protectors of the flag.

THE HISTORY OF THE TRAINING OF AFRICAN AMERICAN PILOTS

As early as 1917, African American youths had tried in vain to join or enlist in the Air Service of the Signal Corps as Air Observers, but with no success. In 1921, there was active lobbying and urging of the War Department to include African American fliers in the Negro Army Air Force Reserve Units. The War Department rebuffed these demands and argued that it was "impossible to establish such units because no Negro officer had previously held commissions in the Air Service. Furthermore, there was no justification for the appointment of Negroes as flying Cadets."[14] This response from the War Department was not surprising since there were several studies in 1925. The most telling study was the one conducted by the Army War College in a 1925 study of Blacks in World War I. This study found that "the Black man was physically unqualified for combat duty: was by nature subservient, mentally inferior and believed himself to be inferior to the White man...could not control himself in the face of danger and resourcefulness of the White man."[15] The War College study had a devastating impact on African Americans being admitted to the Army Air Force. The Army did not take into account the real facts that contradicted the findings of the study. The facts were as follows:

1) Eugene Bullard, a Georgia native had joined the French Foreign Legion

as an infantryman. In 1917, eight years before the Army College Study, he was sworn into France's flying corps, the Lafayette Escadrille. Eugene Bullard was a very effective flyer, in fact, he was known as the "Black Swallow of Death," who flew with a monkey as a companion.[16] Although his service as a fighter pilot was short due to objections from the American pilots who refused to fight along side of him. Interestingly, his efforts and skills as a fighter pilot earned him France's military honor, i.e., the "Croix de Guerre."[17]

2) What was even more telling at that time was the fact that "it was unusual enough for a Negro to fly a plane, but for a Negro woman to do such a thing, it came near being a miracle" (Enoch P. Waters, City Editor, Chicago Defender).[18] This woman was Bessie Coleman who in 1920 went to France and entered a flying school, Ecole d'Aviation des Frers Caudron at Le Crotoy in the Somme, in November 1920. In 1921, she earned the coveted Federation Aeronautique Internationale (FAI) license that gave her the right to fly anywhere in the world. She returned to United States in 1922 and flew in air shows throughout the United States.

3) In addition to Eugene Bullard and Bessie Coleman, there were other pilots, such as, John C. Robinson who started the first Black flying club in Chicago. He also built the first airship in the Black Town of Robbins, Illinois in 1933. Willa Beatrice Brown Chappell, a certified flight instructor and expert aviation and engine mechanics earned her pilot license in June 23, 1938. In 1930s, J. Heiman Banning and Thomas C. Allen became the first Black Aviators to conduct a transcontinental flight. Known as the "Flying Hobos," it took them 41 hours and 27 minutes to complete the flight (Blacks in Aviation, 1996, p.9)

In 1933, Dr. Albert E. Forsythe and C. Alfred "Chief" Anderson took their transcontinental flight from Atlantic City, New Jersey to Los Angeles. In 1934, the first Black aviators, made the first Pan-American flight to promote interracial harmony and debunk the myth in the 1925 Army College study that concluded, "Blacks cannot fly." The initial leg from Miami to Nassau was the first ever flight by a land plane. Up until that time, only seaplanes made the trip to Nassau, Bahamas.[19] Their trip also made stops in Havana, Cuba, Jamaica, Haiti, the Dominican Republic, Puerto Rico, the Virgin Islands, Granada, Trinidad and Guyana, my country of birth located in the tip of South America and next to Venezuela, Brazil, Surinam and French Guiana.

Thus, this was further evidence that African Americans were capable of flying airplanes in the United States, Europe and other parts of the world. However, despite this contradictory evidence proving that African Americans could fly, there was no ray of hope until 1939 when several historically Black colleges and Universities including Tuskegee Institute, established a Cadet Flying Program. It would not be until July 19, 1941 that the 99th Pursuit Squadron was formed. The first class of cadets and officers included Captain Benjamin O. Davis Jr., John C. Anderson Jr., Charles Brown, Frederick H. Moore, Ulysses S. Pannell, George S. Roberts, William Slade, Mac Ross and Roderick Williams.[20] It should be noted that all of these 13 pilots had a four-year degree including Captain Benjamin O. Davis who graduated in 1936 from the United States Military Academy at West Point, New York.

This background of bright, talented men and women pilots distinguished themselves in flying and as courageous, capable and competent pilots who went on to prove themselves as fighter pilots in World War II. One of these pilots who graduated from Tuskegee Flying School was Lt. Col. Hiram Mann who was recognized for his distinguished flying record and service by being awarded one of the highest honors, namely "The Certificate of Valor". This award that is presented on the next page, was given to the then First Lieutenant Hiram E. Mann in recognition of courageous service in aerial combat in March 1945. This campaign was a part of his attachment to the 332nd Fighter Group. There were 48 missions Mann flew over enemy terrorterory including European-African-Middle Eastern, Bronze stars for Balkans, Germany, Appennines, and Po Valley Campaigns, while flying a single engine combat airplane. The certificate of valor was accompanied by the awarding of campaign medals i.e. "Air Medal 3 Oak Leaf Clusters to Air Medal."

On September 3, 1939, Germany invaded Poland, causing Great Britain and France to declare war. Once the United States decided to help in war efforts overseas, many training sites were put into action. West Virginia State College, the University of West Virginia, North Carolina Technical College, Howard University, Delaware State University, Hampton Institute, and the Tuskegee Institute are just a few of the ones that were first established (Holway, 1997).[21] Therefore, it was in 1941, the Official Tuskegee Airmen Pilot Training Program was established at Tuskegee Institute. The first African American pilot trainees landed in Tuskegee, Alabama to begin extensive aviation training. "These combat pioneers began their journey towards redefining America's relationship with Black men in the Air Force. The President of the Tuskegee Training Operation at the time was Dr. Frederick Patterson who wanted his men to succeed. While some considered this a flawed compromise, African American pilot trainees welcomed the opportunity to prove their ability and commitment to the war efforts".[22] In order to equip them to their best, Dr. Patterson hired Charles Anderson who was the first African American to earn his private pilots license in the United States. Before him, all African American pilots had to get their license in a country other than United States such as Canada and England. Charles Anderson was made head of flight training and nicknamed "chief". He arrived on Tuskegee Army Air Field on July 29, 1940 in a new 225-horsepowered airplane painted blue and yellow. Chief Charles Anderson and others were faced with many challenges including "unequal facilities, an incomplete airfield, and an overcrowded institution".[23] The first official flight training began on August 25, 1941. The enlisted African American pilot trainees slept in cold long rooms with bunk beds with a thin blanket. They were allowed one trunk and everything they had was required to be kept in that trunk. They endured harsh circumstances as well as being treated unjustly by the White officers who were in charge of the training.

They had to make the choice to fly for the United States of America and leave behind the people they loved most. Not only these husbands and sons had to sacrifice themselves for this country, but the mothers and wives as well. Little did they realize that some of their beloved men would never return home. Many of these men suffered from depression as they were forced to watch their friends die or wash out in the attempt to learn to fly the planes.[23] The second air field, Moton Field, was under construction, however Tuskegee Institute was having trouble paying for it; the men could use only the one on Tuskegee Training Property. Approximately 150 men lost their lives while in training or during flights in combat.[24] It was expected that the squadron would consist of 33 pilots and 27 aircrafts. The 278 men were expected to receive training at the Tuskegee Institute in a range of complimentary roles including mechanics, weather specialist, and technical clerks.

FIRST LADY ELEANOR ROOSEVELT AND HER ROLE IN 1941

An important turning point for the Tuskegee Airmen pilots was the visit of Mrs. Eleanor Roosevelt, the wife of President Franklin D. Roosevelt. On April 19, 1941, the first lady Mrs. Eleanor Roosevelt arrived at Tuskegee and was responsible for publicizing to the world that these African American Tuskegee pilots could fly. To the surprise of many and as depicted in the HBO movie of 1995, Mrs. Roosevelt requested that she be flown as a passenger by trained Tuskegee Airmen pilots. Chief Charles Anderson obliged and flew Mrs. Roosevelt safely. Thus, this flight demonstrated to the world that the Tuskegee Airmen were well trained, competent and ready for battle in World War II.[25] Mrs. Roosevelt's actions paved the way for the Tuskegee Airmen to achieve their ultimate goal of flying combat missions as part of the Army Air Corps. Following this visit of Mrs. Roosevelt, the training center then received $175,000 of the $200,000 dollars needed to complete the other airfield strip from the Rosenwald Fund, which was commonly known for giving money to help African American causes.

THE TUSKEGEE INSTITUTE AIR TRAINING PROGRAM

The Tuskegee Air Training Program included 480 hours of classes on the ground and more than 100 hours of flying time. Equipment was well maintained and instruction was proven the best, which gave the cadets confidence and the courage they needed to prove to the world they could do it. Colonel Benjamin O. Davis Jr. said "The training at Tuskegee Army Air Field … was the equal of whatever was going on in … any other flying school operated by the Army Air Corps."[26] When Japanese forces attacked the U.S. Naval Base at Pearl Harbor on December 7, 1941, the United States decided it was time to join the war instead of just providing a variety of military assistance. Therefore, the next day, the U.S. entered World War II against Germany, Italy, and Japan. As the war wore on the Army Air Corps, some senior officers did not want the African-American pilots serving in the military and tried to have them discredited. The Tuskegee Airmen pilots continued their training and became competent pilots. The first graduation class of Tuskegee pilots took place on March 7, 1942. The five Army Air Corps pilots were CPT Benjamin O. Davis, Jr., District of Columbia; Lemuel R. Curtis, Connecticut; Charles Debow, Jr., Indiana; George S. Roberts, West Virginia; and Mac Ross, Ohio. These first pilots were in the 99th Pursuit Squadron that was to be used for combat duty in North Africa. Flying along with the 99th Pursuit Squadron was the 332nd Fighter Group, which had bases in Italy. Their first assignments were to fly shore patrol, strafing, dive-bombing, and escort missions in the P-40 Warhawk, the P-39 Aero Cobra, the P-47 Thunderbolt, and the P-51 Mustang. In pilot training, they flew the Piper Cup J-3 in CTD, the PT-17 Stearman (some classes flew the PT-Fairchild) in Primary Training, the BT-13 Vultee Vibrator in Basic Training, and the AT-Texan (also known as the SNJ) in Advanced Single Engine Training. The Medium Bomber Pilots went from the BT-13 to the AT-10, to a trainer-type B-25 Mitchell Bomber in Advanced training, then the actual B-25.[27] These were not huge planes. There was barely enough room to turn around in them. These pilots had to know what was on every side not only their plane, but also the plane they were escorting. It took much courage and intellectual commitment for these men to finish at the Tuskegee Institute flight school. In March of 1942, five Tuskegee men received silver wings meaning they had completed all their classroom hours, and many hours in flying time. These men were the first African American men to receive their Army Air Corps pilot's licenses. Blacks as well as Whites were amazed by this achievement of the Tuskegee Airmen both at home and abroad. They were credited not only by those who loved them at home, but also by President Roosevelt and his wife. Never before and never after have we seen such talented men who put their whole hearts into fighting to preserve freedom of the free world. In August of 1941, twelve Black enlisted men started military flying training as U.S. Aviation Cadets in segregated Tuskegee

Army Air Field. Even in North Africa, the Tuskegee Airmen were again segregated from the White fighter pilots. Very little was known by the White pilots about the Tuskegee Airmen at that time. The Bomber pilots had no idea that their escorts were Tuskegee Airmen fighter pilots. On July 2, 1943, Lieutenant Charles B. Hall was the first Tuskegee Airman to down a FW-190 and damaged a ME-109. This was not the first example of how highly skilled and trained these men were, it was simply another demonstration of the passion and determination of the Tuskegee pilots to defend their country.

In September of 1943, the Tuskegee Institute located in Tuskegee, Alabama implemented an additional training program. However, the war ended before these trainees could graduate. This is a clear example of how long the training process took to be completed. These fighter pilots were already tired and physically exhausted before ever being transferred to Italy or North Africa, but they were certainly not mentally exhausted. Another change came in October 1943. Half of the 99th Pursuit Squadron was put into the 79th Fighter Group of the 12nd Air Force. Their success was also evident on October 9, 1943 when the 79th Fighter Group was taken out of escort duties and assigned to bombing the German strongholds. On July 2, 1943, the 99th Pursuit Squadron joined the 332nd Fighter Group. They were integrated with the 79th Military group. The sudden shock came when the White pilots found out it was African American men flying as their fighter pilot escorts. Although prejudice and hate were a common happening on home soil, they were just as common in the air where most people would have expected trust and collaboration will be necessary in order to stay alive. The White pilots were against the Black fighter escorts and tried to have them removed because they believed the fighters to have no knowledge in flying or combat skills. They quickly learned that the Black fighter pilots of the 332nd Fighter Group were going to save them.[28] The Tuskegee Airmen never lost a single bomber although they did loose 66 pilots to the war and they lost 32 men to the enemy fire of the Nazi in Germany. The last assignment for the 99th and 79th Squadrons known as Operational Strangle was on July 4, 1943. The 99th Pursuit Squadron then joined three other Squadrons which were the 100th, the 301st, and the 302nd to form what is better known as the 332nd Fighter Group which proved that they had the commitment, the technical ability, and the drive to carry out all their military assignments. In August 1944, the 332nd group helped to invade Southern France by flying as escorts. They also participated in escorting bombers as well a conducting ground attacks on several missions in Romania, and Czechoslovakia. These brave soldiers took on this amazing feat of flying combat during the war.[29]

On September 10, 1944, the Distinguished Flying Cross was awarded to four Tuskegee pilots from the 332nd Fighter Group. This marked a new era of recognition for the Tuskegee pilots during a period in American history when segregation and discrimination based on one's color was very rampant in the Armed Forces of the United States of America. However, most of the White fighter pilots still did not know about the Tuskegee pilots. By the time, June 1944 rolled around Colonel Benjamin O. Davis, Jr. was named the commander of the 477th Composite Fighter Squadron. They started training for combat in the Pacific Theater .They were fully aware of the dangers that are involved in war. "There was never a good war or a bad peace," said Benjamin Franklin.[30]

On March 24, 1945, Colonel Benjamin O. Davis Jr. led fifty-four pilots on an escort mission to Berlin, Germany. Not a single bomber was hit or lost that day. The 332nd Fighter Group was awarded the Presidential Unit Citation for their professional skill and determination of the mission. This was a great victory for the pilots who worked so hard to prove themselves to their country. In the spring of 1945, the Tuskegee pilots destroyed 150 enemy aircraft and downed another 111. On their best day, they were able to shoot down over 13 aircrafts. The last four enemy airplanes were shot down over the Mediterranean on April 26. The Tuskegee men had flown over 200 missions and never lost a single bomber.[31]

THE DISMANTLING OF THE 332ND FIGHTER GROUP

On May 8, 1945, the 332nd Fighter Group was disbanded. Some members of the 332nd Fighter Group finally started going home to a country where they were still viewed as second-class citizens. The United States was determined to keep the African Americans segregated and discriminated against in housing, employment, education and other areas. After all of the recognition they had received as pilots overseas, they found it hard to believe that they would be treated so poorly. Luckily, for the Tuskegee Airmen, President Harry S. Truman had been so impressed with the performance of the African American pilots that he promised he would help these African American pilots in the States. He kept his word. On July 26, 1948, President Truman announced Executive Order 9981 calling for an equality of treatment, and opportunity in the Armed Forces and all military regardless of race. This was the beginning of the process that led to the end of segregation, at least, in the Armed Forces.

These brave and gallant pilots known as the Tuskegee Airmen continued their success in military and civilian life. General Benjamin O. Davis Jr. continued in his military work, fought in later wars, and was awarded the rank of a four-star general by President Bill Clinton in 1998. Charles McGee, an original Tuskegee Airman and World War II pilot, fought in Korea and Vietnam. He achieved the highest three-war total of fighter missions of any Air Force aviator, which amounted to 409 missions. From 1998 to the present, McGee has served in leadership positions in the Tuskegee Airmen, Incorporated, which was originally founded in 1972.[32]

FIGHTING JIM CROW

It is critical that the reader understands that the Armed Forces of the United States of America were segregated by law since the case Plessy vs. Ferguson in 1896 which ruled that "separate but equal is legitimate." This meant that the "White only water fountains, schools, restaurants, hotels, colleges and universities and the military were legally separated with the result that "Blacks were subjected to segregation with harsh punishments including being arrested. Therefore, it was in this context that African Americans began the flight training at Tuskegee Army Air Field in Tuskegee, Alabama. A statement of the segregated Armed Forces policy on segregation follow in this original policy statement published in 1940. The Nation during the 1900s was a segregated United States of America and "Jim Crow" was the order of the day in the South and in fact in the Armed Forces of the United States.

SEGREGATION OF THE ARMED FORCES

Lest we forget, it is necessary to observe that the Armed Forces of the United States of America were segregated as a matter of fundamental policy of the Federal government. This fact of segregation made it even more certain that there will be uneven resources and opportunities. For example, there were no opportunities for African Americans to be trained as pilots in the military.

Segregation of the Armed Forces

1. The strength of the Negro personnel of the Army of the United States will be maintained on the general basis of the proportion of the country.

2. Negro organizations will be established in each major branch of the service, combatant as well as noncombatant.

3. Negro reserve officers eligible for active duty will be assigned to Negro units officered by colored personnel.

4. When officer candidate schools are established, opportunity will be given to Negroes to qualify for reserve commissions.

5. Negroes are being given aviation training as pilots, mechanics and technical specialist. This training will be accelerated.

6. At arsenal and army posts Negro civilians are accorded equal opportunity for employment at work for which they are qualified by ability, education and experience.

7. *The policy of the War Department is not to intermingle colored and white enlisted personnel in the same regimental organizations. This policy has been proved satisfactory over a long period of years, and to make changes now would produce situations destructive to morale and detrimental to the preparation for national defense...*

Statement of Policy submitted by Robert P. Patterson, Assistant Secretary of War and approved by President Roosevelt, October 9, 1940.

This sanctioned segregation policy of the War Department of the United States Army created a discriminatory status that affected both Blacks and Whites who served their nation. However, there were several key leaders including Truman, Roosevelt and McGovern and others who objected to these segregationist policies in the military.

The Black press and Black leaders pressed the military and the federal government for fair practices and fair access to the various branches of the military services. After much struggle and discussion, and with the continued opposition of labor unions, business, and other groups resulted in the compromised policy initiative as outline above in the 1940 document entitled "Segregation of the Armed Forces." As you read this policy closely, you will get a keen sense of why the Black community was uneasy with the document and continued their opposition to the Armed Forces policy of "segregation as a deliberate policy to undermine the rights of African American enlisted men and women who believed that such a policy violated the equal rights and freedoms guaranteed by the Constitution of the United States of America.

SENATOR GEORGE MCGOVERN, A FORMER BOMBER PILOT

George McGovern, who was a bomber pilot and who became a senator in the United States Congress said, "It was a wondrous sight to see those escort fighter planes coming up to take care of us, escorting us into the targets, picking us up after the bombing raid, and taking us home. They were flown by men with enormous skill and coordination".

The Tuskegee Airmen proved to the world they had what it took to be competent pilots, but, they also have demonstrated that African Americans were just as smart, hardworking, and loyal to the flag of the United States of America, as the White pilots were. These men fought for a country they truly loved, but also a country that supported Plessy vs. Ferguson (1896), the landmark Supreme Court of the United States case that held "separate but equal" was the standard of treatment for African Americans and other minorities. Jim Crow laws and blatant discrimination continued until the 1954 Supreme Court Case Brown v Board of Education, Topeka, Kansas. The march on Washington 1963 led to the passage of the Federal 1964 Civil Rights Law that put an end to Jim Crow forms of discrimination against African Americans and other citizens. These Tuskegee Airmen won hundreds of awards including one Silver Star. The then Air Force Chief of Staff General Ronald R. Fogleman said, "In the end, the men and the women of the Tuskegee Airmen experience broke forever the myths that allowed segregation, inequality, and injustice to exist..."[33] These great victories paved the way for every citizen of the United States would have equal rights and opportunities.

Although the Tuskegee Pilot Training experience took place over 64 years ago, still in 2007, racial discrimination and re-segregation are persistent problems in the United States today. "No, we don't have separate schools, bathrooms, or drinking fountains, but, this mindset is still pervasive in many communities in the United States of America." African Americans still experience discrimination in housing, equal pay and other areas of American life such as education, access to business opportunities and access to health care and other critical opportunities in the United States of America.

Thus, it is essential that we revisit, teach and learn about World War II. We must tell our youth about the heroic exploits and achievement of the Tuskegee Airmen. They did not only distinguish themselves as African American pilots, but rather they were exemplary as enlisted United States of America Air Force pilots who succeeded in being decorated as one of the finest pilot groups who flew in bitter combat against the Germans during World War II.

"Nothing splendid has ever been achieved except by those who dared believe that something inside them was superior to circumstances"
(Bruce Barton)

CHAPTER IV

Three Crucial Facts that Clarify the Tuskegee Airmen Experience

Understanding the Tuskegee Airmen Context

SINCE 1999, I have had the privilege of spending countless hours with several Tuskegee Airmen, pilots, ground crewmen and women, and other support personnel who were trained at the Tuskegee Army Air Field (TAAF) in Tuskegee, Alabama and other bases. However, what was striking about these discussions was that no one was able to clarify for the record of future generations a puzzle as to who is a "Tuskegee Airman". Nevertheless, a more sensitive issue is who is an Original Tuskegee Airman? My field research, reading of several books and episodes did not satisfy my inquiry until I met and spoke extensively with Ret. Lt. Col. Hiram E. Mann and listened carefully to his articulation on these three facts that follow. "There are essential facts that are crucial to the clarification of the Tuskegee Airmen Experience" according to Ret. Lt. Col. Hiram E. Mann.

DEFINITION OF THE TERM "ORIGINAL TUSKEGEE AIRMAN"

There are five categories that define who are Tuskegee Airmen, namely, 1) Individuals who served as pilots, support staff or other personnel in the Tuskegee Airmen Experience, 2) Associate Tuskegee Airmen (Any person who is not an "Original Tuskegee Airman"), 3) The members of the Heritage Group

31

and 4) Honorary Tuskegee Airmen Incorporated (TAI) members and 5) Life Members who can be anyone from any of the four categories stated herein. The following information describes each of these categories of members.

THE TERMS: TUSKEGEE AIRMEN OR ORIGINAL TUSKEGEE AIRMEN

The clear definition offered by Lt. Col. Hiram E. Mann is that "anyone, male or female, Black or White, military or civilian, who served or worked at least one day on TAAF between 1941, when construction began on the Tuskegee Army Air Field (TAAF) and 1948, when TAAF officially closed, or any unit assigned to the TAAF. Additionally, this definition covers in a particular way anyone who was assigned to the College Training Detachment (CTD), the 99th Pursuit Squadron, the 332nd Fighter Group or the 477th Medium Bombardment Group, between 1941, when construction began on TAAF and 1948, when TAAF officially closed, are eligible to be, or have been, an "Original Tuskegee Airman". If someone claims to be an "Original Tuskegee Airman", that person must provide documentation proving specific assignment and actual participation in the Tuskegee Airmen Experience at the Tuskegee Army Air Field(TAAF), Tuskegee, Alabama, or any unit associated with the Tuskegee Experience located elsewhere.

ASSOCIATE TUSKEGEE AIRMEN

The "Associate" Tuskegee Airman is a person who did not participate in or was not an "Original Tuskegee Airman". However, this is someone who is committed and interested in supporting the Tuskegee Airmen Incorporated (TAI) in all of its policies and procedures to ensure that the contributions of the Tuskegee Airmen is incorporated in the military history and American history. The "Associate" member is a person who is eligible to participate in all of the activities of a local chapter and the national organization Tuskegee Airmen Incorporated (TAI).

HERITAGE GROUP MEMBERS

There are "Heritage Group" Members who are the spouses and descendants of Original TAI members. The critical test is to establish that there is a close familial relationship between Original Tuskegee Air personnel and the Heritage Group members. This link to the Tuskegee experience is one that can be established by birth records, photographs or any other authentic evidence and official documents.

HONORARY TAI MEMBERS

"Honorary" TAI members are individuals who are invited to be Tuskegee Airmen Incorporated (TAI) members. These individuals are recommended by other TAI members because they are deemed to possess those qualities and interests that are compatible with the with the goals of the TAI. Those individuals who are honorary members do not pay dues however they can attend any of the national and local activities of the TAI.

LIFE MEMBERS

It should be noted that any of the members in all four categories can become Life Members by the paying the Life Member Fee subject to the approval of the national organization of the Tuskegee Airmen Incorporated (TAI).

RELEVANCE OF THE TERM TUSKEGEE AIRMEN AND TUSKEGEE AIRMEN INCORPORATED (TAI)

The term "Tuskegee Airmen" is often used retrospectively when referring to the accomplishments and incidents about all the African American pilot groups, which trained at TAAF in Tuskegee, Alabama. This term was not used until 1972; some 30 years later after World War II had ended. So this term "Tuskegee Airmen" is used retrospectively to identity those African American enlisted personnel who participated in the 1940's Tuskegee flying experience that trained African Americans to fly and group support staff to maintain and manage the operations of an Army Air Force Base in Tuskegee, Alabama.

IMPORTANCE OF THE YEAR 1972 AND TUSKEGEE AIRMEN INCORPORATED (TAI)

In 1972, coming from the roots of the Tuskegee experience during World War II, a group of single engine pilots who were all members of the legendary 332nd Fighter Group began an organization in the city of Detroit, Michigan. The pilots called the new organization "Tuskegee Airmen Incorporated."

The primary goals of the organization were two-fold, to ensure that the legacy and documented military achievement of the African American pilots who put their lives on the line in co-combating the Nazis in North Africa and Europe. The concern at that time among these single engine pilots was that there was no national monument built to recognize their achievements and more fundamentally, the Air Force and the other branches of the military failed to publicize the achievements of the Tuskegee Airmen. The second goal and reason for the formation of the organization in 1972 was the deep commitment and desire to educate the youth and the community about the opportunities in the aviation careers.

MEMBERSHIP REQUIREMENTS OF THE TUSKEGEE AIRMEN INCORPORATED (TAI)

As Ret. Lt. Col. Hiram Mann puts it well by saying that, "At the time in 1972 and even before that the pilots and other personnel struggled with the idea of what to call themselves. No one wanted to be known as the Black pilots during a period when segregation in this country was so pervasive. As I have always advocated that the other worse name to be called was the 'Tuskegee Experiment' because that had a negative connotation with respect to the other Tuskegee Experiment which focused on experimentation of syphilis disease that was prevalent in Tuskegee, Alabama and in the nation." The major concern about that "is the fact that the Experiment involved men who were inflicted with syphilis, a dreaded disease. It was important that we set the record straight and make sure there was no confusion about the connection to this disease being studied at that time in Tuskegee, Alabama. "(See Appendix 1 for list of TAI Chapters).

The essential fact was that these African American military pilots had all their military flying training at Tuskegee Army Air Field, Tuskegee, Alabama. Thus, the consensus was that the best name for the keeping of the legacy was the name of Tuskegee Airmen. "Thus, from then onwards in 1972 and until today, we are known as the Tuskegee Airmen." As Lt. Col. Mann recalls it, "As a member of this early association, the cost for dues was $2.00." Today, the cost of membership in the TAI varies around $75.00 annually in some of the chapters. The membership card of an "Associate" member, Patrick C. Coggins is displayed herein. There is an opportunity for anyone to become an "associate" member of the TAI, thus, fulfilling the dream of the Tuskegee Airmen that their legacy will be discussed and celebrated by generations long after they depart from this world.

Certificate of Membership

Patrick C. Coggins

1 June 2003
DATE

Brian Rhodes
PRESIDENT

The charter group and organization was initially established for the fighter pilots only. Later on, in the year 1972, it was decided to broaden the classification of membership to include first the bomber pilots and still later, the support personnel who included the ground crew that operated and serviced the airplanes, the doctors, nurses and medical staff. The Judge Advocate General personnel, mess hall (now called the Dining Facility) employees, motor pool, bandleaders, the Women's Auxiliary Corps or WACS, clerical and everyone that maintained or worked on the Tuskegee Army Air Field (TAAF) in Tuskegee, Alabama.

Lt. Col. Hiram E. Mann supported the broadening of the membership due to two very important issues. First, "The bomber pilots were well trained to fly airplanes, but were never allowed to go into combat despite their proven abilities and training on the same level of competence as their White counterparts and bomber pilots. This bothered me a lot and I am still upset about the pain and suffering these pilots had to endure at the hands of a segregated Army and Air Force who had difficulty integrating the military to allow Blacks to have access to every aspect of combat experience like their White bomber pilots."

The second group that really should be in the Tuskegee Airmen Incorporated (TAI) organization was the ground and support personnel. "It was also their efforts that contributed to the success of the pilots. Therefore, together we will do all we can to take care of the planes and keep them flying. In pilot jargon, we say 'it took about 10 people on the ground (support personnel) to keep one military airplane in the air."

A further reality is "there are only a few of the Original Tuskegee Airmen who will be able to carry on the legacy of the Tuskegee Airmen. Thus, Lt. Col. Mann said, "There are very few of us living and all of us who are alive are well over 80 years old. Most are in their 80s and a few in their 90s. When you look at us, you see faces that are no longer young. Yet, beneath the stares and the smiles is the heart and determination of each one of us to tell the story of how we became an original Tuskegee Airman."

Thus according to Lt. Col. Hiram Mann an Original Tuskegee Airman is:

> "Anyone, male and or female, Black and White, military and civilian, who served/worked at least one day on Tuskegee Army Air Field(TAAF): Or the Tuskegee Institute College Training Detachment(CTD) or any program stemming from or related to the Tuskegee Experience, between the years of 1941 and 1948, is by designation, an Original Tuskegee Airman."

Keep in mind that this definition not only includes pilots who graduated from The Tuskegee Airmen Flight Program (i.e. fighter pilots and bomber pilots), "It also consists of those pilot trainees who were admitted to the flight training program and either left on their own or were officially eliminated from the program and never received their wings." This point is critical for the `many individuals who have been and will continue to produce pictures in flying gear and papers that say they were admitted to the Tuskegee Airmen Flying School in the 1940s. "However, the critical issue is whether they really graduated from the Tuskegee Army Air Field Advanced Flying Training School. According to my research and the words of many Tuskegee Airmen that were interviewed for this book, about 992 pilots graduated and received their wings from the Tuskegee Army Air Field Flying School. "While there is no exact count of total numbers who entered the flying school, it is estimated that this figure represented one third (the wash out rate was a much higher percentage) of those who completed the program that means that two thirds were washed out. Of 992 pilots trained, 450 were single engine fighter pilots who went overseas, 66 were killed in combat and 32 were shot down and became prisoners of war".

HOW TO KNOW WHO IS AN ORIGINAL TUSKEGEE AIRMAN

Another controversial issue is the fact that many individuals are claiming to be part of the " Tuskegee Airmen" experience and to have had fighter pilot experience as a Tuskegee Airman and the famous "Red Tails" that were very successful as fighter pilots. These pilots were feared by the German enemies and revered by their American counterparts both White and Black. According to the visual depiction in the HBO special on the Tuskegee Airmen and also from my interviews with many original Tuskegee Airmen fighter pilots including Ret. Lt. Col. Hiram E. Mann US Air Force , Lt. Col. Leo R Gray, Captain Charles Hill, Lt. John B. Turner, all of whom I have personally met, listened to their claims and verified their official status by reviewing the published list in the book by Lynn Homan and Thomas Reilly (2001) with 42 pages listing the original Tuskegee Airmen who satisfactory completed the Military Flying Training Program at the Tuskegee Air Field (TAAF), Tuskegee, Alabama.

Lt. Col. Hiram E. Mann said that "one of our members has compiled a data base on a compact disc with more than 14,900 names of people who are qualified to be, or could have been, Tuskegee Airmen. There were also others who were not directly associated with flying like hospital staff, doctors, nurses, dentists, ordinance and motor pool personnel, billeting, band members, clerical and administrative cadres required to run a military installation. This list of individuals also includes and embraces the White officers and civilian employees who trained us to fly the planes and performed some of the functions mentioned before." Lt. Col. Hiram E. Mann said that based on this definition, "Col. Frederick Von Kimble, the second TAAF Commander who was staunch segregationists would still be eligible to be an "Original Tuskegee Airmen,". Col. Noel F. Parrish, the third and final commander at the TAAF was a supportive military leader who demonstrated public and private respect for the abilities and flying skills of the Black pilots. I believe that it was due in part to his urging and support of us, that we were able to see combat duty in the air during the war of World War II. Even after the war ended, he joined our National Tuskegee Airmen organization and was one of the first Caucasian/ White Original Tuskegee Airmen. His widow, Dr. Florence Parrish St. John, continues to attend the national conventions of the TAI, even after Col. Noel F. Parrish's death in 1987 and her subsequent marriage to General St. John."

FORMATION OF THE NATIONAL ORGANIZATION'S LOCAL CHAPTERS

The national organization was formed in 1972 to make sure that legacy of the achievement is secured in the minds of future generations. In addition, this organization desired to "provide motivation for all of our youth especially minority youth to learn from our achievements and see that they can enjoy a successful career in the many careers in aviation". Thus, there are categories of members that were approved, namely 1) The first or "Original Tuskegee Airmen" that meets the definition that was set forth in this book. This means that these individuals, directly or indirectly, were involved for one day or more in learning to fly as pilots, or were involved in one or more support tasks such as ground crew or administrative services such as medical services, clerical or technical services. 2) The "Associate Tuskegee Airman" is a person who did not participate in or was not an "Original Tuskegee Airman", but someone who is committed to supporting the Tuskegee Airmen Incorporated (TAI) in all of its efforts to perpetuate the valuable African American history, which was an integral part of the military and American history. The "Associate" member is able to get involved in the local chapter in their hometown and the national organization in carrying out educational programs that celebrate the rich history of the Tuskegee Airmen. Col. Parrish's widow, Dr. Florence Parrish St. John, remarried and married Retired General St. John. They both joined as Associate Members and are currently involved in the association. 3) There is a third category of membership "Honorary Tuskegee Airmen". This category of membership is bestowed on those individuals who have supported the organization. According to Lt. Col. Mann, USAF, Ret. some of the honorary members include Lena Horne, the late Ella Fitzgerald, Joe Lewis, and all Presidents Ronald Reagan, William Clinton, George Bush and current President George Bush have been designated as honorary Tuskegee Airmen. This special membership group provides validation and recognition for the Tuskegee Airmen's legacy.

The fourth category of membership is the fact that there is a "Heritage Group" whose purpose is to perpetuate the legacy of the "Original Tuskegee Airmen". These individuals are direct descendants of the Tuskegee Airmen. The national organization hopes that this group commits to the maintenance of the history of the Tuskegee Airmen because of their closeness to the Original Tuskegee Airmen. It is important that this "Heritage Group" would see fit in their hearts and heads to continue the military legacy that their family members have achieved during World War II. As Ret. Lt. Col. Hiram Mann said, "this 'Heritage Group' can sustain the legacy of the Tuskegee Airmen through speaking engagements, attendance at national and local meetings and activities, to mention a few things." The fifth group is

"Life" Members who are eligible upon the payment of the required fees and approval by the national organization. The 2007 membership card is the evidence of the fact that Lt. Col. Hiram E. Mann, USAF, Retired is an active member of the Tuskegee Airmen International Incorporated (TAI). This also means that Lt. Col. Hiram E. Mann, USAF, Ret. can participate in all of the deliberations at meetings and conventions, provide input and suggestions to the national organization and represent the local chapter and the national organization when required. A copy of the recent design of the national membership card is included for Ret. Lt. Col. Hiram .E. Mann and this cards shows that he is a member of the General Daniel "Chappie" James Chapter. A full listing of the TAI Chapters throughout the United States of America is provided in the Appendix I.

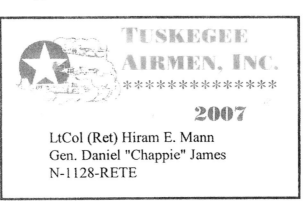

It is important to note that this author is an "Associate" member. This chapter includes both the membership card here of an "Original Tuskegee Airmen" and the membership card of an "Associate Tuskegee Airman" member. It is recommended that historians, former military personnel, and all ethnic groups join the National Tuskegee Airmen Incorporated (TAI). Even Jamaicans, Haitians, and other citizens of several countries sent Pilot Trainees to the Tuskegee Army Air Field, Tuskegee, Alabama (TAAF) to learn how to fly combat airplanes. Among the members who were "Original Tuskegee Airmen", "it is our desire to see that all good meaning people of all races in our nation join in celebrating and perpetuating the legacy of the Tuskegee Airmen whether they are card carrying members or not."

THE CONFUSION ABOUT WHO WERE THE ORIGINAL TUSKEGEE AIRMEN THAT WERE TRAINED AS PART OF THE TUSKEGEE AIRMEN

Ret. Lt. Col. Mann puts it well when he said, "The time has come to set the record straight about the pilots. There was 1) the single engine fighter pilots who were trained on the following aircrafts Piper Cub J-3, Stearman PT-17, Vultee BT-13, and North American At-6. These planes were used during WWII for the different missions. 2) Then you had the multiengine or medium bomber pilots who were trained on the North American AT-10 aircraft. 3) The support personnel for each of the single engine and multiengine planes did everything to keep the planes in the air in good efficiency and maintenance. They were the pilot's eyes and ears on the outside and inside of various systems of the plane. It took about 10 ground personnel to service and keeps a single plane running. (This figure includes *"all personnel"* including, mechanics, maintenance, medical technicians, nurses and medical staff, medics and others.) The pilots will always respect them and thank them for their efficient work on the ground."

CONGRESSIONAL GOLD MEDAL IN 2007

On a pleasant note, it is important to share that the Congress of the United States of America and President George W. Bush approved and awarded the Original Tuskegee Airmen, one of the highest honors and recognition that can be earned by citizens, namely, the "Congressional Gold Medal" on March 29, 2007, at a ceremony in the Capitol Rotunda, Washington, D.C. President Bush was joined by Congressional leaders of both parties and other dignitaries, including Retired Army General Colin Powell, in presenting the Congressional Gold Medal to the Tuskegee Airmen including Col. Charles E. McGee, Lt. Col. Lee Archer, Lt. Col. Alexander Jefferson, Lt. Col. Harry T. Stewart, Lt. Col. Woodie Crockett, and Capt. Roscoe C. Brown, Jr., and Lt. Col. Hiram E. Mann. About 300 Original Tuskegee Airmen and their guests attended the ceremony.

Capt. Brown accepted the Medal for the Tuskegee Airmen Incorporated (TAI). The original medal will be permanently displayed in the Smithsonian Institution. Each Original Tuskegee Airman (OTA) present received a replica of the medal. Ret. Capt. Roscoe Brown Jr. said, "We are overjoyed and proud today, and I think America is proud today." President Bush said, "For all the unreturned salutes and unforgivable indignities...I salute you for your service to the United States of America." This tribute and honor is on behalf of the over thousands of African American men and women who participated in the Tuskegee Airmen Experience at Tuskegee Army Air Field at Tuskegee, Alabama during the early 1940's.

It was President Franklin D. Roosevelt who had overruled his top generals and ordered that such a program to train Black pilots begin at Tuskegee Institute in Tuskegee, Alabama. During World War II, these Tuskegee pilots distinguished themselves by painting the tails of their planes red. Thus, many of the White pilots, the German enemies and the allied forces knew the Tuskegee pilots only as the "Red Tails" fighter pilots.

Hundreds of these Tuskegee Airmen had to overcome blatant racism and discrimination from White commanders and military personnel who persisted with the perception that they did not possess the intelligence, courage and patriotism to do what was being asked of them, including flying an airplane and fighting the feared enemy of the free world, the Nazi Germans. Yes, indeed as Ret. Lt. Col. Hiram Mann said, "Several hundreds of the Tuskegee Airmen saw fierce combat throughout Europe, the Mediterranean and North Africa on missions that included taking out enemy targets and escorting bombers on missions to destroy enemy targets. The record shows that less than 100 died in combat, others were captured as prisoners of war while others were injured defending the flag of the United States of America and the freedom of the world."

However, a significant message was echoed on this glorious day of March 29, 2007 by Ret. Army General Colin Powell who thanked the Tuskegee Airmen for "paving the way for his career". "You caused America to look in the mirror of its soul and you showed America that there was nothing a Black person could not do."

Since the end of World War II, the Tuskegee Airmen believe that their accomplishment warranted some special recognition by Congress and the military branches of the United States of America. The intrinsic pain endured in the minds of the Tuskegee pilots who knew that the very members in the walls of the United States government including the Congress were ambivalent at best about their support for the training of African Americans as fighter pilots in the United States Army Air Force in the 1940s. Rumors of the Congressional Gold Medal being awarded started under the Presidency of William Clinton. The Congressional Gold Medal was awarded in 2007 as an important national recognition for all of the pilots and ground personnel who participated in the original Tuskegee Airmen Experience from 1939 to 1948 at the Tuskegee Army Air Field (TAAF) in Tuskegee, Alabama.

CHAPTER V

The Tuskegee Airmen Experience of the 1940s

How Did The Tuskegee Airmen Experience Begin?

THE TUSKEGEE AIRMEN Experience began in 1940's as a government funded Experience to prove that "Blacks" could not fly airplanes. It is important to place this Tuskegee Airmen Experience in a period of this country's history, marked by blatant segregation in the United States of America and even in the military where Blacks were attempting to gain entrance into the Army Air Corps since World War I. Senators Harry Swartz of Wyoming and Styles Bridges of New Hampshire were among a few of those members in Congress who championed the cause of the "Blacks" interested in serving as pilots in the Army Air Corps.

In 1939, two pilots from the National Airman's Association comprised of Black pilots met with Senator Harry Truman from Missouri and persuaded him to sponsor a bill that allowed Black pilots who met the requirements to serve in the Civilian Pilot Training Program. On April 3, 1939, Senator Truman along with other supportive senators passed Public Law 18. The new law that provided for large-scale expansion of the Army Air Corps. One section of the law authorized the establishment of training programs in Black Colleges, also to employ Blacks in various areas of Army Air Corps Services. (Communication Committee, HQDA, SACC, Pentagon, Washington, D.C, 1989)

The Tuskegee Institute in Tuskegee, Alabama was designated as a training center for Black pilots. The Army Air Corps submitted a plan to the War Department for an "Experience" which was comprised of an all Black Fighter Pilot Squadron of about thirty-three pilots. The War Department accepted the general intent of the plan and its location, at the Tuskegee Institute, Tuskegee, Alabama.

FORMATION OF THE 99ᵀᴴ PURSUIT SQUADRON

On January 16, 1941, the War Department of the United States of America announced the formation of an all Black unit, the 99th Pursuit Squadron, to be trained at Tuskegee Institute, Tuskegee, Alabama. After the selection of the first men, the training began in earnest. However, there were two major issues, namely, the first issue was the lack of an airfield at Tuskegee Institute, Alabama and secondly, the process of developing a training program for the Tuskegee Airmen. Thus, 400 or more men of the 99th Pursuit Squadron arrived at Tuskegee Institute, and devoted much of their energy to the construction of the airfield. The photo, which follows, shows the early construction of the Tuskegee Airfield in Tuskegee, Alabama. This construction of the airfield was an essential milestone in the successful training of the African Americans who were in becoming fighter pilots as part of the Armed Forces of the United States of America.

Tuskegee Airfield, Tuskegee, Alabama

CONSTRUCTION OF THE TUSKEGEE AIRFIELD

The following aerial picture shows the original site where the Tuskegee Army Air Field was constructed. This airfield became the training site for the "Original Tuskegee Airmen" who trained as pilots and went on to fight in World War II. This Air Field was later called the Tuskegee Army Air Field, Tuskegee, Alabama. Of course this facility became one of the primary locations for the training of the African American cadets who later became known as the Tuskegee Airmen. The picture below shows the ground breaking ceremony and the White commanders of the Tuskegee Army Air Field who provided the initial training and leadership, not only for the construction of the airfield, but also for the training of the "Tuskegee Pilots". As the Tuskegee pilots often stated, "This facility was the proving ground as to whether African Americans can fly airplanes. Despite some delays the ground breaking did happen."

Groundbreaking ceremony at Tuskegee Field, Tuskegee, Alabama.

GROUND BREAKING FOR THE TUSKEGEE AIRFIELD

The major issue confronting the men in the Tuskegee Pilot Training Program was receiving adequate pilot training. The fact that there were no high-ranking Black officers to train them worried the new recruits. It meant that they had to be trained by White officers in the Air Corps Flight Training programs. Indeed, eleven White senior officers were assigned to train the 429 enlisted men and 47 officers as part of this first Military Black Flying School at Tuskegee Institute, Tuskegee, Alabama.

Ground breaking visitors at ceremony, Tuskegee, Alabama

The previous picture shows those individuals who were at the groundbreaking ceremony for launching the Tuskegee Army Air Field at Tuskegee, Alabama. It should be noted that there were loud protests from the Whites who lived nearby in Tuskegee, Alabama. For many Whites, this new Air Field was seen as bringing in a high concentration of African Americans who will then be living on the base, as well as in nearby communities.

THE FIRST GRADUATION CEREMONY AND PROMOTION OF THE FIRST CAPTAIN

The army was at least sensitive to the concern of the Tuskegee Airmen who pushed for the promotion of Captain Benjamin O. Davis, Jr. who could relate in a respectful and sensitive way to the African American enlisted personnel. Furthermore, in March 7, 1942, the first graduation ceremony of the 99th Pursuit Squadron was held and the Army promoted Captain Benjamin O. Davis, Jr. to Lieutenant Colonel. He had proven his stripes as able and competent and led the flight-training program with distinction. This promotion was hailed as a positive step in demonstrating to the African American community that its enlisted men were talented and qualified. The information that follows describes the very trying circumstances that the personnel experienced in the Tuskegee Airmen Experience as embodied in the 99th Pursuit Squadron and Air Base detachment.

Graduating Class of 1943 Tuskegee Airmen

GRADUATING CLASS OF 1943, TUSKEGEE AIRMEN

Following the graduation class in March, 1943, the picture depicts the euphoria, which was high as these African American men earned wings as pilots.

This represented the second step in breaking the color barrier by being accepted in the Army Air Corps and completing the training as fighter pilots. Thus, the "Black Eagles" as the Black pilots called they, became a reality when on August 24, 1942, Lt. Colonel Benjamin Davis Jr. took full command of the 99th Pursuit Squadron, ending the exclusive leadership of White commanding officers over the now 99th Pursuit Squadron. This transfer of power and leadership took place with little or no incident. This was another notch in breaking the color barrier in the military. On April 15, 1943, there was excitement in the air, but all was not well, though, the segregated Black unit under Lt. Colonel Benjamin Davis, Jr. command, headed for the war zone in Europe. It should be noted that this Squadron of Black fighter pilots arrived in North Africa later that month, and went on to serve in Europe.

THE ULTIMATE VINDICATION FOR THE RACE AND TUSKEGEE AIRMEN

"The 99th Pursuit Squadron which was later assigned to the 332nd Fighter Group fought throughout the Mediterranean and European countries and became respected pilots. If we had failed, there would have been a termination of the pilot training program. If the 187 enlisted personnel and five Cadets failed, then the War Department, the doubting Senators, and the nation would have lambasted us as being incapable of flying airplanes. We had proven the government and others wrong." The final vindication was on the day Lt. Charles B. Hall became the first Black pilot to shoot down an enemy aircraft on July 21, 1943.

Charles B. Hall

On July 21, 1943, Lt. Hall while escorting B-25 bomber over Italy on his eighth mission, two FockeWulf (Fw 190) were seen approaching after the bombers had dropped their bombs on the enemy target at Castelvetrano Airfield.

He quickly maneuvered in the space between the bombers and enemy fighters and turned aside the Fw190s. Hall fired on the Fw190s and made a direct hit and one aircraft crashed on the ground. That display of extraordinary flying earned him the respect of White pilots and others in his squadron for his skills and boldness. Lt. Charles B. Hall was among the first Tuskegee pilots to receive the Distinguished Flying Cross for being the first Black pilot to shoot down a German Aircraft. This achievement was the third step in breaking the entrenched prejudice and stereotypes that existed in the Army Air Force and the military in general. As Lt. Col. Hiram E. Mann recounted, "We made believers of everyone in the world, and thus, you can see that the failure of this Flying Experience would have had far-reaching implications for the struggle of equal justice for African Americans (Blacks)." It is clear that as we examine the drive for equality and freedom from discrimination experienced by African Americans, the success achieved from the Tuskegee Airmen Experience sent a clear message to the "White" society and the "White" power structure in the military that there can be no rational reason for discrimination against the African American pilots and enlisted service personnel. They had many successful missions in terms of protecting the bombers. The myth that Blacks cannot fly was proven to be unsupportable." As Lt. Col. Hiram E. Mann said, "We did not lose any bombers we escorted to enemy aircraft. We were too good for the enemy. We were very well prepared as fighter pilots." These words represent the essence of the character of the Tuskegee Airmen who had a real sense of purpose, a vivid determination to succeed, coupled with a deep sense of courage in the pursuit of their military service.

WHAT WAS THE DIFFERENCE BETWEEN THE 99TH PURSUIT SQUADRON AND THE 332ND FIGHTER GROUP?

August 1943 was the day of the departure of Lt. Colonel Benjamin O. Davis Jr. from the 99th Pursuit Squadron to assume command responsibility for the newly formed 332nd Fighter Group. This all Black unit comprised of Black pilots and service members from the 99th, 100th, 301st and 302nd Fighter Squadron which became the 332nd Fighter Group. Lt. Col. Hiram E. Mann said that the "332nd Fighter Group was formed because of the excellent flying skills of the 99th Pursuit Squadron, that showed Black pilots can fly well." Many enlisted African American men were sent to Selfridge Air Field located in Michigan, while others were sent to Tuskegee Air Base, in Tuskegee,

Alabama. "We had different hats to wear because there were so few of us; however, they started allowing more cadets to be trained in 1943." This push for more Black pilots resulted in the 332nd Fighter Group being formed. "I believe that the 'US Army,' started accepting more Blacks in the 99th Pursuit Squadron of the Tuskegee Airmen Experience. They proved that they could fly and run airfield operations with the same efficiency as their White pilots and ground support personnel counterparts.

Lt. Hiram E. Mann in flight gear.

According to Ret. Lt. Col. Hiram E. Mann, "This was a typical day on the European Theater while we were stationed at Ramitelli, Italy in 1945. The expression on my face is not of worry, but rather, the intensity and reflection on each flying mission and the numerous details that I had to remember about the targets and the enemy terrain".

REFLECTIONS ON THE FORMATION OF THE 332ND FIGHTER GROUP

It is important to reflect on the formation of the 332nd Fighter Group which was activated on October 13,1942 at the Tuskegee Air Field, Tuskegee, Alabama, in accordance with a letter from the Adjutant General's Office, Washington, D.C. As Ret. Lt. Col. Hiram E. Mann said, "The 332nd consisted of the 100th Fighter Squadron, the 301st Fighter Squadron and the 302nd Fighter Squadron. In order to ensure that the 332nd was at full strength, additional personnel were brought in from the 318th Air base Squadron, Tuskegee, Alabama and the 8th Aviation Squadron, McDill Field, Tampa, Florida. On October 19, 1942, the 332nd Fighter Group was fully constituted and became the second official "Negro Fighter Group" following the 99th Pursuit Squadron, which was organized and activated on March 21, 1941. The 99th Pursuit Squadron, operated as an independent unit until June 29, 1944 when it was transferred to and merged with and was fully integrated into the 332nd Fighter Group.

On November 30, 1942, Lt. Col. Sam Westbrook was appointed Commanding officer of the 332nd Fighter Group, the number of enlisted personnel reached 948 persons. Thus on March 27, 1943 the 332nd Fighter group departed from Tuskegee Army Air Field for its new home at Selfridge Field, Michigan. After being fully settled in at Selfridge Field, a month or so later, on April 13, 1943, the 100th Fighter Squadron and the 301st were relocated to Oscoda, Michigan. Col. Robert R Selway succeeded Lt. Col. Sam Westbrook as commanding officer.[33]

In the midst of these shifts, the 332nd Fighter Group continued its intensive combat training in anticipation of being sent overseas for combat assignment in World War II. At the height of this combat training, a critical decision was made to replace the White officers with the first Black officer named Col. Benjamin O. Davis, Jr. who assumed the position as commander of the 332nd Fighter Group on October 7, 1943. The group was able to benefit from the overseas experience that Col. Benjamin O. Davis, Jr. had with the 99th Pursuit Squadron that was fighting overseas since April 2, 1943 as part of the 12nd Air Force in the Mediterranean Theater of Operations.

On January 3, 1944, during a very cold spell, the 332nd Fighter Group departed from the United States for Europe. "I can remember the day of January 29, 1944 when the first boat containing Tuskegee pilots and other personnel and me arrived at Taranto, Italy. That same day I witnessed the first campsite with other personnel into World War II. Being in the combat zone was a delight for all of us who had trained hard to perform well as fighter pilots and other support personnel."

"Yes, we missed home but there was no time to think about that, we had to get busy preparing for briefings and other requirements for combat wherever we were to be sent by the commanding officers."

Tuskegee Pilots at Walterboro Army Air Field. L to R: Rupert Johnson, Robert Murdic, Hiram Mann, George Lynch, and Lincoln Hudson.

"This picture is important to me," said Lt. Col. Mann, "as I stand in the center with two fighter pilots flanking me on my right and left. This was one of the many moments, when I realized that my survival, efficiency, and accomplishments as a pilot were linked intricately to the souls, experiences and mutual efficiency of my peers and fellow pilots. I knew that my success was dependent on the positive and reliable expertise and relationships that I maintained with my fellow pilots and the ground crew."

DISTINGUISHED COMBAT RECORD OF "TUSKEGEE AIRMEN"

The discussion of the Tuskegee pilots will be incomplete without careful documentation of the combat record of the "Tuskegee Airmen" during World

War II. While there are many figures and accounts available, those provided by Charles E. Francis (1988) were the best documentation of the accomplishments of Tuskegee's Black Pilots.[34] Francis' (1988) records are generally accepted based on my interview of twelve Tuskegee Air personnel, who were a part of the Tuskegee Flying Experience. The aircrafts operated in combat were P-39, P-40, and P-47 and P-51. It should be noted that these airplanes were very efficient and reliable for maneuvers in enemy territory. (Black Knights by Homan and Reilly, 1997).[35] As Lt. Col. Hiram Mann said, "The reason for the achievement while spectacular should not be overshadowed by the critical fact that we the "Original Tuskegee pilots" were well trained by the best instructors who often told us that we are well prepared with long hours of flying. The rest of the process is execution that is grounded in efficiency, following set procedures we faced at that time in Europe and using the God given skills to win the battles with the enemy that we faced at that time in Europe."(Charles Frances, 1988). The combat record that follows is clear and convincing evidence of the extraordinary flying skills and combat experience that the "Red Tails" demonstrated on the battlefield thousands of miles away from their homes in the United States of America.

COMBAT RECORD OF BLACK AIRMEN
(June 9, 1945)*

	Destroyed	Damaged	Total
Aircraft Aerial	111	25	136
Aircraft (ground)	150	123	273
Barges and Boats	16	24	40
Boxcars and Other Rolling Stock	58	561	619
Building & Factories	0	23	23
Gun Emplacements	3	0	3
Destroyers	1	0	1
Horse drawn Vehicles	15	100	115
Motor transports	6	81	87
Power Transformers	3	2	5
Locomotives	57	69	126
Radar Installations	1	8	9
Tanks on flat cars	0	7	7
Oil & ammunitions Damps	2	0	2
Total	423	1023	1446

The above chart shows a small taste of the achievement of the Tuskegee pilots. The Tuskegee Pilots destroyed or damaged over 1446 military targets.

OTHER ACCOMPLISHMENTS*

Total Missions	12th Air Force	1,267
Total Missions	15th Air Force	311
Total Sorties	12th Air Force	6,381
Total Sorties	15th Air Force	9,152
Grand Total Missions		1,578
Grand Total Sorties		15,533
Total number of pilots sent overseas		450
Total number of pilots graduated at Tuskegee		992

These other accomplishments indicate that the Tuskegee Airmen were actively involved in World War II and actively fought the Germans and other enemies. The data also suggest that the Tuskegee Airmen were busy fighting in many settings of the war in Europe during World War II. The meritorious awards that follow in the table below show that the Tuskegee Airmen also known as the "Red Tails" were a well decorated flying unit with the Legion of Merit, the Silver Star, the Soldier Medal, at least 8 Purple Hearts, 95 Distinguished Flying Crosses, 14 Bronze Medals and 744 Air Medals and Clusters.

AWARDS*

Legion of Merit	1
Silver Star	1
Soldier Medal	2
Purple Heart	8
Distinguished Flying Cross	95
Bronze Medal	14
Air Medals and Clusters	744

(Number of Distinguished Flying Crosses and other medals awarded to Black pilots, according to Charles E. Francis, the Tuskegee Airmen, 1988)[36]

The above figures are evidence as to why the United States Military had no choice but to integrate the military. Breaking the color barrier in the military was slow, but the Tuskegee Airmen success provided the impetus for the "Road to Brown in 1954" and the Civil Rights marches of the 1950's and 1960's. Colin Powell's appointment as Chief of Staff of the United States of America military was a final vindication for people of African descent in the United States. Like the Tuskegee Air Pilots and Personnel, he had proven himself to be capable, competent and an ardent protector of the flag of the United States of America.

THE SPECIAL CITATION OF THE 332ND FIGHTER GROUP

This special citation from the Headquarters Fifteenth Air Force US Army was dated 9 August 1945. The citation that follows describes the depth and importance of the recognition of the 332nd Fighter Group, which comprised of the Original Tuskegee Airmen pilots of World War II.

RESTRICTED

HEADQUARTERS FIFTEENTH AIR FORCE
APO 520   US ARMY

ORDERS }   9 August 1945

NUMBER   3674

CITATION OF UNIT

Under the provisions of Circular No. 333, War Department, 1943 and Circular No. 73, MPO, 12 May 1945, the following unit is cited for outstanding performance of duty in armed conflict with the enemy.

332ND FIGHTER GROUP. For outstanding performance of duty in armed conflict with the enemy. On 23 March 1945, the group was assigned the mission of escorting heavy bombardment type aircraft attacking the vital Daimler-Banz Tank Assembly Plant at Berlin, Germany. Realizing the strategic importance of the and fully cognizant of the amount of enemy resistance to be expected and the long range to be covered, the ground crews worked tirelessly and with enthusiasm to have their aircraft at the peak of mechanical condition to insure the success of the operation. On 24 March 1945, fifty-nine (59) P-51 type aircraft were airborne and set course for the rendezvous with the bomber formation. Through superior navigation and maintenance of strict flight discipline the group formation reached the bomber formation at the designated time and place. Nearing the target, approximately twenty-five (25) enemy aircraft were encountered which included ME-262's, which launched relentless attacks in a desperate effort to break up and destroy the bomber formation. Displaying outstanding courage, aggressiveness and combat technique, the group immediately engaged the enemy formation in aerial combat. In the ensuing engagement that continued over the target area, the gallant pilots of the 332nd Fighter Group battled against the enemy fighters to pervent the break up of the bomber formation and thus jeopardizing the successul completion of this vitally important mission. Through their superior skill and determination, the group destroyed three (3) enemy aircraft, probably destroyed three (3) and damaged three (3). Among their claims were eight (8) of the highly rated enemy jet propelled aircraft with no losses sustained by the 332nd Fighter Group. Leaving the target area and enroute to base after completion of the primary task, aircraft of the group conducted strafing attacks against enemy ground installations and transportation with outstanding success. By the conspicuous gallantry, professional skill and determination of the pilots, together with the technical skill and devotion to duty of the ground personnel, the 332nd Fighter Group has reflected great credit upon itself and the Armed Forces of the United States of America.

A Presidential Unit Citation that was given by the War Department on 8 August 1945 was very significant since it was intended as a special recognition for the entire 332nd Fighter Group that distinguished itself as outstanding fighter pilots during World War II. This citation, while special for the 332nd Fighter Group, was also important as a Nation as it focused on the contributions of other African Americans who served in other branches of the military services of the United States of America.[37]

PRESIDENT TRUMAN'S EXECUTIVE ORDER

The Tuskegee Airmen Experience provided evidence, which exposed the depths of racism in the United States. It represented the convincing evidence that for Black men and women serving and defending the flag was not enough to gain equal treatment and protection in the military and their hometown. Despite the open discrimination in a society steeped in institutional racism, the Tuskegee Airmen and other military personnel who participated in the Experience, found a way to make a difference in their individual lives, while defending the United States of America. As Lt. Col. Hiram Mann said, "We understood that failure was not an option, we worked hard helping each other and continued to push each day for equal treatment as enlisted military personnel." The achievements of the Tuskegee Airmen came at a critical time in the history of the United States. It was one of the many demonstrative efforts of African Americans in the military, which led President Truman to declare the military must be integrated in 1948. President Truman said, "No person serving in the military should be discriminated against based on their race or national origin." Thus, we see the first major institutional push for equality in the United States Military services.

President Truman's Executive Order 9981 laid the foundation for more sweeping changes in the Civil Rights of African Americans in other areas and institutions in the United States. As Lt. Col. Benjamin O Davis Jr. said, "The Tuskegee Airmen's contributions are beginning to influence the general population of this country to understand how the Tuskegee Airmen revolutionized the military operations and relationships in the military." Truman's order prohibited discrimination against African Americans and others solely on race and ethnicity.

"The Tuskegee Airmen were special because they knew how to fight to be an American. They knew what it meant to fight to be treated as a person with dignity and the same ability as others known for flying an airplane. The Tuskegee Airmen are the epitome of the American Dream. Their childhood daydreams of flying transcended into the making of American war heroes, which transformed world history."

As Mann often said, "The accomplishments of the Tuskegee Airmen are not simply the accomplishments of African Americans for footnotes in African American history. In fact, these accomplishments are part and parcel of American military history, American history and World history." By telling the story of the accomplishments of the Tuskegee Airmen, it is one way to ensure that the history and contributions of all Americans are included in the history books, including the discourse of World War II. This inclusion of contributions of the Tuskegee Airmen will ensure that history is not disjointed, but rather, it is inclusive of stories and events that are factual and historically accurate at all times. The key point of contention is a rather fundamental thought that African American history is American history. Therefore, the inclusion of the Tuskegee Airmen achievements in World War II is also simply the history of the United States of America in the 1940s and during World War II.

"Try not to become a person of success alone, try to become a person of value"
(Albert Einstein)

CHAPTER VI

Ret. Lt. Col. Hiram E. Mann's Life Before and After the Military

A Dream of Serving in the Military

ALTHOUGH THE MILITARY was not always easy for Ret. Lt. Col. Mann, it was voluntary. As you will see from the story in this book, Ret. Lt. Col. Mann had several options to pursue in his life, but he decided to join the military so that he could fly for his country in the midst of World War II and the dire conflicts in Europe.

Lt. Col. Mann said, "As Hitler was taking over various parts of Europe; he did not want him to come to America". Lt. Col. Mann said, "I could not imagine my wife, my mother, or my grandmother wanting me to join the military." Furthermore, "I was convinced that I did not want to be on the ground and serve as an infantry soldier, nor, did I want to be a sailor." "I remember having numerous discussions with my wife who argued against my flying and let me tell you, her objections were very loud." "I had to follow my own mind and to pursue the dream that I have had since I was a child and that was to fly an airplane." "As I remembered those trying and critical days in my life, I was torn with my decision. Because there was no military draft at that time, it meant that I was volunteering with my own free-will. I was convinced that I could best serve my country by joining the pilot training program of the military."

DEALING WITH REJECTION

In order "to carry out my decision I did the research and found out the appropriate address and wrote a letter to the War Department requesting information on how I could get into the military flying training program." "I was very excited to get a response from the War Department. However, little did I know that the news would not be good news? I readily opened the envelope and after a few lines I realized that this was a letter of rejection." "The letter stated and I quote, *"There were no facilities to train Negroes to fly in any branch of the military service."*

The fact of the matter was that before "the war started, early in 1941, there were no military places for training of the Black enlisted men who were interested in becoming pilots." As Ret. Lt Col. Hiram Mann said "I was angry, disappointed and concerned about what to do so the first thing I did was to ball up the letter and threw it away." Later on, some months had gone by and in speaking with some friends, I was told that there were going to be a special training program for the preparation of the Blacks "to fly at Tuskegee Institute, Tuskegee, Alabama. After checking around, I was able to confirm that such a program would be established to train Blacks to fly (to prove that Blacks couldn't fly)." "I was delighted at the news and decided to apply the second time." After receiving the first letter of rejection, I did not realize that one of the requirements was to be a college graduate. I had only my high school diploma at the time. So "I went back and reviewed the original requirements and did confirm that in addition to rejecting me, the letter also said, *"For anyone to get into a flying training program one must have completed a minimum of two years of college, be single ."*

"I was baffled and had a long discussion with my family and other members of the community. To my surprise they, too, agreed that maybe one of the reasons I was rejected was that I was married and was not a college graduate. As the war progressed they dropped the two of the key restrictions, namely, 1) The applicant had to have completed a minimum of two years in college and 2) Be single, that is, be unmarried." For me the biggest hurdles were that if anyone passed the rugged mental and physical examination they could get into the program. I felt strongly that I could pass the rugged mental, physical and other intelligence tests that they required for admissions to the pilot training school at Tuskegee Institute. I then applied again and this time my application was accepted for the flight training school at Tuskegee Institute, Tuskegee, Alabama. "

MAKING IT INTO THE MILITARY

"My application was received and 18 months later, I was ordered to report to be sworn into the US Army Air Corps. The procedure for the Blacks was different from the Whites, for many of them went directly into service within a week or two. The Blacks were sworn in and placed in the Army Enlisted Reserve Corps. My military time began on December 14, 1942. I did not go on active duty in the military until March 22, 1943."

THE EARLY LIFE OF HIRAM E. MANN

So one might ask: who was Hiram E. Mann before his military career? Hiram Eugene Mann was born on 23 May 1921, in New York City and raised in Cleveland, Ohio. "I was a depression baby and the only child born to Carrie Ann Matthews Mann and John Wesley Mann. My dad died in 1931, when I was only 9 years old. Thus, I was raised by a God-fearing Christian single-mother. My mother worked at several jobs to support us and these jobs included domestic worker, box factory worker and any other menial work to support us. This economic reality led my mother to rent a one–room with kitchen privileges since we could not afford a bigger apartment or a house. As my parents told me often that, we left Athens, Alabama to escape the southern oppression and domination for a better economic and life of equality and dignity. When I was only two years old, my parents moved to Cleveland, Ohio to be near other friends." I began kindergarten in 1926 at Bolton Elementary School and later attended Fairmont and Rawlings High Schools. "A critical turning point in my life was when I started to take trumpet lesson during the eighth grade at Rawlings Junior High School. This love for music and playing instruments, earned me the first seat trumpet in the school band and orchestra. I played trumpet in the Adolph Brandon Jazz (dance) band when I was in my senior year. Sadly, I had to give up my band activity as I took a job as a bellhop at the Hotel Cleveland in 1939. I was very happy when my guidance counselor told me that I will be able to graduate one half year ahead of the class I started with. The reality of graduating from Central Senior High School came in January 1939.

I continued working as a bellman at the Hotel Cleveland in February 1939. The take home pay at that time was $3.86 a week and (4 cents [1%] was withheld for social security). I was happy to work and help my mother and myself as I was contemplating going to college in the future. But, it was in this same year 1939 that my mother married to my stepfather whose name was James Blanton Simmons. This marriage took place just months before I left home to attend Philander Smith College in Little Rock, Arkansas."

"I resigned the bellman job in Cleveland, Ohio to go to College at Philander Smith College, in Little Rock, Arkansas. I was able to complete my first year at Philander Smith College, but, my grades were not to my liking. One reason was that this was my first experience of real freedom and being on my own and away from home. I was reminded by my best friend in high school, Thomas Reese, who was indirectly responsible for me going to Philander Smith College. He was a year older than me. He graduated from Central High in 1938, the year before me and attended Philander Smith College. One reason was that his cousin was Marquis Lafayette Harris who was the president of Philander Smith College. Thus, with his urging I wrote for and received a work-permit scholarship. After I was there for a while, I advanced to the position of a student assistant to a French Professor. The Professor told me that I had advanced French in high school in Cleveland. The Professor selected me to write and direct the 1939/40 play for the freshman Follies, "*A Wedding in Swing*" and the French play "*Le Medcin Malgre Lui*" by Molguire. I was also fortunate to be selected to be a part of the 1939/40 Ohio Club. The seven members of the Ohio Club included faculty and students." These experiences enhanced my interest in majoring in romance languages.

MY RELATIONSHIP WITH MY WIFE, KATHADAZA

Kathadaza Marie Henderson was born in New Orleans. She was raised in Chicago, Illinois. She transferred to Philander Smith College in 1939 as a junior from Chicago Junior College, in Chicago, Illinois. She earned work permit scholarship and worked in the College library.

"Our relationship started as brother and sister. Remember, I did not have a sibling. Thus, she became that sibling at first. She listened to my complaints about my girlfriend and my struggles in life with school and work- study. I cannot recall the specific circumstance when Kathadaza and I stopped being brother and sister and moved into the realm of boyfriend and girlfriend. After the end of the school year in May 1940, Kathadaza went home to Chicago and I went home to Cleveland. I began writing her more and more telling her passionately how I missed her and wanted to be with her for the rest of our lives. Her replies were equally stimulating and showed interest in each other. In the three months between May and September, when classes were scheduled to resume, we decided to elope instead of returning to Philander Smith College.

"Therefore, on September 3, 1940, Kathadaza and I were married after two semesters of my freshman year. This marriage was not compulsory. It was a Romeo and Juliet fairytale, which still goes on today. Of course, the rumor spread among our classmates and friends that our marriage was a shotgun marriage. However, as time passed, that rumor was proved false because we did not have a baby to show after several months. In fact, our first and only child was not born until 1949, or nine years after our marriage."

"Life as a married couple was financially a challenge for us. I went back to being a bellman to sustain my wife and me until I went into the military, two years later in 1943. When I shipped out in 1944, Kathadaza returned to Philander Smith College and graduated in May of 1945 with her bachelor's degree. When she graduated, I was unable to attend since I was stationed in Italy in the midst of World War II. After graduation, Kathadaza took a teaching job in Cleveland, Ohio and as an educator for the Ohio State Teachers Retirement System in August 01, 1974."

THE MILITARY DRAFT

Just before America entered World War II, the United States began drafting able-bodied males 18-37 years old for what was supposed to have been a single tour of active duty to establish a reserve military force as a ready source to deter aggression from our shores. "I was not drafted immediately because I was married. I later volunteered for pilot training to fulfill my childhood desire to fly military airplanes for my country. It was thought that working in the defense plants would be a cause for deferment from being drafted. Thus, I left the hotel to work at American Steel and Wire, Coke Plant, as a laborer. I did not care for shoveling cinders from the coke ovens and left to go to Wellman Bronze and Aluminum as a chipper. I chipped the rough edges from newly poured aluminum airplane wheels after they were shaken from their sand moulds. "I really did not like that job because it was a little too messy for me." "I reminisced about my previous job which required that he wear clean and well trimmed bellman's uniform and a sparkling White shirt." Therefore, I applied to different hotels. Although, I could not get my job back at Hotel Cleveland, I did get the opportunity to work at Holland Hotel, to once again, work as a bellman. Then while working there, I finally, made the transition to participate in the Tuskegee Pilot Training Program at the Tuskegee Army Air Field. Thus, I left my family and headed for Tuskegee, Alabama."

"After I was separated from the military service in 1947, I went back to college under the GI Bill, which paid him $90.00 a month. I went to College fulltime until I had to find a fulltime job working for the Federal Civil Service at the Finance Center of the Veterans Administration at the bottom of the employment scale, then a CAF 2 (the Federal grade scale was changed to General Service (GS) soon after I started."

"I held several other positions over the years, such as file clerk in the Veterans Administration, a fiscal accountant in the Liaison Officer at the Air Force academy, Office of Price Stabilization, and Army Ordinance which was later changed to the Defense Supply Agency, GS 4 thru GS 13, from Property Accountant until he received a position as a Supervisory Program Analyst (Management Analyst). When I started working full time, I attended school in the evening and did complete my lifelong goal, which included my Bachelor's degree from Fenn College, in Cleveland, Ohio in 1953. In 1957, after much hard work , I received my Masters Degree from John Carroll University, in Cleveland, Ohio."

However, "I can say that my dream of receiving a doctorate was realized on February 23, 2006 when Tuskegee University conferred the Honorary Doctor of Public Administration degrees on the fighter pilots in WW II as part of the famous Tuskegee Airmen. This was a moving day for my family and me. For me it was very nostalgic to look around the Tuskegee University campus and imagine my first graduation in 1944 as a cadet and pilot in the Tuskegee Institute Pilot Training Program. My return to Tuskegee University this time was happier and full of contentment for knowing that I and other African American pilots succeeded in flying; succeeded in completing flying school in the United States of America." "Like all of the other Tuskegee pilots we went into the Army Air Corps Reserve and succeeded in performing admirably as fighter pilots in several theaters in Europe and North Africa during World War II."

You can not expect roots to grow if you don't plant the
seed.
(Gary Byrd)

CHAPTER VII

Military Experience of Lt. Col. Hiram E. Mann

My Acceptance Letter in 1941

T HE PERSISTENT DREAM and desire of Hiram Mann was to become an Army Air Corps pilot. However, the road to Tuskegee Institute was bumpy at first. "In response to the Tuskegee Pilot Training requirements, he was determined to submit my first application to enlist in June 18, 1941. The stark reality of a real rejection was experienced by me when a letter dated June 19, 1941, W.L. Blum 1st. Lt. Ac Personnel Officer wrote to me (See Appendix II), Mr. Hiram E. Mann, living at 2484 E. 84th Street, Cleveland, Ohio and said:

> *"Your letter of June 18, 1941 making application for enlistment in the 99th*
> *Pursuit Squadron has been received. We are sorry to advise that the quota*
> *has been filled for sometime. However, we will keep your letter of applica-*
> *tion on file, and in the event any opening at a future date, we will advise*
> *you accordingly."*

(1st LT. W.L. Blum, June 19, 1941)
c. c. Tuskegee Institute,
Tuskegee, Alabama

This was a time of hurt and setback for me and my family whom were supportive of my application to pilot training. After speaking with my wife and family, I decided that I must pursue my goal of entering the Tuskegee Pilot

Training Program. With this goal in mind I carefully reviewed once more the Tuskegee Pilot training requirements," which stated:

The Requirements for Pilots
May 12, 1941
Division of Aeronautics
Tuskegee Institute, Tuskegee, Alabama

Overview
"It is the desire of Tuskegee Institute to accept for training students from other Negro Institutions not having a Civilian Pilot Training Program in order that as many of our youth as possible may avail themselves of this opportunity. There may be at your institution one or two students desiring to make aviation a career, and to them we extend an invitation to participate in our summer session private course of the Civilian Pilot Training Program. The summer session will start approximately June 15, 1941. We invite you to post this notice and select as many as two candidates from your student body. Subsistence (room, board and laundry) at Tuskegee Institute would approximate $100.00 during the course. Students meeting the requirements or otherwise prepared to pursue training, and who are accepted must report for training approximately June 15. Applications must be forwarded to Tuskegee Institute c/o G.L. Washington, Coordinator, CPT, Tuskegee Institute, Alabama, on or before June 1, 1941."

The qualifications that an applicant had to meet included the following:

Requirements

1. Those meeting requirements below first report to the nearest C.A.A medical examiner for physical examinations to secure the necessary student pilot certificate of commercial CPT grade. (This examination costs $5.00. Wire Tuskegee Institute, Division of Aeronautics for location of nearest medical examiner and application blanks if necessary).

2. They must be a citizen of the United States.

3. They must have reached their nineteenth but not their twenty-sixth birthday on or before July 1, 1941.

4. They must neither hold or have held a pilot certificate of private grade or higher.

5. Applicants who are undergraduate still in college must be fully matriculated for a degree at the participating institution and must have satisfactorily completed at least one full year of accredited college work acceptable to sponsoring institution.

6. <u>Those who are no longer enrolled in college</u> must have satisfactory completed at least two full years of accredited college work acceptable to the participating institution. Students coming to Tuskegee Institution and planning either to carry part schedule or no schedule of classes may qualify under this provision.

7. They must meet the physical requirement for STUDENT PILOT CERTIFICATION OF COMMERCIAL CPT GRADE as determined by a designated civil aeronautics medical examiner.

8. If under 21 years of age, they must have written consent from their parents or legal guardian to take the training.

9. They must never have been disqualified from participation in the Civilian Pilot Training Program by advisory board action.

(Tuskegee Institute Admission Policy, May, 1941)

Black Colleges and Universities). In fact, the requirements that include numbers five and six appeared to be relevant to me. However, the requirement number six appeared to fit me much closer since I had completed two years of college. I felt I was ready and qualified. Thus, I submitted another letter of application to the Tuskegee Pilot Training Program.

A JOYOUS DAY OF ACCEPTANCE TO THE PILOT TRAINING PROGRAM

On December 7, 1942, he received a letter from Major David. C. Hale, which stated,

> *"With reference to your application for aviation appointment, you are advised that you have been found qualified for Fighter Training School of the Army Flying School, Tuskegee, Alabama. Your enlistment in the Air Force Enlisted Reserve has been recommended to the Adjutant General this date and your nearest recruiting officer will advise you when to report for such enlistment. Wait at least five days before making inquiry to the recruiting officer regarding your enlistment.... Orders will then be requested by the adjutant office for your call to active duty, appointment as aviation cadet and assigned to a class..."*

Signed:
David C. Hale, Major
Army Air Corps
Assistant Chief, Aviation Cadet Section
Military Personnel Division, O.D.P.

Thus, "I was notified by the United States Army Air Forces that I was accepted to the Army Flying School, Tuskegee Airfield, and Tuskegee, Alabama. Thus, my life long dream was fulfilled when I was assigned to the 99th Pursuit Squadron. However, I was sworn into the enlisted reserve on December 14, 1942 in Cleveland, Ohio for the Tuskegee Pilot training Program."

"Thus, on December 14, 1942, special orders No. 85 was received with my assignment to the 99th Pursuit Squadron at Tuskegee Institute, Tuskegee, Alabama. I traveled by train and arrived at Tuskegee Institute on December 16, 1942. I participated in the pilot training at Tuskegee Air Force Base, and this resulted in my successful graduation in the 99th Pursuit Squadron on September 18, 1943. But what I remembered as important was that the Board met on May 22, 1944, comprised of Col. Noel F. Parrish 019992 AC; President Maj. Donald G. McPherson 0395259, AC member, Maj. Gabe C Hawkins, 0376771 AC, Member, Capt. Harold D Martin, 0904648, AC, member, 1st Lt. Thomas J. Collins, 0565072, AC, member, 20 Lt. George E. Burton, 0577036 AC Recorder." These board members recommended that I was eligible to graduate from the Tuskegee Pilot training program in 1943 along with a list of other individuals."

Lt. Hiram E. Mann

WHAT THIS GRADUATION MEANT?

"To see my name among the distinguished group of Aviation Cadets on September 18, 1943 provided me a deep sense of pride and job. I was even more excited to receive my wings and my first commission of 2nd Lieutenant, Air Corps, Army of the United States and appointed Flight Officer, Air Corps, Army of the United States of America. Furthermore, I was elated to receive the designation, "rated pilot" effective upon graduation, on or about 27 June, 1944."

CLASS OF 44-F TUSKEGEE PILOTS

The official picture of the Class of 44-F below shows Hiram E. Mann seated in the first row from the left to right.

CLASS 44-F   06-27-44

Left to right:

Seated:

Hiram E. Mann, John B. Turner, William T. Jackson, Yenwith K. Whitney, Laurel E. Keith, Harry T. Stewart, *Hugh J. White, *Samuel L. Washington, *Frank N. Wright

Kneeling:

John R. Perkins, *George A. Lynch, *James T. Mitchell, *Wyarain T. Schell, Charles A. Hill, Leon W. Spears, Carl F. Ellis, Rohelia J. Webb, Robert W. Lawrence

Standing:

*Frank Lee, *James T. Ewing, *Lincoln T. Hudson, *James W. Wright, Rupert C. Johnson,*Richard Smith-Alfred Armistead, Lewis J. Lynch, *Robert J. Murdic

FLIGHT HELMETS DENOTE SINGLE ENGINE PILOTS
OVERSEAS CAPS DENOTE MULTI-ENGINE PILOTS

*PCS (11 of 26) TO "LONELY EAGLES SQUADRON" (DECEASED) AS OF JANUARY 2008

ORDERS FOR OVERSEAS COMBAT

On September 18, 1943, after intense training as a fighter pilot, Hiram Eugene Mann AC15134652 saw his rank changed from students graduating from the College Training Detachment to that of Aviation Cadets of the Class SE-44-F. On 27 June 1944 Mann was commissioned 2nd Lieutenant, Air Corps, Army of the United States and rated pilot (See Certificate AAF Form No. 8). This meant that 2nd Lieutenant Hiram E. Mann could be deployed any day to fight on the front lines of the World War II in Europe and North Africa.

A TRUE COPY   A TRUE COPY   A TRUE COPY

"M" SQUADRON
LOCKBOURNE ARMY AIR BASE
Columbus 17, Ohio

16 August 1946

CERTIFICATE

The undersigned hereby certifies that HIRAM E. MANN, 1st Lt,
AC, 0 835 329, reported to the 302d Fighter Squadron, 332d
Fighter Group, APO #520, c/o U S Postmaster, New York, on 13
January 1945, pursuant to authority contained in Movement Orders
from Hampton Roads POE, Norfolk, Virginia, effective 30 November
1945.   Officer was assigned Shipment No FF550CT.

s/ VERNON V. HAYWOOD
t/ VERNON V. HAYWOOD
Captain, Air Corps
Commanding Officer 302d
Fighter Squadron
(13 Jan 1945)

A TRUE COPY

s/ HIRAM E. MANN
t/ HIRAM E. MANN
1st Lt AC
0 823 529

This is the evidence that Lt. Hiram E. Mann AC 0835329 reported to the 302nd
Fighter Squadron, 332nd Fighter Group APO # 520 on January 13 Vernon V.
Haywood Commanding Officer 302nd Fighter Squadron approved this order
for overseas assignment. The letter above clearly provides the significance and
essence of the order to become an active member of the fighter pilot group
overseas.

ONE SUCCESS OF THE "RED TAILS": PROMOTION TO CAPTAIN

It is essential to understand that Lt. Hiram E. Mann was determined to move
up the ranks in the military. Becoming a Captain was important since it
was evidence of his flying skills and combat experiences. The Certificate of
appointment as Captain, Air Corps is displayed in the document provided
hereafter.

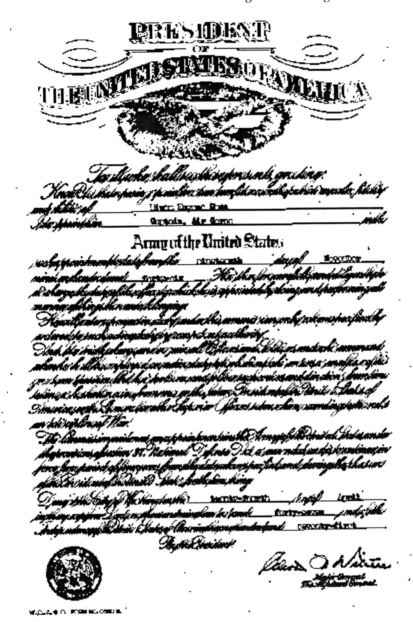

"On November 19, 1946, I was delighted to be promoted to Captain in the Army Air Corps of the United States (Par 3, WD Cir IAQ, 1946). This achievement was cherished and gave me the inspiration to continue my study and focus on doing the best job ever while being a member of the Army Air Corps."

74   *Dr. Patrick C. Coggins*

ARMY AIR FORCES AWARD

In order to achieve this award, Captain Hiram E. Mann had to demonstrate that as a pilot, he had been efficient and effective in carrying out all of his duties during the war. The citation indicates that he was regarded as an efficient pilot and serviceman in the United States Army Air Forces.

On November 19, 1946, Captain Hiram E. Mann 0-835329 received the coveted Army Air Forces "Honor of Efficiency of Fidelity Achievement Award" in appreciation for valued services with the Army Air Forces. This special award was earned based on honor, efficiency and fidelity as a pilot and as an enlisted officer who served diligently during World War II.

CERTIFICATE OF SERVICE

The United States Army on 3rd January 1947 awarded Lieutenant Hiram Eugene Mann 0835329 of 318th Army Air Force Base Unit, the "Certificate of Service for honorably serving in Active Federal Service in the Army of the United States until June 27, 1947". A careful examination of this certificate will show that Lt. Col. Hiram Eugene Mann was honored for three Oak leaf Clusters with Air Medal, Distinguished Unit Citation Certificate of Valor, EAME Ribbon, ATO Ribbon, and a World War II Victory Ribbon.

HONORABLE DISCHARGE

The goal and desire of every member of the Tuskegee Airmen Experience was to be honorably discharged. Therefore, it was essential that after all the intensive pilot training and the dangerous, but challenging pilot experiences in World War II, one's discharge would be honorable. Lt. Hiram E. Mann was honorably discharged on January 3, 1947.

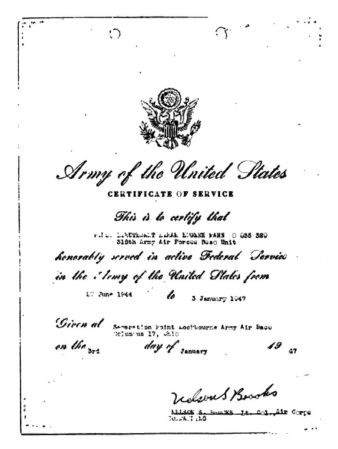

Having served with distinction from June 27, 1944 to January 3, 1947. As Ret. Lt. Col. Hiram Mann said, "This Certificate of Service in the United States Army represents a triumph over doubts, an achievement of a lifelong dream to fly an airplane, and a realization of the special desire to be a Combat pilot in the United States Army Air Corps." Thus, to graduate from the Tuskegee Airmen Flying School in 1944 was "an accomplishment that was a personally happy experience for me as well as a most satisfying moment for my family members and fellow pilots who were supportive of me."

STILL HAVING THE MILITARY BUG

"Like many of the Tuskegee Airmen pilots, the idea of serving in the Officers Reserve Corps Army of the United States of America was a priority for me. I saw this opportunity as a Reserve Officer to continue what I was trained for and that is to either fly a plane or teach young people to fly. While I was not worried about assuming the responsibility of a Reserve Corps officer in the United States Armed Services, I was a little anxious about the kind of reception I will receive from enlisted personnel as well as other officers." Nevertheless, "I had to pursue my career desires to remain in the military and move up in the ranks to the highest level that was attainable by me at that time. Bear in mind that this was a period of continued civil rights struggle where there was still several pockets of blatant discrimination and segregation that permeated every town, county and state in the United States of America. Don't get me wrong, the military was integrated, but, that did not mean that it was easy for African Americans to be promoted into key management and leadership positions in the military."

SQUADRON "K"
318TH AAF BASE UNIT (SEPARATE ON POINT)
LOCKBOURNE ARMY AIR BASE
COLUMBUS 17, OHIO   18 November 1946

SUBJECT: Appointment under Section 27,   A. Captain Air Reserve
Nation Defense Act, as amended

TO   : Capt Eugene H Mann
10525 Anthoway Avo. Cleveland Ohio   B. O-835 329

1. The Secretary of War has directed me to inform you that by direction
of the President, you are tendered appointment in the Officers' Reserve Corps
Army of the United States, effective this date, in the grade and section shown
after A above. Your serial number is shown after B above.

2. There is inclosed herewith a form for oath of office, which you are
requested to execute and return promptly to the agency from which it was
received by you. The execution and return of the required oath of office
constitute an acceptance of your appointment. No other evidence of acceptance
is required. Upon receipt in the War Department of the Oath of Office, properly
executed, a commission evidencing your appointment will be sent to you.

3. Prompt action is requested since the regulations require cancella-
tion of the tender of appointment if acceptance is not received within a
reasonable time.

4. You will not perform the duties of an officer under this appointment
until specifically so directed by competent orders.

5. Whenever your permanent address is changed, it is important that you
notify all concerned, using the inclosed Personal Report form.

NELSON S DROOKS
Lt Colonel, Air Corps
Commanding

Inclosures:
Form for Oath of Office
Personal Report form.

I certify that;
Captain Eugene H. Mann   O-835329)
          and   } Are one in the same.
Captain Hiram E. Mann   O-835329)

Hiram Eugene Mann
O-835329
Captain, Air Corps

Therefore, Captain Mann with a patriotic zeal for serving his country, decided
to re-enlist in the Air Reserve and on November 18, 1946, he received his
appointment. This appointment as a Reserve Officer in the United States Air
Force was critical. He was stationed at the 318th AAF Base Unit Squadron "K"
Lockbourne Army Air Base, in Columbus, Ohio. "As I reflected on this appointment, I observe that there was a significant change from being a Captain
in the Army Air Reserve to being a Captain and Officer in the newly formed
United States Air Force." This difference meant that for the first time "I had
a rank in a newly formed Air Force in an era of an integrated military. I felt
a deep relief that I was now serving in a branch of the military where there
were no signs, like in the past, "Whites Only" officer's quarters."

This picture is important since Capt. Hiram E. Mann like other military personnel had to juggle their loyalty to the military service while being at that time, committed to their wife and family. This challenge was a difficult one in 1946 and it was even more challenging for married personnel in the military services of the United States of America.

LT and MRS HIRAM E. MANN
TUSKEGEE, ALABAMA
1946
****

Lt. Hiram and wife Kathadaza Mann" In 1946, the World War II was over and all of us pilots, Black and White, were able to return home. You can see from the positive and warm expression from my wife Kathadaza that she was happy that God spared my life despite flying and fighting in the war in Europe. Yet, I signed up as a Reserve Officer in the United States Air Force."

TRAINING AIR COMMAND AND STAFF COLLEGE

In 1956, the participation in the Air Command and Staff College was only available to a few people. "Thus, I was determined that I will do all that I could to make sure that my application was accepted by the military for the Air Command school." This Air Command and Staff College trained military officers from over 24 allied countries in the world.

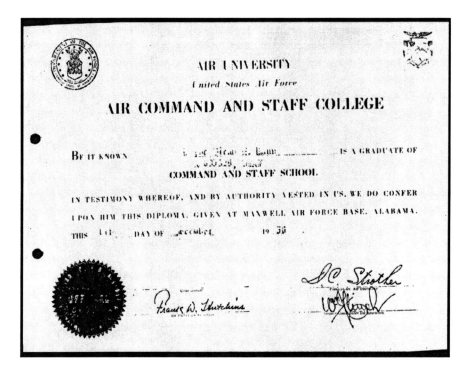

HEADQUARTERS
AIR COMMAND AND STAFF COLLEGE
Maxwell Air Force Base, Alabama

ACPD-PP   12 March 1956

SUBJECT: Reporting Instructions

TO: Each Officer Scheduled to Attend Class 57,
         Command and Staff School

1. Orders on officers scheduled to attend Class 57, Command and
Staff School normally will direct them to report during the period 0800,
28 August 1956 to 1600, 31 August 1956. Authority has been delegated to
this headquarters to establish the specific date and hour within this
four day period that each officer will report for processing and duty.

2. Processing must be programed carefully and controlled on a very
strict schedule. During the period students are enrolling, peak work-
loads develop which could result in great inconveniences to the individual student officer. Deviations from the schedule for the convenience
of an individual cannot be approved.

3. You are scheduled to report to the Personnel and Processing
Division, Room 278, Building 1401, at the time and date shown below:

Reporting Time   Reporting Date

1400   *29 AUG 56*

4. It is requested that you bring the following items with you
when you report for processing:

   a. At least five copies of your orders and all amendments re-
assigning you to the College. If you are arriving from overseas, also
bring all orders and amendments issued in connection with your reassignment and travel from your permanent overseas station to the ZI.

   b. All Field Personnel Records which are in your possession.
These include your Unit Personnel Records, Health Records, and Individual Flight Records (if on flying status).

   c. Military Pay Record (DD Form 113).

   d. Your copy of all UNCLASSIFIED Air Force Manuals in the
1-series (Air Doctrine) which by now should have been issued to you

Hq AC&SC ACPD-PP Subject: Reporting Instructions

through normal supply channels. Authority for this distribution is in
the Foreword of each manual and paragraph 5a (2), Air Force Regulation
5-22.

    c. A copy of this letter.

    5. Attached is your copy of our booklet titled "Student Orienta-
tion." This booklet contains complete, detailed, current information
and will provide answers to most of your questions concerning the Air
Command and Staff College, Maxwell Air Force Base, and the city of
Montgomery.

    6. It is strongly requested that you have your personnel records,
particularly Form 66, adjusted if necessary and brought up to date prior
to departure from your present command. Special attention should be
given to the AFSCs listed in Item 24 of your Form 66. While attending
Command and Staff School you will be shown as performing duty in your
primary AFSC as it is indicated on your Form 66 (paragraph 13c (2) (c),
Chapter 4, Air Force Manual 36-1). CLASSIFICATION ACTION CHANGING THE
PRIMARY, AWARDING OR UPGRADING AN AFSC WILL NOT BE TAKEN WHILE YOU ARE
ATTENDING COMMAND AND STAFF SCHOOL. Therefore, the AFSCs you hold when
you depart your present command will be the ones used in reporting you
for reassignment upon graduation.

    7. You will be "signed-in" for duty at this base when processed.
Do not sign-in on any other registers located at this base.

      FOR THE COMMANDANT:

1 Incl
    Student Orientation Booklet
                   H. H. GOURLEY
                   Lt Colonel, USAF
                   Director of Military Personnel

Having a burning desire to enhance his military and flying skills, Hiram
enrolled in the Air University, United States Air Force, Air Command and
Staff College, where he successfully completed the VARTUS training between
January 11, 1952 and December 14, 1956, given at Tuskegee Air Force Base,
Alabama. The scope of this training involved in depth examination of the
administrative and policy dimensions of Air Command tactics affecting the
United States and strategic regions of the world.

APPOINTMENT AS MAJOR

The experience of the officers training program at the Air Command and
Staff College training brought him in contact with officers in the United

States as well as from different parts of the world. Captain Hiram E. Mann was appointed Major on July 1, 1955 a rank he held until June 27, 1965.

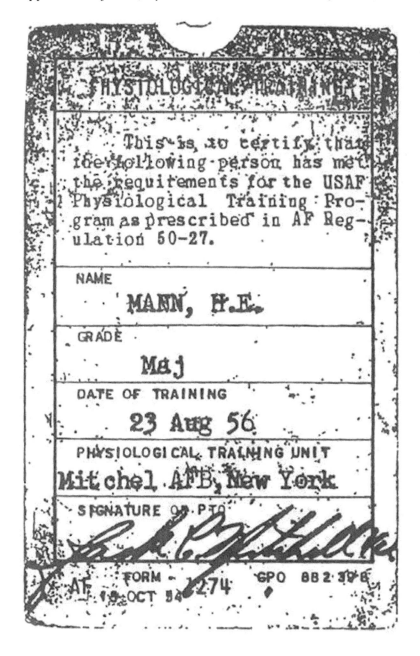

This rank was achieved with his successful participation in the Air Command and Staff College training course in 1956. There were 51 officers from 24 allied countries including Brazil, Chile, China, Colombia, Denmark, Ecuador, Germany, Greece, Iran, Italy, Japan, Mexico, Netherlands, Nicaragua, Nigeria, Norway, Pakistan, Peru, Philippines, Republic of Korea, Spain Thailand, Turkey and Venezuela. There were four African Americans including Daniel "Chappie " James ,two others and myself with the rank of Major. "I felt that my career goal was achieved with the promotion to the rank of major. I dreamed about making this rank but never in my wildest did I think that it would become a reality given the difficulties that African Americans had to face living in a segregated society that discriminated against Blacks. The ironic point is that even though the military was integrated, there were still major pockets of blatant discrimination that flourished in the South. "

ORDNANCE MANAGEMENT ENGINEERING TRAINING AGENCY

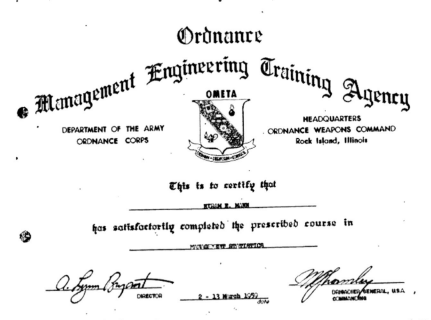

During the period of March 2-13, 1959, Major Hiram E. Mann successfully completed an intense two-week management statistics course held at the Ordinance Management Engineering Training Agency Department of the Army Ordinance Corps, Headquarters Ordinance Weapons Command Rock Island, Illinois. "This course provided me with knowledge and skills in the many areas."

AIR FORCE INSTRUCTOR SCHOOL

According to Lt. Col. Mann, "My academic preparation had provided me with the skills and competencies to become an instructor in the public school or colleges in my community. However, I had this burning desire to become an instructor in the military schools so I enrolled in the Air University, Extension Course Institute Gunter Air Force Base, Alabama. I successfully completed the "Academic Instructor Course" No 7521 and was awarded the certificate on 23 May, 1962."

"This course provided me with essential skills and competencies that enabled me to be an effective instructor of others. I realized that being an effective academic instructor will require additional advance training and study leading to a master or other graduate degrees. I believed at that time that the goal of advance study was attainable and within my reach and means. Thinking about that time, I remembered the saying and encouragement from my parents and family who often said that education and training in marketable skills will make it easier to compete effectively and secure one's future career opportunities."

EXTENSION COURSE INSTITUTE
AIR UNIVERSITY
GUNTER AIR FORCE BASE, ALABAMA

Certificate

THIS IS TO CERTIFY THAT   Date **23 MAY 1962**

MAJ H E MANN   A00895329   has successfully completed

ACADEMIC INSTRUCTOR   Course No. **7521**

through correspondence with the

EXTENSION COURSE INSTITUTE, USAF

Officers, Airmen and U. S. Civil Service employees are authorized entry in appropriate qualification or personnel records.

Wilfred W Wagner
WILFRED W. WAGNER
Lt. Colonel, USAF
Commandant

Active duty Air Force personnel and U. S. Civil Service employees submit this certificate to their base education office for coordination prior to entry in qualification or personnel records.

EDUCATION OFFICER

PROPERTY DISPOSAL CERTIFICATION

It is clear from the record that Major Mann was committed to enhancing his education in order to sustain a competitive edge, and in his words,"My curiosity continued about learning the methods used in the disposal of military materials. I had read articles on surplus materials and disposal of excess military property. So in December 30, 1965. I successfully passed the examination to Sub course ALM 61 Property Disposal Methods" and received a rating of excellent. "I considered pursuing a career in the disposal of military waste as well as working in a civilian enterprise that disposed waste."

DEPARTMENT OF THE ARMY
HEADQUARTERS
UNITED STATES ARMY LOGISTICS MANAGEMENT CENTER
FORT LEE, VIRGINIA 23001

30 December 1965

Lt Colonel Hiram E. Mann
332 East 140th Street
Cleveland, Ohio 44120

Dear Colonel Mann:

You received a rating of Excellent on your examination to Subcourse ALM 61, Property Disposal Methods. Your records have been referred to our Processing Section for issuance of a letter of subcourse completion and diploma for successful completion of the Defense Property Disposal Management Extension Course. Inclosed is a copy of letter of subcourse completion for Subcourse 60 for use by your DO.

We do not return examination papers to the student, but I am happy to state that you did a very fine job.

Sincerely,

JOHN F. FREUND.
Instructor
Nonresident Instruction Department

JFF/ca
1 Incl
Copy of S/C Comp Ltr
S/C 60

PROMOTION TO LIEUTENANT COLONEL

Being a Lieutenant Colonel in the Military was a prestigious rank. "This rank was evidence that I had earned the requisite skills and knowledge to walk in the footsteps of my mentor and role model General Benjamin O. Davis, Jr., who achieved the rank of Lieutenant Colonel when I was a member of the Tuskegee Airmen Pilot Training in 1944." "As my role model I always aspired to walk in part in his footsteps. I learned from him that in order to be successful in the military, you have to function at your best potentials every day. So, my achieving the Lt. Colonel promotion was a tribute and promise to myself that I would secure the coveted rank of Lieutenant Colonel."

HEADQUARTERS
AIR RESERVE RECORDS CENTER (CONAC)
United States Air Force
3800 York Street
Denver, Colorado 80205

RESERVE ORDERS)
NUMBER E-5748)   27 JUN 65

MAJ MANN HIRAM E   A00835329
3332 E 140TH ST
CLEVELAND,OH 44120

BY DIRECTION OF THE PRESIDENT YOU ARE PROMOTED AS A RESERVE OF THE AIR FORCE TO THE GRADE SHOWN BELOW.

COMPONENT   GRADE

   AFRES   LIEUTENANT COLONEL

EFFECTIVE DATE   CURRENT PROMOTION SERVICE DATE

   27 JUN 65   27 JUN 65
AUTHORITY

   SECTION 8366   TITLE 10 US CODE

FOR THE COMMANDER:
          R. E. LOCKE
                    , USAF
               Chief of
          Administrative Services

DISTRIBUTION:

   E-PLUS
9518 AIR RESERVE SQ   (CNC) 2494 AFS
685 NORTH HAMILTON ROAD
COLUMBUS 19,OHIO

   2 - RPR-R

"My desire was to retire from the military with the rank of Colonel. I had worked very hard and came through the ranks with a stellar record as a pilot and officer. Thus on June 27, 1965, I was notified that, *"By the Commander that is promoted as a reserve officer Air Force to the grade shown below."*

Component:AFRES
Grade: Lieutenant Colonel
Promotion Date: 27 June 1965
Authority: Section 8366, Title 10 US Code

Because of this promotion to Lieutenant Colonel, I was then assigned to the USAF Academy Liaison Officer in Colorado.

USAF ACADEMY LIAISON OFFICER

"This United States Air Force (USAF) Academy Liaison Officer detail required that I be transferred from the 9023 Air Reserve Squadron, to the 9767 Air Reserve Squadron (ARPC/RPR-S) (CONAC), Denver, Colorado. On January 6, 1966, I was assigned to the 9767 Air Reserve Squadron, Denver, Colorado as the USAF Academy Liaison Officer, Position Control Number CNX 00802A, Position Grade, and Lieutenant Colonel. The responsibilities included recruiting, advising, counseling and conducting a number of workshops for aspirants on the requirements and expectations of those who were selected as cadets in the Academy. I remained in this position until 1972. It should be noted that very few African Americans and other minority groups were aware of the possibilities that were available for them to apply and be selected to the Academy."

"I, like other African Americans, believed that unless we were prepared to compete at every level in the military branches, we as a people would not be able to make substantial progress and attain higher level positions with substantial influence and higher pay grades. The bottom line for me was that in assuming the position of Liaison Officer with the United States Air Force Academy (USAFA), I would be able to influence decisions that will benefit our African American people especially the youth. Upon being accepted to become the Liaison Officer of the USAFA , I felt a real sense of achievement of a dream that came through not just for me but for other African Americans who strived to be promoted to higher positions in the military services of the United States of America."

Lt. .Col.. Hiram E. Mann, USAF Liaison Officer

The decision to become the USAF Academy Liaison Officer in 1966 was a real challenge. It became apparent to me that the opportunity would afford me the chance to play a significant role in the recruitment and selection and admission process to the United States Air Force Academy in Denver, Colorado. I believed at this time that there were talented youth in all of our inner cities who could be identified and selected for the USAF Academy in Colorado. I also believed that this was a position of a lifetime that very few African Americans had ever been given the opportunity to apply for prior to this time." "I remained in this position of recruiter for the USAFA until mandatory retirement in 1972."

CERTIFICATE OF APPOINTMENT

AS
A

UNITED STATES AIR FORCE ACADEMY LIAISON OFFICER

LT COL

is hereby appointed a United States Air Force Academy Liaison Officer and is authorized to represent the United States Air Force Academy as an official spokesman of the District Commander Advisory Service

THOMAS S. MOORMAN
LIEUTENANT GENERAL, USAF

"In retrospect this USAF Academy Liaison Officer detail required that I moved from Columbus, Ohio to 9767 Air Reserve Squadron. (ARPC/RPR-S)(CONAC), Denver, Colorado as the USAF Academy Liaison Officer, position control number CNX 00802A, Position Grade Lieutenant Colonel. The responsibility included recruiting young people for the USAFA and making presentations to these youth and parents regarding the career opportunities in the military. Additionally, I had the opportunity to target minority students and parents who also needed to know about the many opportunities that were available in the United States Air Force Academy and more so in the United States Air Force, in general."

FINAL COURSE IN DEFENSE SUPPLY

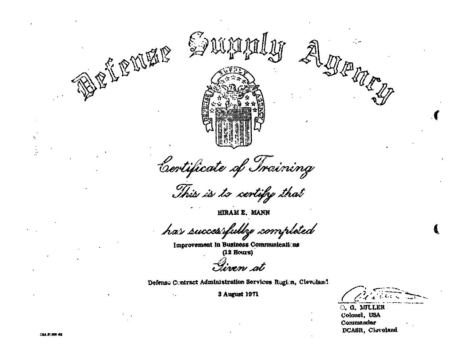

The certificate of completion shown above indicates that "I completed my final training course in the military on August 3, 1971. The Defense Supply Agency Certificate of Training in 'Improvement in Business Communications (12 hours)' given at the Defense Contract Administration Service Region, Cleveland, Ohio. This course provided me with insights into the following areas, effective communications, both oral and written, the psychology of motivating people, conflict resolution skills and general office management."

A SAMPLE EVALUATION OF MY SERVICE RECORD

The report that follows is a sample evaluation of my performance as the Liaison Officer for the United States Air Force Academy.

It is important to share a sample evaluation of his service, skills and competencies both as a pilot and as an officer who survived 48 combat missions defending the USA bombers during World War II. This distinction of being a Black Academy Liaison Officer in Northeast Ohio earned him high praise for counseling twenty candidates, four nominees, and two appointees to the USAF Academy. Having a Masters Degree in guidance and counseling earned in 1961 from John Carroll University while in the military service, was identified as an important factor in his success as an Academy Liaison Officer and as military personnel.

A closer review of the evaluation document will glean that Lt. Col. Mann was credited as being one of the most active Academy Liaison Officer. He supervised several employees and travel led over 740 miles to counsel 20 individual candidates. Being the only African American Liaison Officer at the Academy, he voluntarily took on the added task of contacting minority groups and organizations as well as the predominantly Black Colleges and Universities in order to reach all disadvantaged young men who might be encouraged to apply for nomination to the Academy. He was also commended for his community activities which included in 1971-72 serving on the Mt. Pleasant Community Council, Masons, Red Cross, Federal Employees Association, NAACP , United Torch Drive and other organizations.

FINAL JOURNEY-TIME FOR RETIREMENT

DEPARTMENT OF THE AIR FORCE
HEADQUARTERS AIR RESERVE PERSONNEL CENTER
3800 YORK STREET
DENVER, COLORADO 80205

28 FEB 1972

REPLY TO
ATTN OF: DPRAR

SUBJECT: Maximum Service

TO: Lt Colonel Hiram E. Mann, 277-12-7473, USAFR
3332 East 140th Street
Cleveland OH　44120

1.　Our records show that you will complete 28 years of commissioned service on 26 June 1972. The law requires that 30 days after this date you must:

　　a.　Transfer to the Retired Reserve, or

　　b.　Be discharged from your Reserve appointment.

2.　You are eligible for transfer to the Retired Reserve and will probably desire to select this option in lieu of discharge. If so, complete and return your application, through your unit of assignment, not later than 10 June 1972. This will allow sufficient time to process your retirement before the mandatory discharge date. If your application is not received by the above date, we will proceed with discharge action.

3.　Please feel free to write us if you have any questions with regard to this matter, your present or your future Reserve status.

FOR THE COMMANDER

LEWIS R. BARRETT, JR., Colonel, USAF
Director of Personnel Actions

2 Atch
1.　AF Form 131
2.　Return Envelope

Copy to:　RTU/9001 ARS
　　　　　w/o atch

ADDRESS CORRESPONDENCE TO "AIR RESERVE PERSONNEL CENTER" —NOT TO INDIVIDUALS
INCLUDE YOUR SOCIAL SECURITY ACCOUNT NUMBER

"In February 1972, I received a letter from the Department of the Air Force, Air Reserve Personnel Center, informing me that I must prepare to transfer to the Retired Reserve or be discharged from my Reserve appointment. After discussing the options with my wife Kathadaza M. Mann, I decided that it would be in my best interest to transfer. Thus, I applied on July 26, 1972 to be classified as to the Retired Reserve." This request was granted by the Department of the Air force of the United States of America. "I must say that I had mixed feelings about retirement, however, I also felt that I must be realistic and accept the final chapter of my career in the military. I had no regrets since I have achieved all of my goals including that of flying an airplane as a fighter pilot and moving through the ranks to Lieutenant Colonel."

These reflections in this chapter indicated that the journey Ret. Lt. Col. Mann took since joining the military in December 14, 1942, included a successful military career that saw him rise from the rank of "Buck" Pvt., to Aviation Student, to Aviation Cadet, Tuskegee Army Air Field, Alabama, to 2nd Lieutenant, 1st Lieutenant, Captain, Major and ultimately Lieutenant Colonel, the rank with which he retired from the military. There are several insights that are shared with the readers especially our youth:

1)   "Setting goals were essential to me and all of my colleagues in the Tuskegee Airmen Experience: I believed at that time in the 1940's that every one of us had one goal in mind and that was to be the best pilot and fighter pilot ever in the military service of the United States of America."

2)   As Lt. Col. Hiram, E. Mann often said. "Failure was not an option; each of the Tuskegee pilots and personnel understood the significance of the struggle in that, we knew that for every failure, the opportunity to fly an airplane would be more difficult for African Americans in these United States of America." As a member of the 332nd Fighter Group, led by Lieutenant General Benjamin O. Davis, Jr., the first African American General escorted bombers on many air combat missions over Europe, flying into the teeth of some of the Nazi Luftwaffe's most tenacious defenses (Martin Weil, The Washington Post, 2002).[40]

3)   "I am proud to have been a fighter pilot who was able to complete 48 of those grueling missions that tested every sense of my being. However, the most important goal we achieved as Tuskegee Airmen Pilots was shared as a collective achievement and that was the fact that not one of the bombers that 'Red Tails' escorted and protected was lost to an enemy fighter."

This unmatched achievement was due in part to the excellent educational background of the pilots, the extraordinary pilot training skills that were taught to each of the pilots who were trained in the Tuskegee's Pilot Training Program. Additionally, it is essential to attribute this success to the exemplary leadership of Lieutenant General Benjamin O. Davis Jr. who instilled in each of us that "we must set goals, believe that we can achieve our goals and then set out to use our talents and skills to achieve them. I can assure you that this advice was reflected by me and other pilots during each moment and day of our involvement in the European theaters and serving in the military."

4)   The additional factor that impacted on our determination and success as pilots was the early realization by each of us that our involvement in the Tuskegee Airmen Experience was the sense and realization that there was an ultimate responsibility to the African American Community who supported us in every phase of our trials and tribulations as Tuskegee Pilot Training Program. The Black Press insisted that we be given the equal opportunity to fly military planes like our White counterparts. People like Dr. Mary McLeod Bethune, President of Bethune Cookman College, Mrs. Eleanor Roosevelt, and others who argued that the African American pilots be afforded not only the same opportunity to fly but also to be involved in combat missions overseas as defenders of the liberty enjoyed by the free world at that time (Martin Weil, "How Many Tuskegee Airmen?" The Washington Post 2002)[41]

INDIVIDUAL COMBAT AND FLIGHT RECORD

The actual "Individual Flight Record" of Lieutenant Hiram E. Mann is fascinating for it will show when examined closely that he flew P 51-B, C and D in combat during World War II. The flight records in Appendix V provide additional information on the distinguished combat record . These reports indicate that Lt. Col. Mann was a very busy and competently trained Tuskegee pilot whose combat record involved the flying and execution of several types of fighter planes and targets. Like other Tuskegee pilots, he had several close calls that could have involved the loss of his airplane and possible the loss of his own life. These escapades are discussed later in the chapter on the epistles. This thrilling account of his plane "Boss Lady, No. 26" was lost in combat when another pilot on a certain day used his plane only to have it shot down and both the plane and the life of the pilot were lost forever. As Col. Mann puts it, "Only by the grace of God this loss was not me."

INDIVIDUAL FLIGHT RECORD

(1) SERIAL NO. O-835329   (2) NAME Mann, Hiram E.   (3) RANK 1st Lt   (4)
(5) PERS. CLASS 13   (6) BRANCH Air Corps   (7) STATION APO #520
(8) ORGANIZATION ASSIGNED IV   XV F   306th F   332nd   100th F
(9) ORGANIZATION ATTACHED   AIR FORCE   COMMAND   WING   GROUP   SQUADRON   DETACHMENT
(10) PRESENT RATING & DATE Pilot 6-27-44   (11) ORIGINAL RATING & DATE Pilot 6-27-44
(12) TRANSFERRED FROM   (13) FLIGHT RESTRICTIONS None
(15) TRANSFERRED TO   (14) TRANSFER DATE

(17) MONTH April 19 45

Day	Aircraft Type, Model & Series	No. Landings	Command Pilot C CA	Co-Pilot CF	Qualified Pilot Dual GO	First Pilot	Rated Pers. Non-Pilot / Day	Night / N OR H	Non-Rated Other Arms / Other Crew	Special Information
1	C-5		11	22	23	3:00 4:45	26	*Type of Mission*		*Target*
3	P-51D20NA	1				1:15				Army
5	"	1				4:00		Bomber Escort		Poggia
6	"	1				3:30		Ferry Plane		Poggia to Ramitelli
7	"	1				5:00		Target Cover		Udine
8	"	1				4:00		Bomber Cover		No. Italy (Germany)
9	"	1				4:00		Route Cover		Verona
12	"	1				2:45		Bomber and Area Cover		Brenner Pass RR
14	"	1				4:15		Bomber Escort		Northern Italy
15	"	2				6:15		Bomber Escort		South Germany
16	"	1				3:15		Strafing		Brenner Pass RR
17	"	2				4:15		Return to Home Field		Munchen & Linz
19	"	1				4:15		Bomber Escort		Ramiti vs Raw
20	"	1				4:15		Flt Leader Bomber		Bologna
21	"	1				3:45		Bomber Escort		West Germany
22	"	1				3:45		Supply Drop Escort		Northern Italy
24	"	1				4:45		Bomber Escort		Yugoslavia
25	"	1				5:15		Bomber Escort		Northern Italy
26	"	1				4:00		Rescue Escort		Pilson - Salz
30	"	1	Last Comb. Mission			11:30		Flt Leader Bomber		Northern Italy
10								Training Flight		Local
								Certified Correct		1:00

Roscoe C. Brown, Jr.
1st Lt., AC
Opns O

| | | 22 | | | | 78:15 | | | | 1:00 |
COLUMN TOTALS

	(42) TOTAL STUDENT PILOT TIME	(43) TOTAL FIRST PILOT TIME	(44) TOTAL PILOT TIME
(37) THIS MONTH		78:15	78:15
(38) PREVIOUS MONTHS THIS F.Y.		274:15	273:50
(39) THIS FISCAL YEAR		350:30	352:05
(40) PREVIOUS FISCAL YEARS	208:00		208:00
(41) TO DATE	208:00	350:30	560:05

Aircraft	INL	Card No. 1	Card No. 2	Card No. 3
	19	20 21 22 23 24 25 26	27 28 29 30 31	32 33 34 35 36
P-51D	22	78		

TFT   338:45

The flight records also indicate that Lt Hiram E. Mann flew 48 combat missions using a variety of P-51's and other aircrafts. The types of missions as part of 302nd, 332nd and 100th included 1) Bomber Escort, 2) Strafing, 3) Supply Drop Escort, 4) Test Hop and, 5) Other flight assignments. These flight combat missions were directed to targets at Prana, Linz, Munchen, Vienna, Zagreb, North Yugoslavia, North Italy, Brenner Pass, Engles Abort, Munchen-Linz, Geoggnitz, Germany, St. Profens, Munchen-Regensburg and

Wels to mention a few. See Appendix V for additional flight records.

A JOURNEY WELL SPENT IN THE MILITARY

As Sgt. Lorenzo D. Harris, Airman, staff writer, in his article "All Guts, Little Glory," recorded that Lt. Colonel Samuel Wade Watts Jr. said, "Just before the war and its early days, most Blacks in the military were in support organizations such as supply civil engineering or food services." The essence of this point was that the Black Community was fully aware that the success of the Tuskegee Airmen as pilots will have a positive impact on integration of the military and increasing the respect of Whites for the innate abilities of African Americans.

Hiram and Kathadaza Mann at the P-51 Mustang Pilots' Association Reunion, Metairie, LA, August 2005

LIFE AFTER A FULL AND SUCCESSFUL MILITARY CAREER

The current and future links to the community has been expressed Mann who said, "We should be the first to set a positive example for young men and young women who are pursuing careers in aerospace and aviation." The second link to the community is the formation of the Tuskegee Airmen Incorporated, a national organization with local chapters that are committed to providing scholarships for students, speakers bureau and networking with community organizations and regional and national conferences opened to anyone in the community. Lt. Col. Hiram E. Mann is the historian and charter member of the General Daniel "Chappie" James Chapter. He devotes time to sharing the history of the Tuskegee Airmen Experience with civic organizations, public and private schools, and with colleges and universities. The community focus of the Tuskegee Airmen's legacy for the future is best expressed by his wife, Kathadaza "Kitty" Mann, a retired school teacher, living in Titusville, Florida. She said, "Despite the negative aspect of segregation, they took it because they were proud men including my husband, who wanted to learn to fly and fight for America. But more so, they wanted to erase the myth that Blacks were not intelligent enough to fly and maintain airplanes." "We were not glory seekers, but we believed that the accomplishments of the Tuskegee Airmen should be recognized and celebrated not only in the Black community but also throughout every community in the United States of America." (Francis, 1985).[42]

"Life after the military has been enjoyable and full of excitement with my family. On August 10, 1980, we enjoyed a special reunion with my family. The picture shows me, my wife Kathadaza, older granddaughter Cheryl seated and son Eugene with his wife Linda holding the younger granddaughter Krista standing."

Lt. Col. Hiram Mann enjoying a festive moment with his wife Kathadaza and son Eugene

It is always a beautiful sight to see the Tuskegee Airmen like Ret. Lt. Col. Mann with their medals and their officer jackets being worn with a sense of pride coupled with a special touch of African American and Military history of the United States of America.

Picture in 2003 at TAI Conference

As Ret. Lt. Col. Hiram E. Mann said, "I continue to be active in Civic work by educating everyone about the unique racial challenges that were overcome by the African American pilots who were part of the Tuskegee Airmen Experience of the 1940s. I want to make it clear that I never ordered or in any way coerced my son to join the military. The decision to join the Armed Forces was made of his own free will."

Son Eugene who joined the Marine Corps

"It is important to state that my wife Kathadaza and I encouraged our child and our grandchildren to go into the military. However, my son Eugene joined the military branch of Marine Corps and spent from 1968 to 1970 in the service. He chose not to make the service a career. He made a decision to not pursue a lifelong career in the military like his father. He was comfortable with his decision. Both of his parents embraced and supported his decision. However, as his father said on a few occasions that "I wished he had tried to attend the US Air Force Academy since I was a Liaison Officer at the Academy."

However, one thing was obvious, and that is, Eugene always admired his father's achievements in the military, especially the fact that his father was an Original Tuskegee Airman with a distinguished flying record that included fighting and flying in the European Theater as a proud member of the United States Air Force. He has been involved in all of the activities of the local General Daniel "Chappie" James Chapter located in Central Florida.

A grandchild joined the Navy Junior Reserve OTC in Senior High

"The thought of a grand child entering one of the military branches was never in our wildest dreams. Upon her graduation in 1999, Krista joined the Navy on June 18, 1999. I had the proud moment of being there and I swore her into the US Navy. This was a moving moment of joy coupled with a deep dose of pride. Yet, I must admit that I was nervous about her being involved in a war or international conflict."

Krista Mann spent from June, 1999 until November, 2006 in the military. Her experiences enabled her to develop her leadership skills and self-confidence. She knows as she often says, "I can achieve anything I put my mind to and work hard for. She left the service and secured a position as a Computer technician in Maryland I gave her the dickens for not transferring to the US Air Force."

"Our older granddaughter, Cheryl, joined the Army in 1997 and served honorably for ten years. She left the service and accepted a position as a Radiologist in Maryland

KADAZA and HIRAM MANN
SPRING 1942

As you examine the life of Ret. Lt. Col. Hiram Mann, you will see a very close military family that began with Hiram Mann's joining the Tuskegee Pilot Training Program, Tuskegee Institute, Tuskegee, Alabama in 1942 with the support of his wife Kathadaza Mann, shown in the pictures that follow. These pictures also provide a glimpse into Mann's close connections to his family and his consistent devotion to supporting the individual careers of his grandchildren whom he speaks very fondly of in almost every conversation about his immediate family. Hiram and Kathadaza Mann made sure that they were involved in the lives of their son and grandchildren including being a part of their decision to join the military services.

SPRING 1942, KADAZA
the "HAWAIIAN PRINCESS"

In case the reader is wondering why Kathadaza is called "Kadoka" and also the "Hawaiian Princess," as depicted in this spring of 1942 picture. She is called the "Hawaiian Princess" because as Hiram puts it "She looked Hawaiian with the long beautiful hair with the flowers in her hair." Obviously, these words were ones of endearment expressed by Hiram Mann as he described his wife Kathadaza, "The success I achieved in the military was directly related to the unconditional love and support I received from my wife Kathadaza Mann and my other family members."

This picture that follows of Kathadaza and Hiram Mann is another illustration of the unwavering support that his wife Kathadaza provided to her husband who was juggling his time between being a pilot in the Army Air Corps and being a supportive and responsible husband. As Hiram puts it," She too had to juggle her school and work with the civil service. Despite the challenges that she faced as a mother and a wife of a husband who was serving in the military, she never wavered in her endless commitment to Hiram to ensure that he succeeded in his goal to become a fighter pilot and achieve his childhood dreams of one day flying an airplane

"This picture shows the support I received from my wife Kathadaza who wore a pilot jacket while she visited me at the Tuskegee Airfield Base in Tuskegee, Alabama. In 1942, when I was an Air Cadet enrolled in the Tuskegee Army Air and Pilot Training Program at Tuskegee Institute, Tuskegee Alabama." In case it is not clearly stated, "I must confess that I succeeded only in part due to my wife Kathadaza unselfish and unconditional support of my career in the military. She eventually quit her civil service job with the Treasury Department and came to be with me at the Tuskegee army Air Field."

"Life in the military as a Cadet. Kathadaza was always there for me, every step and phase of my training."

"Life in the military as a Student Cadet was great for me for the most part. Kathadaza was always there for me during every step and phase of my training. I can safely say that all of my successes were because of the blessings of the Almighty God who looked over me as I flew the planes and fought in World War II. However, my personal support also came for the most part especially from my wife, Kathadaza, my son Eugene and all of the other members of my immediate and extended family. I also want to reiterate again that my success as a pilot was intricately linked to the fellow pilots who flew beside me and were looking out for me at all times. In addition, I owe much thanks to the ground crew and all of the support personnel whose tiring work kept our airplanes and the airfield in the best working condition. "

"Unlike many of my colleagues in the Pilot Training Program at the Tuskegee Institute Army Air Field, I was married with the added responsibility of thinking about my wife. It is important to note that very few of the Tuskegee Air Students and Air Cadets were married, most, if not over 95% were single men. In fact, the criteria for admissions to the Tuskegee Institute's Pilot Training Program emphasized, being single as a critical requirement for each applicant to the flight training program."

CHAPTER VIII

Timeline of the Tuskegee Airmen Experience

THESE TIME LINES provide a quick look at the key events that tell the story about the Tuskegee Airmen Experience of World War II. The information will tell the story and give insight into the critical events that shaped the lives of the men involved in the Tuskegee Airmen Experience at Tuskegee Institute, Tuskegee, Alabama. Other African Americans were in a grim struggle for justice and equality as enlisted personnel in the United States military. The timelines will also tell the events during the Tuskegee Airmen Experience and the events since the end of the Experience during World War II. The information will also provide the reader with events that will trigger further research that answers one's curiosity and thirst for knowledge about one of the most important periods in African American history in the United States of America. These African American men fought gallantly to protect the flag of the United States and to defend the freedom of the world especially Europe that was under siege from Nazi Germany and Hitler in the 1930's and 1940's. The ironic fact is that these African American men knew that when they returned to the United States of America, they did not have any legal and civil rights. They were returning to "Jim Crow" and a society whose modus operandi was that of segregation of the races in housing, public accommodations, water fountains, hospitals, schools, colleges and the military to name a few segments of American life. In fact, all of them were enlisted and fighting in segregated Armed Forces of the United States of America in the 1940s. All faced the reality of fighting an enemy abroad while being segregated and discriminated in the United States Army Air Corps.

EVENTS LEADING UP TO THE FOUNDING OF TUSKEGEE INSTITUTE AND THE ACHIEVEMENTS OF THE TUSKEGEE AIRMEN

- 1861-1865 – Civil War- Blacks comprise 12% (178,895) of the Union Army and 25% (30,000) of the Union Navy, Thousands more served as laborers in the various service units. About 2,751 Blacks were killed in battle: another 65,427 died from disease and other causes.
- 1866-1891 – Over 5,000 Blacks served in the all Black 9th and 10th cavalry and the 24th and 25th infantry regiments of the Buffalo soldiers. Blacks made up about 10% of the total troops who guarded the Western frontier.

UNITED STATES CONSTITUTIONAL PROVISIONS

- 1865 – Abolition of slavery in Amendment XIII – This provided African enslaved persons with legal and constitutional right to be free of slavery and/or involuntary servitude.
- 1868 – Amendment XIV – Protection of the equal rights and due process for all persons born or naturalized in the United States as citizens of the United States and of the State in which they reside.
- 1870 – Amendment XV – The right of citizens of the United States to vote shall not be denied or abridged by the United States or by a state on account of race, color, or previous condition of servitude.

TUSKEGEE INSTITUTE IS FOUNDED

- 1881, July 4 – Booker T. Washington opens the Tuskegee Institute after the state legislature grants charter. Washington was selected as the first principal of Tuskegee Institute, a segregated school. Other historically Black Colleges and Universities were founded throughout the United States to fulfill the need to educate African Americans in segregated Colleges and Universities.
- 1890-1920s – African Americans established a network of approximately 200 Black hospitals and nurse training schools.
- 1895 – Booker T. Washington makes his famous speech at the Atlanta Exposition and publishes his autobiography, "Up from Slavery."
- 1896 – The Supreme Court of the United States of America rules that separate-but- equal is legal in the treatment of Blacks and other groups.

This meant separate facilities, schools and of course separate Black units in the military. This famous case was Plessy Vs. Ferguson (163 US. 537, 16 S. Ct. 1138, 1896).

WARS IN WHICH BLACKS PARTICIPATED

- 1898 – Spanish American War: Four Black regular regiments fought in Cuba. These regiments comprised 12% of the forces on the island. Another 2000 or 7.65% comprised the sailors in the Navy.
- 1899 – Philippines War- while the numbers are not exact, four African American regular regiments plus two volunteer regiments of Blacks fought in this colonial campaign in the Philippines.

FOUNDING OF NATIONAL ADVOCACY ORGANIZATION

- 1909 – The National Association for the Advancement of Colored People was formed to advocate for the legal and civil rights of African Americans and disenfranchised persons.
- 1910 – The National Negro Improvement Association was formed by Marcus Garvey who ultimately returned to Jamaica.
- 1911 – The National Urban League was formed as an educational and economic development entity for African Americans.
- 1915 – Booker T. Washington dies; trustees select Robert Russa Moton as principal. Moton served as commander of cadets at Hampton for 25 years. He had ideologies different from Washington; He saw himself as "occasionally a race leader, and only rarely as a political boss."
- 1915 – Tuskegee Institute is well established as a vocational training school for teachers, tradesmen and farmers, while providing courses at the post high school level.

FOUNDER OF BLACK HISTORY WEEK/MONTH

- 1915 – Carter G. Woodson forms the Association for the study of "Negro Life and History."
- 1916 – Mexican Punitive Expedition- The all Black 10th Cavalry comprised 12% of the Armed Forces that pursued Pancho Villa in the famous desert expedition as shown in the video named "Buffalo Soldiers."

- 1917- Pan African Congress is organized by W.E.B. Dubois to advocate for the rights and unity of Africans in the Diaspora.

WORLD WAR I

- 1917-1918 – World War I – Over 200,000 Black soldiers made it to France, equaling 9.2% of the American Armed Forces. Blacks limited to support units. The all Black 92nd and 93rd Infantry Units had 773 members killed in action and 4,408 wounded.
- 1918 – Eighteen Black nurses admitted to the Army Nurse Corps after the armistice of WWI and assigned to Camp Shermen, Ohio and Camp Grant, Illinois.
- 1920 – Moton introduces college courses although no degrees were conferred at Tuskegee Institute.

TUSKEGEE INSTITUTE

- 1925 – Moton introduces ten million dollars by having a joint campaign fund-raiser with Hampton; this allowed the construction of buildings for a new collegiate division.

FIRST NEGRO HISTORY WEEK

- 1926 – The First Negro History Week was organized by Dr. Carter G. Woodson. This week was the forerunner for the "Black History Month" as celebrated today.
- 1927 – Moton organized collegiate level courses and majors. Courses included topics in education, agriculture, and home economics. He argued that such changes were needed in order to train the future graduates to teach and work in a competitive workforce.

TUSKEGEE ARMY AIR FIELD

- 1934(May 22) – The first airplane lands on the ground in an airfield at Tuskegee, Alabama.
- 1934 (September) – Moton and administration support plans for two Black aviators to do an air tour (Pan American). A used plane christened

as the Booker T. Washington. For the first time, Tuskegee Institute is linked with a major aviation venture publicly.

- 1935 – Moton retires and Frederick Douglas Patterson becomes Tuskegee's third president. Unlike his predecessors who graduated from Hampton, Patterson brought professional and academic credentials.

TUSKEGEE INSTITUTE OFFERS AVIATION COURSES

- 1936 – Newspapers announced that Tuskegee planned to offer courses in aviation. Tuskegee was considered an ideal place for aviation training for many reasons; it was situated in the deep-South afforded excellent year round flying weather, the rural setting afforded ample underdeveloped land for an airfield. Aviation complemented the school's traditional emphasis on task-oriented vocational education. Credibility of the Tuskegee Institute made it easier to enter into a field that many Whites felt Blacks could not master flying an airplane.

FIRST INTEGRATION OF THE MILITARY

- 1939 (April 3) – Public Law 18 was passed by Congress. This law provided for the large-scale expansion of the Army Air Corps, with one section of the law authorizing the establishment of flight training programs in Black Colleges to employ various areas of Army Air Corps support services. Tuskegee Institute was one such college designated as a training center for Black pilots and support personnel. Race and color were obstacles because there were elements of racial integration due to the fact the instructors were not Black.

- 1939 – United States Congress enacted legislation to expand the Army Air Corps and train thousands in flying. There were amendments to Public Law 18, which allowed the Army Air Corps to be expanded to include African Americans as regular Air Corps personnel.

- 1939 – About 20 African American pilots came together and formed the National Airmen's Association. They hoped to change the policies that limited their options as pilots by gaining public attention to the struggle for equal treatment.

- 1939 (May) - The National Airmen's Association sponsored Chauncey Spencer and Dale White on a 10-city tour. While in Washington D.C., the pilots met and found an ally in a senator from Missouri, Harry S. Truman. Truman put through legislation that permitted a Black Training Program.

- 1939 (August)- Dr. Frederick Patterson, President of Tuskegee Institute was given approval to make an application to the Civil Aeronautics Authority for participation in the Civilian Pilot Training (CPT) program at Tuskegee Institute.
- 1939 (September)-Tuskegee Institute began publicizing the Civilian Pilot Training (CPT) program.
- 1939-Tuskegee Institute establishes the aviation course. The aviation course was a direct result of the Blacks crusade to be included into the nation's military. Component to crusade was admitting Blacks into the Air Corps. Ulysses Lee characterizes wide spread pressure campaign.
- 1940 (January) – Roundtree appointed as Alabama's Aviation Commission's Director of Airfield Development.

TUSKEGEE ARMY AIR FIELD BUILT

- 1940 (April) – G.L. Washington presented a proposal to President Patterson, the Board of Trustees and the Alumni of Tuskegee Institute to construct an airfield at Tuskegee Institute for a total cost of $220,900.

TUSKEGEE AIRMEN EXPERIENCE BEGINS

- 1940 (May) – The first class of students trained at Tuskegee Institute under the Civilian Pilot Training (CPT) program were tested and received their certificates.
- 1940 (Summer) – C. Alfred "Chief" Anderson began as a flight-training instructor at Tuskegee Institute.
- 1940 (Early October) – Ten secondary students' ground and flight training had been completed. Refused aviation course campaign to get Blacks into the Army Air Corps.
- 1940 (December 18) – The Army Air Corps submitted a plan to the War Department for an "Experience" forming an all Black fighter squadron with thirty-three pilots.
- 1941 – Lt. Della Raney Jackson became the first Black nurse to enter military service during World War II.

WORLD WAR II

- 1941-1945 – World War II - 500,000 Black troops stationed overseas or 4% of the 11 million Americans who served on foreign lands. The all Black 92nd Division in Italy had 616 killed and 2187 wounded. The 93rd division in the South Pacific lost 17 soldiers and 121 wounded in action. 2500 soldiers formed the Black infantry in Battle of the Bulge. Three all Black units flew overseas: the 99th Pursuit Squadron, 332nd Fighter Group and 477th Bombardment Group. There were 66 African American pilots killed in action. Over 140,000 African Americans served in the Army Air Forces; about 150,000 African Americans served in the Navy. Of the 12,000 or more Marines, 9 were killed in action.

- 1941 (January 6) – General Hap Arnold told the Assistant Secretary of War for Air Support that African Americans could be trained at Tuskegee Institute. This Black College was selected because it was the only possible place to start an African American training school in the shortest amount of time. The major facilities were already available. There was no question of air congestion and this allowed the school to start with minimal delay. Thus, it was close enough for control and supervision by Tuskegee Army Air Field, Commanding General.

- 1941 (January 9) – The Plan received formal approval of the Secretary of War "… the era of the all White Army Air Corps has ended, and the day of the non-segregated Air Force had arrived"

- 1941 (January 16) – The War Department announced the formation of the 99th Pursuit Squadron, a Black flying unit, to be trained at Tuskegee, Alabama, the home of the Tuskegee Institute. Eleven White officers would be assigned to train 429 enlisted men and 47 officers as the first Black military personnel in the flying school.

99TH PURSUIT SQUADRON

- 1941 (July 19) – Tuskegee Army Air Field officially opened in Tuskegee, Alabama.

- 1941 (March 21) – The 99th Pursuit Squadron was activated. It was expected that this squadron would consist of 33 pilots and 27 aircrafts. The total of 278 men was selected to receive training at Tuskegee Institute in a range of complementary roles including mechanics, weather specialist and technical clerks.

- 1941 (July 19) – The Tuskegee Institute began a program in Alabama to train African Americans as military pilots. The Division of Aeronautics of

Tuskegee Institute, the famed school of learning founded by Booker T. Washington in 1881, conducted primary flight training.

- 1941(August 25) – The members of the 99th Pursuit Squadron group received their first flight instruction.

- 1941(November) – Only 10 weeks of training, drew to an end, only six of original thirteen remained in the program. The flight training was only one phase of the training of the 99th Pursuit Squadron at Tuskegee Airfield, Alabama.

- 1942 (March 1) – Captain Benjamin O. Davis, Jr. was promoted to Lieutenant Colonel.

- 1942 (March 7) – The Class of 42-C, the first five Army Air Corps pilots African Americans earned their wings and graduated from Tuskegee Institute. The five Army Air Corps pilots were Capt. Benjamin O. Davis, Jr., District of Columbia; Lemuel R. Curtis, Connecticut; Charles Debow Jr., Indiana; George S. Roberts, West Virginia and Mac Ross, Ohio. The Tuskegee Airmen flew the P-40 Warhawk escorting bombers in North Africa.

- Among the aircraft flown by the pilots were the PT-17, Stearman, BT-13, AT-6 Texan, Piper Cub J-3, PT 19 Fairchild, P-39 Aerocobra, the P-40 Warhawk, P-39, P-47 and P51 Mustang.

- 1942 (March)- Tuskegee Army Air Field, Tuskegee, Alabama saw the five (5) men received the silver wings of Army Air Force pilots; George S. Roberts, Benjamin O. Davis, Jr., Charles H. DeBow, Jr., Mac Ross, and Lemuel R. Curtis. These men completed standard Army flight classroom instruction and many hours of flying time. This was a milestone in US military Aviation. Since these were the first African Americans to qualify as military pilots in any branch of the Armed Forces.

- 1942 (August 24) - Lt. Col. Benjamin O. Davis, Jr. took command of the 99th Pursuit Squadron.

- 1943 (April 15) - The 99th Pursuit Squadron (The Lonely Eagles) heads for North Africa.

- 1943 (June) - Lieutenant Charles Hall of Indiana became the first member of the 99th to shoot down a FW190 German plane, which was in the area at the time. All of the Black flyers were in the 332nd Fighter Group, which consisted of the 99th Pursuit Squadron; the 100th, 301st, 302nd Fighter Squadron, Capt. Hall and Lt. Weld sank a German destroyer with machine gun fire from their P-47s.

332ND FIGHTER GROUP

- 1944 (June) – The 332nd Fighter Group was attached to the 15th Air Force. The designation of the 99th was changed to Squadron. Their integration with the newer 332nd officially ended the existence of the 99th Pursuit Squadron as a distinct military pilot group. Members of the 99th Pursuit Squadron voiced opposition to being reassigned to this new all-Black squadron. As the 332nd Fighter Group had only arrived in the war zone in February 1944, they had no significant battle experience. The 99th Pursuit Squadron considered the change regression to segregation policies, one that held no positive or strategic military merit.

- 1944 (August) – The 332nd Fighter Group participated in the invasion of Southern France by escorting bombers and on ground attack mission in Romania and Czechoslovakia.

- 1944 (September 10) – Four pilots of the 332nd were awarded the Distinguish Flying Cross.

- 1944 – The 477th Bombardment conducted training missions, but winter conditions reduced flying time.

477ᵀᴴ BOMBARDMENT GROUP

- 1945 (March 15) – The all Black 477th Bombardment Group was moved from Godman Field, Kentucky to Freeman Field, Indiana.

- 1945 (April 1) – The men of the 477th protested the strict segregation policies ordered by base commander Colonel Robert Selway in a document called Regulation 85-2.

- 1945 (April 5) – Some 101 Black Officers and pilots led by 2nd Lt. Marsden Thompson tried to enter the segregated Officer's Club. These enlisted men of the 477th Bombardment Group organized a peaceful protest against the strict segregation policies ordered by Base Commander Robert Selway. These charges included the "Regulation 85-2."Several of the African American officers tried unsuccessfully to enter the Segregated Officers Club in Freeman Airbase in Indiana. These 101 Tuskegee Airmen were arrested. These "Black Pilots and Officers" were all charged with a felonious act for refusing to obey a direct order. There charges and military record was expunged by President Bill Clinton on August 25th, 1995.

- 1945 (April 9) – Base Commander Colonel Robert Selway ordered all of the African American officers to sign a statement that they have read and accept Regulation 85-2. The 101 Tuskegee Airmen officers refused to do so in what was called the Freeman Field Mutiny.(see book *Freeman Mutiny by Col. C. Warren)*

COLONEL BENJAMIN O. DAVIS JR.

- 1945 (June) – Colonel Benjamin O. Davis Jr. was named Commander of the 477th Composite Group, which included member of the 99th Pursuit Squadron and 100th Fighter Group. They began training for combat in the Pacific Theater.
- 1945 (August 12) – The court martial proceedings resulted in the so-called "Freeman Field Mutiny Group." was cleared by the Air Force and charges were dropped except charges against Lt. Roger Terry.
- 1945 (August 25) – World War II ended with the surrender of Japan.
- 1945 (September 2) – World War II finally came to an end, the members of the 99th Pursuit Squadron and 332nd Fighter Groups' valuable contribution was proudly acknowledged.
- 1948 – Armed Forces officially integrated. The Tuskegee Airmen continued under the command of Colonel Benjamin O. Davis, Jr. 450 Black Pursuit Squadron pilots were sent to fight in the African/European/Mediterranean Theaters of War.
- 1948 (July 26) – President Truman issued two Executive Orders. The first Executive Order - 9980 stated, "*All personnel action taken by federal appointing officers is authorized and directed to consist of appropriate steps to insure that in all such action there shall be no discrimination because of race, color, religion, or national origin.*" He submitted a similar proposal in February, 1948 to integrate the military, but was strongly opposed by Southern Congressmen. The second Executive Order - 9981 specifically focused more on the requirement that "military *personnel have full access to every branch of the services and be free from any form of discrimination based on race, color religion or national origin.*"

KOREAN WAR

- 1950-1953 – Korean War - About 195,000 Blacks were in Korean Company 13% of the US Troops. About 3, 223 or 9% of the total enlisted Blacks were killed in action. Korea saw the end of the segregated units in all of the United States Armed Forces.
- 1954 (October 27) – Col. Benjamin O. Davis, Jr., was promoted to Brigadier General, the first Black American to wear one star in the USAF.
- 1955 (May 15) – First edition of Tuskegee Airmen – The story of the Negro in the U.S. Air Force by Charles E. Francis was published, Boston, MA.

VIETNAM WAR

- 1961-1973 – Vietnam War- There were 275,000 Blacks or 10% of all forces that served in Vietnam. Hostile deaths were 5,711 or (12.1% of the total deaths) and 1530 non- hostile deaths
- 1967 – Eugene Mann, son of Lt. Col. Mann was honorably discharged from the Marine Corps.

PROMOTION OF AFRICAN AMERICANS TO TOP MILITARY POSITIONS

- 1967 – Lawrence Washington became the first male, Black or White, to receive a regular commission in the U.S. Army Nurse Corps.
- 1971 – Dr. Lauranne Sams, former Dean and Professor of Nursing at Tuskegee University, became a founder and first president of the National Black Nurses Association.
- 1971 (August) – Under the impulse of Charles Francis, the Tuskegee Airmen formed their first national organization, now widely known and accepted as the prestigious Tuskegee Airmen, Incorporated (TAI). This National Organization was organized in 1972 and legally chartered in 1975.
- 1975 (September) – Daniel "Chappie" James promoted to General, the first African American to wear four stars as a general in the military services of the United States of America.
- 1979 – Brigadier General Hazel W. Johnson-Brown became the first Black

woman in the Department of Defense to become a Brigadier General and the first Black to be Chief of the Army Nurse Corps.

- 1982 – Fostine Riddick became the first Black nurse appointed to the board of trustees of a major academic institution, Tuskegee University, Alabama.

- 1991 – Brigidaire General Clara Adams-Ender became the first Black woman and nurse to be appointed Commander General of an Army Post. As the highest-ranking woman in the Army, she commanded more than 20,000 nurses serving in the Persian Gulf War.

- 1991 – Persian Gulf War erupted and approximately 104,000 (24.5% of the total) Armed Forces were African Americans who served in Saudi Arabia. About 27 died during the military invasion of Iraq, called Desert Storm.

FREEMAN FIELD MUTINY PARDON REVISITED

- 1995 (August 12) – The Air Force cleared the service records of Tuskegee Airmen involved in the so-called "Freeman Field Mutiny," vindicating their stand for equality and justice as officers in the United States Military.

TUSKEGEE AIRMEN HONORED

- 1996 – President Clinton Honors Tuskegee Airmen and other World War II veterans in a ceremony at the White House, Washington, D.C.

- 1997 (August 18) – Tuskegee Airmen who were all Officers at the time of the mutiny, revisited Seymour, Indiana where they were arrested 52 years ago for trying to enter a segregated Officer's Club.

- 1998 (December 10) – General Benjamin O. Davis, Jr. who was born on Dec. 18, 1912 in Washington D.C. Commander of the Tuskegee pilots received his fourth star. President William Clinton made Benjamin O. Davis Jr., Commander of the famed Tuskegee Airmen, a Four Star General. He did not lose a single Bomber during 200 escort missions in World War II. This fourth star was received 28 years after his father; the nations' first African American Brigadier General joined the Army.

TUSKEGEE AIRMEN HONORED NATIONALLY

- 2005 – Congressional approval for the awarding of the Congressional Gold Medal to all of the original Tuskegee Airmen including support personnel.

- 2006 (February 23) – Tuskegee University Conferred Honorary Doctorate Degrees on the Fighter Pilots who participated in World War II as part of the famous Tuskegee Airmen.

- 2006 (April 11) - President George W. Bush signed into law the awarding of the Congressional Gold Medal to the Tuskegee Airmen who participated in the Tuskegee Experience during World War II.

- 2007, (March 29) The Congress of the United States and President bestowed the highest honors given to the Tuskegee Airmen and that was the "Congressional Gold Medal ".

THE IMPORTANCE OF USING TIMELINES

After more than 66 years, the history of the Tuskegee Airmen Experiences of World War II remains quite obscure. These timelines are intended to demonstrate that African Americans have always fought in defense of their country, the United States of America.

During the era of World War II engagements, the Tuskegee Airmen faced the contradiction between fighting for democracy and freedom for others, especially Europeans overseas while they were being discriminated against in the military, while serving in segregated units and being faced with the reality that at home their human and civil rights were limited and blatantly denied in every aspect of life.

The Tuskegee Airmen and African Americans who served in the segregated and non-segregated military have established key standards for the struggle for universal civil and human rights in the United States of America and in the world. These standards of action for freedom and equality include, but are not limited to the following lessons:

1. Success in a segregated society is realized by the setting of specific goals and measurable objectives that are attainable in the face of discrimination, segregation, and prejudicial behaviors.

2. The Tuskegee Airmen and the leadership at Tuskegee Institute and other Historically Black Colleges and Universities (HBCUs) emphasized the value of education as the central means to assuring success in one's cho-

of academic college courses. These courses include history, geography, English, higher mathematics, (the humanities) and of course the ever present physical training. I was fortunate enough to make it there but I was in the group, which had to receive the five months in the College Training Detachment (CTD).

In the CTD, we were not co-mingled with the civilian college students. In CTD, we received our first flying lessons, which were a minimum of 10 hours in a Piper Cub, J-3, and airplane. This was the first time in my life I had been close enough to any airplane of any type to touch. Academic elimination from the training program began here.

There were aspirants who suffered from astraphobia, claustrophobia, motion sickness, extreme anxiety, and/or other disorders, physical and mental. Those of us in my class who completed flight training in CTD were designated as Class 44-F. We graduated as Aviation Cadets. We were transferred to Tuskegee Army Air Field (TAAF), all of about four miles away, for two months of pre-flight ground school. Then it was back to TI for the two months of primary flight training and ground school. My class was the first to fly the Fairchild PT-19 aircraft. Classes before mine flew the Stearman PT-17 aircraft.

After primary, we went back to TAAF for two months plus of Basic Flying Training in the Vultee BT-13, and two more months of Advanced Flying Training in the North American AT-6. The Class 44-F graduated from the Tuskegee Army Air Field Advanced Flying Training School on 27 June 1944. There were 26 pilots in my class, 19 single engine combat pilots and 7 multi-engine pilots.

All of our training was accomplished at TAAF. Upon graduation, we received our first leave. For me that amounted to 15 months of training without an approved weekend pass or other leave. The single engine pilots were ordered to return to TAAF after the leave to perform our Tactical Aircraft Training in the Curtis Warhawk P-40. The multi-engine pilots were ordered to Goodman Army Air Field, KY, to do their training in the twin-engine Billy Mitchell B-25.

The only difference in the training between White and Black pilots was that the White aviation cadets received each phase of their training at different airfields that were especially built for that phase of their training. The Black pilots completed their training; I mean all of it at the Tuskegee Army Air Field (TAAF) in Tuskegee, Alabama. In as much as TAAF was the only field where Negroes were trained, everything was done from one field. All of our

flying training instructors were White. Our chemical warfare, physical training, and other ground school officers were colored. There had been no Black
military pilots before Class 42-C, the first class to graduate from TAAF Flying
School. As veteran Black pilots of the 332nd Fighter Group completed their
"extended" tours of duty, they were returned to the United States of America
and re-trained as instructor pilots and were assigned to TAAF. At that time,
Black pilots could not teach White student pilots to fly.

This is my recollection of that wonderful day as I wrote about it in "Too
Short? Too Tall?"

TOO SHORT, TOO SMALL - GRADUATION DAY CLASS 44-F

The next morning dawned bright and clear. A perfect day 27 June, 1944
for a graduation parade and wedding. Today was our day. Class 44-F would
lead the parade. Since it was summer the uniform for the day was our new
khaki colored gabardine shirts and trousers and our officers' dress caps. Not
the dashing "Fighter" with its "50 mission crush" but the more formal stiff"
Luxemburg." It didn't matter; we'd have worn buckets if necessary. Today was
graduation day.

The cadets formed their formation in the street alongside the cadet barracks
as usual. This time the three cadet officers leading the formation were Hugh
J. White, Carl F. Ellis, and Lewis J. Lynch. I was the one who stepped forward
this time and called the formation to attention and took the report from the
Flight Commanders. I reported to the Cadet Captain and took my place to his
left. The three of us marched to the head of the column behind the base band.
Hugh gave the command, "FORWARD MARCH," the band struck up the stir-
ring strains of "The Air Force Song," and off we went.

That was the proudest moment of my life up to that point. As the formation
turned the corner Hugh gave Carl and me and "Eyes Left" command. This
allowed us to look back at the rest of the formation as it rounded the corner.
What a sight that was. The entire cadet squadron moving as one man, brass
shining, arms swinging in perfect unison, a perfect formation, a perfect day. As
usual on graduation day, the streets were lined with spectators.

As the formation approached the chapel we could see our family members
standing outside, awaiting our arrival. Seats had been reserved for them so
they didn't have to worry about seating after the graduates entered the building. We went through the ritual of change of command, turning the squadron
over to the Captain of Class 44-G, then we entered the chapel and took our
seats. The building filled very rapidly after we were seated. The graduation

ceremony went smoothly with speeches by the Base Commander, Colonel Noel F. Parrish, and I don't remember who else.

THE HASSLES TO SEE MY WIFE

I was inducted into the Army at Ft. Hayes, Columbus, Ohio, and shipped to Keesler Army Air Field (KAAF) outside Biloxi, Miss. There I received 28 days Army Basic Training in the 1169th Basic Training Unit.

It was the rule at KAAF that all neophyte basis soldiers should be restricted to the field for the first 30 days that they were assigned there. (Written, un-written, or VOCO [Verbal Order of the Commanding Officer], I don't know.) We were told, however, that upon presentation of a written letter from any member of our families, we could receive an overnight pass on the weekend to visit them.

Kathadaza was in New Orleans with her mother, only about 70 miles away. I had written this information to her as soon as I had heard it. Her Dad had worked in Biloxi, and knew a lady who rented transit rooms to tradesmen who were in town for short stays. She had contacted her for a reservation. Kathadaza wrote the required letter. I presented it to the Commanding Officer and the pass was approved.

The procedure was after duty hours and dinner on Friday evening, sol-ders whose pass-requests had been approved by the Squadron Commander would report to the Orderly Room to pick up their passes. On that particular Friday after all duty and freshening-up necessities had been accomplished, I readied myself to meet my wife whom I had not seen for approximately for two months. I reported to the Unit's Orderly Room and requested the pass for Private Mann, Hiram E. The sergeant in charge informed me that I would have to purchase a package of protective devices before he would issue my pass. The NCOIC (Non-Commissioned Officer in Charge) was the headman after duty hours. He was an NCOIC, a tall, light complexioned man, about 25 years old.

I told the sergeant that my pass had been approved for me to visit my wife and I did not need any protection to see her. The Sergeant informed me that if I did not purchase the protective devices, I would not be issued my pass. Of course, I bought the protective devices. (In as much as I was a Basic Recruit, I knew that the Army Air Corps issued protective devices freely to soldiers who requested them).

This happened in April of 1943. One evening, about July or August of

1946, we were in the Officers Club at Lockbourne Army Air Field outside Columbus, Ohio, when I happened to look up and across the large room my eyes fell upon none other than the sergeant. When I realized who he was I remembered what he had done to me. I gave out a loud explicative and said, "That's the NCOIC officer who harassed me before he would give me a pass to see my wife. " I was tempted to go over and talk to him about the procedure he had in place. However, my wife was able to talk me out of it.

DO-DO VERSES (NON-SENSIBLE "BABBLE" LEARNED FOR DISCIPLINE)

"How's the cow?" Sir! The cow, she walks, she talks, she's full of chalk the lacteal fluid extracted from the female of the bovine species is highly prolific to the nth degree, sirrrrre!

"Have you had enough to eat?" Sir! My gastronomic society admonishes me that I have reached that state of deglutition which is highly consistent with my every dietetic state, sir!

"Do you understand?" Sir! My head is made from a thick layer of Vermont marble and African ivory, covered over with a thick layer of case-hardened steel, which forms an impenetrable barrier to all which seeks to impress itself upon the ashen tissues of my poor brain. Hence, sir, I am very dumb and do not understand, Sirrrrre!

"What time is it Sir?" Sir! The inner workings and hidden mechanisms of my poor chronometer are in such a state of discord with the great ciderial movement by which all time is commonly reckoned that i cannot with any degree of accuracy state the correct time; however, sir, without fear of being too far off and too far wrong, I will state that it is approximately "blank" ticks, "blank" seconds, and "blank" minutes past the "blank" hour, Sirrree!

HIGH NOON, JULY 1944

Congress had finally, grudgingly over some vehement protests, approved the bill, which would admit "Blacks" into the Army Flying Training Program. The site for conducting the training was an area outside the small township of Tuskegee, Alabama, near Tuskegee Institute. At the Institute Civilian Pilot Training had been a course taught by all Negro civilian pilots' staff, before WW II began.

Tuskegee is deep in the heart of Dixie with a small population consisting of approximately 80% Black and 20% White. The White community surrounded the base site. They did not welcome the segregated airfield in their area, especially since it was for training colored soldiers to be pilots.

The first Tuskegee Army Air Field (TAAF) Commander, was Major Jas A. "Straight Arrow" Ellison. He was sort of middle-of-the-road type. After a few months, he was replaced by Lt. Col. Frederick H. Von Kimble, a staunch segregationist." He worked to appease the restless, frightened, White Alabama community.

Lt. Col. Parrish replaced Von Kimble when morale on the base was at very low ebb. Although being a Southerner, he used his knowledge of human relations and persuasive powers to keep peace among the restless citizens. The separation of the races was the condition, which overshadowed all in the South.

When TAAF opened in 1941, its mission was to train "Blacks" to fly military aircraft. The military and civilian personnel responsible for maintaining and conducting operations at the field were predominately White. The "Black" officers had been trained at Chanute and Selfridge Army Air Fields, to conduct maintenance, ground school, and communications. They had been transferred in to train the Negro enlisted personnel in these specialties.

The atmosphere on TAAF was as it had been since the training of "Blacks" began in late 1941, apparently gratefully tranquil. No one seemed to object to the racial separation in all instances except the flying training. After all, "Blacks" were finally being trained to be pilots in the United States military service.

No one appeared to be overly concerned that Blacks and Whites did not socialize or eat lunch together on the base, since this was the condition, which prevailed outside the base. There was no White Officers' Club, mess hall, dining room or theater on the base. The base had been configured for the "Blacks". White Officers either went to their homes in the city for these things, bought their lunches in the cafeteria next to the Base Exchange, or brown-bagged and ate lunch in their offices privately. It was assumed that this cafeteria was a White Officers' Mess. One day before they entered the cafeteria, took trays, selected food paid and sat down at their tables and ate their lunches. I noticed that the White officers spent some of their time observing the Black officers and sometime they would invade the area where the Black officers were sitting and take their napkins and throw them on the floor and sometimes with food in them and simply walk off. I spoke to one of my friends and said it is clear that they are trying to provoke an incident. We, the Black officers never really responded to this behavior because we had one single goal and that was to fly airplanes. Gradually, Black and civilian employees were hired to serve the Black enlisted personnel of the air base hospital, mess hall, tower, cadre, mechanics, crew chiefs, parachute riggers, telephone, sentries (MPs), post exchange, commissary, all support personnel required to operate an air base.

There were no Black military pilots in any of the American Armed Services prior to the 1940's. Therefore, there were no Black Military Instructor Pilots to teach the Black trainees to fly.

Many of the White instructor pilots accepted their assignments in the name of the army and did the best they could to help their charges earn their coveted silver wings. These wings carried with them a commission as a Second Lieutenant (or Flight Officer) in the Army of the United States. Of course, there were those instructors who were opposed to Negroes flying from the beginning. They did not appreciate their assignments and covertly, and some blatantly overtly, placed obstacles in their trainees paths.

Unrest began to fester among some of the Black permanent part of the officer personnel who were non-trainees. The medical, legal, maintenance, ordinance, chemical warfare, supply, motor pool, etc. officers. The "Clubhouse Lawyers" whispered dissatisfaction with the situation and caused adverse reactions and irritation to permeate their ranks.

The whispered word was that according to military documentation there should be no segregation, or segregated facilities, on military installations. Low self-esteem among the Blacks and racial tension between Blacks and Whites ran rampant throughout the base. Information about this discontentment filtered into Col. Parrish. He posted word for an Officers call at 1200 hours in the Base Chapel on a never-to-be-forgotten-day in July 1944.

The Single-Engine pilots of Class 44-F had recently returned to TAAF after the first leave that was allowed to its members since they entered the Aviation Cadet Corps. They were given 15 days post graduation leave. They had been ordered to return to TAAF to transition into the P-40, Warhawk.

It was a typical warm sunny day in July 1944 at TAAF, Alabama. The Base Commander, Col. Noel F. Parrish, had gotten word of the discontentment and undercurrent situation, which was causing the waves. He had issued an Officers call for 1200 hours on that particular day in July of 1944.

The meeting would be in the Base Chapel, which was the largest assembly hall with seats. All officers stationed at TAAF were required to be present: cadre, administration, school commandants, doctors, nurses, flying personnel (both instructors and trainees), and the whole gambit. The only officers exempt from attending the call were officers whose posts required manning on a mandatory basis.

We were all "in place and on time." We sat in tense apprehension, wondering why the Officers' call had been issued. No one appeared to be deeply troubled or overly concerned those Blacks and Whites did not socialize or eat lunch together on the airfield.

The Chapel bell began its slow peal, twelve times, and then deafening silence prevailed. A short while after the bell ceased to ring; the Chapel door was opened with such force that everyone snatched their heads around to see what had caused the commotion.

It was Col. Parrish who approached. Attention was shouted! Then Col. Parrish walked rapidly down the isle, removing his garrison cap with his right hand and apologizing as he walked. He had three large notebook binders under his left arm. He walked to the podium on the dais pulpit, placed the binders on the podium, and gave the, "At ease." He flipped the first binder open to a place he had flagged and began: According to War Dept Directive "umpti-ump", it reads; according to War Circular "umpti-ump", it reads; according to "umpti-ump", it reads. He read from each binder, one after the other, as he completed reading the particular paragraph.

Then he announced, "Therefore, there will be *NO SEGREGATION ON THIS BASE!* Thank you very much!" and he abruptly left the pulpit within less than two minutes. It only took a little while for the message to sink in. However, the atmosphere took longer to clear up. When we were sent back to TAAF. In December of 1945 and January of 1946, after WWII had ended, practically all of the White flying instructors had been replaced by African-American flying instructors.

FIRST ANNIVERSARY, PLUS ONE DAY: CLASS 44-F GRADUATION (D 2)

Twenty-seven members of Class 44-F graduated from Tuskegee Army Air Field Advance Flying Training School of 1944. There were 19 Single Engine (SE) and 8 Twin Engine (TE) Pilots. The separation of the Twin Engine Pilots from our Single Engine Pilots happened immediately after graduation on 27

June 1944. They were ordered to return to different airfields for transition into fully equipped B-25 "Billy Mitchell" Medium Bombers, after the graduation leave when the Single Engine Pilots were ordered to return to Tuskegee Army Air Field for transition into P-40 Warhawk aircraft after the 15 days of graduation leave.

When we shipped out from Hampton Roads, POE Norfolk, VA, for APO #520, aboard the Liberty Ship S.S. Patrick Henry we left Flight Officer (F/O) Yenwith Whitney behind. He shipped over with Class 44-G. We picked up Lt. Ralph Orduna from Class 44-E. Lt. Richard S.A. Armistead was removed from flying status soon after graduation. The Flight Surgeons determined he was "too apprehensive for combat duty" right after graduation.

Upon arrival at our campsite at Ramitelli, Italy, the members were given another physical examination to determine whether or not they were physically fit for combat. Combat anxiety for one class member, F/O Robert Murdic, his hypertension and anxiety in anticipation of combat were so great that his blood pressure kept racing and could not be lowered. He was returned to the United States of America immediately.

During training, we left Lt. Robert Lawrence and F/O Wyrain Schell behind at Walterboro, SC. They had been involved in an automobile accident and hospitalized. They were held back to Class 44-G, also. The remaining 17 class members who had been together in training were distributed among the four squadrons of the 332nd Fighter Group.

There were Negro Liaison Pilots (spotters) for the 92nd Infantry Division (who had been trained to fly at TAAF) stationed north of our campsite in Italy. Some of the pilots had flown to our field in their L-5 Observation Piper Planes for no particular reason on the 27th of June 1945. Our pilots went up and flew the planes. It was an amusing sight to see these planes "crabbing" through the air. Our men where overcorrecting in handling the lightweight planes.

That evening, 27 June 1945, my classmates held a first anniversary of the class graduation at the Officers' Club. Chairs were leaned against the table for missing class-members who were no longer with us. We drank to them, wherever they were: Frank Wright had been killed in combat; Jim Wright had been killed in Myrtle Beach, SC, in that freak accident situation; Hugh White, Leon Spears, James Mitchell, and Lincoln Hudson had been shot down and had become POW's.

The 11 Fighter Pilot Members of Class 44-F who remained at Cattolica,

Italy, got together in the Officers Club to celebrate the first anniversary of the graduation of Class 44-F. We sat around the table drinking a salute of the "fermented barley and corn" to each of the up-turned chairs. They were: Carl Ellis, Charles Hill, Rupert Johnson, Robert Lawrence, George Lynch, Lewis Lynch, Hiram Mann, Wyrain Schell, Harry Stewart, Samuel Washington, and Yenwith Whitney. (Whitney did not drink!)

Our Military Operation Specialty (MOS 1055) was Single Engine Combat Fighter Pilot. In as much as our war in Europe had ended on 08 May 1945, there was no combat for us to participate in. Each pilot was scheduled, and expected, to fly regularly to get in his flying time and to maintain his flying proficiency. Schedules were made and posted and we were expected, and required, to comply with the posted schedules.

The 100th Fighter Squadron Flying Schedule for 28 June 1945 had been posted. I was scheduled to fly after lunch. In addition, a schedule had been posted for firing our .45s at the firing range that afternoon. I was scheduled to participate in each, first the firing range, then to fly. I had overdone it celebrating the night before at the OC. At the Firing Range, each time the hammer of my .45 struck its chamber, my head felt as though it would jump off. I announced that I was not in any condition to fly, that I was returning to my tent to "sack-time." My head was too messed up. The men from my area draped their 45s over my shoulder for me to carry back and hold until they returned from flying.

After the Firing Range some of our guys decided to fly up to the 92's camp area and "ring it out," which amounted to buzzing down on their site and pulling up into a roll-off-the-deck (a very dangerous maneuver). To put a good air show for them. Lt Floyd Squires decided he would fly in my place that afternoon. The guys went up and really wrung-out the 92nd. Tragedy was a big part of that show!! Somehow, during Squires' roll, when he was inverted, his plane went into the ground. In this maneuver, when inverted, one must operate the controls the opposite of right-side-up flying: to go up the joystick must be pushed forward. To pull back on the stick, pulls the plane toward the ground. What actually happened, no one will ever know, but Squires went into the ground!

AP – 40 WARHAWK THRILLER

The Class of 44-F was graduating from the 2143rd Army Air Force Basic Unit Flying Training School, Tuskegee Air Field, on 27 June 1944. Most of us had not had a day leave since we entered military service. In my case, it had been 15 months. When we graduated, we were granted 15 days leave and ordered to return to the Flying Training School for transition into the P-40 Warhawk tactical aircraft. The P-40 is a Curtis aircraft, with an Allison 1150 horsepower engine. If one stands directly in front of the propeller spinner and looks at the landing gear, it appears to be "knocked-kneed" with a very narrow landing gear. The P-40s at our flying school were relics. The logs showed that some had actually been used by the Flying Tigers in the China/Burma Theater. They were hand-me-downs from the "Flying Tigers" and still had the shark's tooth paintings on the cowls. We were flying them with under-octane gasoline. A pilot had to be extremely attentive when landing. It "ground-looped" easily.

A high school acquaintance from my home City, Cleveland, Ohio who was ahead of me in flight training Class 43-H, had an accident in a P-40 about a year before. His story was: "When he approached for a landing he had a problem and wanted to go around for another approach. There was a workman on a ladder painting a building. As he applied the throttle, he lost control of the aircraft. The plane missed the building, but hit the man on the ladder and knocked his legs off. The plane crashed and caught fire. The pilot was saved but he suffered severe burns."

I was flying my first or second transition flight in a P-40. I had performed the prescribed maneuvers I was to accomplish that session. I had been cleared and was going in for a landing. My downwind and crosswind legs were satisfactory. I turned on to my approach and descended in altitude. I lowered my landing gear and flaps, retarded the throttle, trimmed the plane, lowered the nose and then in front of me I observed a group of workmen crossing the runway carrying a ladder.

I must have had a flashback of my acquaintance's accident. An accident I had not seen, but in anxiety of handling a plane I was not familiar with, it came to mind. I rammed my throttle full forward to perform a go-around for another landing approach. The engine would not accept the sudden introduction of under octane gasoline. It caught, roared, and then sputtered. I retracted the throttle and tried again.

I passed over the beginning and more of my runway as I tried again, and again, and again, with the same result. All the time I was passing over the well-needed landing runway with my gear and flaps still in the down position, in preparation for my landing. (An old pilot's adage, "You cannot use the runway you leave behind.") .There was a clump of trees a short distance ahead, from the far end of the runway.

At some time, I had the presence of mind to retract my gear and flaps. I pulled the nose of the plane up in time to clear the treetops as I passed over the end of the runway, but I did not have sufficient flying speed and the plane settled behind the trees in a clearing on the far side. The engine caught and roared smoothly. I was able to maneuver into a proper climb to re-enter the traffic pattern for another attempt to land.

In the meantime, while I battled this sputtering airplane over the runway, some of my classmates were in the operations room and heard the noise. They rushed out on the porch to see who was causing it. They were just in time to see the plane disappear behind the trees. Later I was told that one classmate started up the hill to tell my wife I had crashed. He did not wait to see the plane climb from behind the trees. Luckily, she was not home. I was also told that the fellows who saw the plane climb to altitude emitted a resounding yell for me. I didn't get weak or nervous until after I landed, taxied back, parked the plane, and stepped out onto the wing of the plane.

CASE OF THE MOVING SHIRT POCKET

Class 44-F returned to Tuskegee Army Air Field in July of 1944, after we were granted 15 days graduation leave. We had returned for our transition into the tactical, 1150 horsepower, Curtiss P-40 Kittyhawk airplane. My classmate, 2nd Lt Robert W. Lawrence, and his brand-new, childhood sweetheart, bride, 1st Lt Mary Rickerds Lawrence, a Nurse at the Base Hospital; and my bride of almost four years and I were sitting at a table eating lunch in the Post Exchange lunch room (the Base Cafeteria was used exclusively by the White officers on the base at that time).

I saw Mary and Bob were opposite Kathadaza. Bob, Mary, and I were in our military summer khaki uniforms. I noticed Mary's left breast pocket moving. I attempted to avert my eyes and not stare at what I thought I was seeing. Our conversation was small talk, casual, as we enjoyed our lunch. Each time I saw the pocket move, my eyes would be attracted to that area. I do not remember how it came about, whether I was caught staring or if I asked about it; but, Mary smiled and reached into her left breast pocket and removed a baby squirrel. Mary had found the baby squirrel on the ground and her nursing instinct would not permit her to leave it to die. She wanted to save the baby squirrel's life. She had placed it in her pocket. That's what the movement was all about.

FIFTY MISSION CRUSH AND SNAPPY SALUTE

Paragraph # 52, Special Orders #24, HQ from Army Air Forces Eastern Flying Training Command, Tuskegee Field, Alabama, dated 17 June 44 delegated authority to grant Aeronautical Ratings which determined who was supposed to graduate in Class 44-F from the 126th, Tuskegee Army Air Field, Alabama, on 27 June 1944. Every pilot wanted his salute to be sharp and snappy and his cap to have the 50-mission-crush look from the very first time he wore it officially, after graduation. And, he wanted his salute to be sharp and snappy.

We could use a copy of this Special Order (SO) to order and buy our tailor-made officers' pink and green uniform. After receipt of the SO we bought our flight caps and we would soak them with water and let them dry. We would place the caps in the inside of our knees when seated. This was to do away with the "new look" and make our caps look like veteran pilots' caps. (Or to give them the 50-mission look.)

We neophyte military pilots-to-be would stand in front of mirrors in the latrine and salute ourselves, practicing snappy salutes. We would jokingly refer to each other. As Lieutenant and say sir, and "throw rank" based on serial number, which, of course were issued alphabetically. The Flight Officers were not quite Lieutenants, yet. They had to be promoted to the rank of Lieutenant.

YOU CAN FIGHT, BLEED, AND DIE, BUT YOU CAN'T EAT HERE

The nineteenth Single Engine Combat Pilots, members of Class 44-F, completed Overseas Replacement Training at the 2246 Basic Training Unit at Walterboro Army Air Field, SC, (WAAF) in November of 1944. The graduates were granted four days pre-embarkation leave in order to visit their families before shipping out to combat in the European Theater of Operations.

Some class members were close enough to travel by bus or train to get home and back in forth in the four days allotted. Others had to fly because of the distant cities, Los Angeles, Detroit, St. Louis, Chicago, Cleveland, New York, etc. During the war, air passengers were assigned priority for space on airplanes depending on urgency. Those of us flying home had been assigned A-1 priority, the highest.

Ten or twelve of the pilot officers were bussed to the civilian air terminal near Walterboro in an army bus. WAAF was situated about 40 miles west of Charleston, SC, which was where the nearest commercial air terminal was located.

As planes departed with classmates aboard, the wind-down came and only two of us were left: Frank Wright, a very fair complexioned Negro, who was assumed to be Caucasian, and me, an unmistakably colored person.

We decided we wanted to eat. We located a place and went into the cafeteria. We hung our coats, placed our caps on the coat stand, and seated ourselves at the counter as any law abiding American citizen should do. The cafeteria was not crowded. About five waitresses huddled in the back by the doors to the kitchen, whispering among themselves. After a while, one came toward us and bent over and said to me, "I'm sorry, we don't serve coloreds in here." Frank and I got up, retrieved our garments, and started for the door. The cashier called, "Lieutenant, Lieutenant!" Both of us turned and looked at her. She beckoned for us to come toward her. Frank went back; I continued to walk ahead. The cashier told Frank she was sorry, since we were officers in the United States Army she had called upstairs to management and asked them if we could be served. Management had said, "No!" Frank asked the cashier where we could get something to eat. The cashier told Frank there was a coffee shop across the lobby. We could eat there. Therefore, we left for our respective destinations. I went home to Cleveland, Ohio.

The four days at home in Cleveland, Ohio passed rapidly, much too fast, and the 10 or 12 of us began to filter back into Washington, D.C., air terminal to catch planes to our respective homes. About six or eight of us assembled and someone suggested we go to the cafeteria to eat. Frank and I told them we would not be served there; we had to go to the coffee shop. We entered the coffee shop, as decent people should, ordered coffee and donuts, paid and were served`. While we were eating, there was a terrible commotion at the entrance doors. There was a little, grey-haired, old White lady standing in the doorway with her hands on her hips shouting, "I'll be glad when they put up signs saying they can't eat in here". "They don't know the Washington Air Terminal is on the Virginia side of the Potomac River and they're not supposed to eat with White people." Lincoln Hudson spoke up and said, "I hope those bullets have colored and White on them also!" No incident followed the insult.

Ironically, Frank Wright was killed in aerial combat; Lincoln Hudson, James Mitchell, Leon Spears, and Hugh White were shot down and became prisoners of war during World War II. These heroic African Americans served their country in the military, yet, they never experienced equal justice, equal treatment and the liberty that they were fighting for.

GERMAN AND ITALIAN PRISONERS OF WAR

I cannot include every degrading incident that we were exposed to during the various developments of our training. I will bring up a very poignant situation, which occurred in Walterboro, S.C., in 1944, also 12 years later in Montgomery, Alabama, in 1956 while I was attending the Command and Staff College of the Air University. Italian and German prisoners of war (POWs), our combat enemies during WWII, had been brought to America.

The stockades in Europe were still overcrowded with POWs. They were transported across the ocean to do menial work around some bases and camps in the USA. On weekends, various organizations, the Chambers of Commerce and White fraternal organizations, would sponsor the prisoners at the USO facilities for recreational activities, socialization, entertainment, and dancing or to the movies.

I know about these two towns because I was there and witnessed it. It was done in other cities too. We, American Negro military personnel, could not, or were forbidden, to enter these premises or attend these activities. When my classmates and I completed our three months of overseas replacement flight training at WAAF, we were allowed 4 days per-embarkation leave. We were given "A-1" priority travel category for plane trips home. Most of us flew into Washington, D.C., air terminal hub to transfer to planes to go to our respective residence cities.

The enemy POW's brought into the United States because of stockade shortage over there is a well-known fact of any personnel who served at installations where these prisoners were kept. The German and Italian POW's ate with the White soldiers, but the Black Soldiers were kept segregated for eating and recreation.

ATLANTIC CROSSING

The Class 44-F completed its Overseas Replacement Single Engine Combat Fighter flying training at Walterboro Army Air Field, SC, in November of 1944. I flew my last training flight in the P-47 Thunderbolt aircraft (built by Republic with a 2300 horsepower Pratt-Whitney engine) on 14 November of 1944.

Fifteen of us were released from assignment to the 126th Air Force Base Unit Walterboro, SC, and transferred by train to Camp Patrick Henry, VA, on 25 November 1944. We were billeted in a segregated area. Second Lt. Robert W. Lawrence and Flight Officer Wyrain T. Schell, had both been injured in an automobile accident and Flight Officer Yenwith K. Whitney for some reason, and were left behind. We were transported to the Hampton Roads Port of Embarkation (POE), Norfolk, VA, by train. We shipped out from the Newport News, VA, Shipyard, aboard the USS "NATHAN HALE," a lightweight Liberty ship, on 01 December, 1944. We were part of a 115-ship convoy to cross the Atlantic Ocean.

It took 19 days, and Blackout nights, for the convoy to cross the Atlantic Ocean, navigating a zigzag route to avoid Nazi submarines, which were prevalent at that time. Destroyers and other American minesweeping ships darted in, out, and around as they escorted the convoy and to protect it from the German ships. There were 39 Black Miscellaneous Troops aboard our ship. (A Miscellaneous Troop was a soldier with no specialty, who was illiterate. Some could not read or write their own names.) En route, some asked us to write V-Mail (Victory Mail) letters to wives, relatives, sweethearts, and friends.

The main cargo on our ship, not counting the 15 Black Army pilots and the 39 Black Miscellaneous Troops, was Post Exchange supplies. Since we were not loaded with heavy equipment, our ship rode high on the water. This is significant because it added to the pitch, roll, and yaw of the ship.

In addition, a convoy can travel only as fast as its slowest ship. Whether or not ours was the slowest, I do not know. I'm certain we contributed our share in retarding the convoy's speed. When we passed through the Straits of Gibraltar, our ship's crew announced we were in one place on earth where one was relatively close to three continents at one time Europe, Africa, and Asia.

The evening of the 19th day, part of the convoy docked at a harbor in Oran, North Africa. We knew (were positive!) from the past experiences of our predecessor Black pilots who had traveled this way before us that this was the route we were to take. Therefore, we assumed that we were going to disembark that evening or the next morning.

The ship's officers induced our class leader to play a joke on the remaining 14 of us. He told seven us would be permitted to go ashore, at 1900 hours that night in a tender. In order to determine which seven, we pulled slips of paper with "go" or "stay." The "go's" shaved, showered, and spruced-up for an evening ashore after the long period at sea. I don't remember what my slip was. The time arrived – and then it passed. The "go's" were told to be patient the tender was running late. Eventually it occurred to everyone that this was a hoax. Angry thoughts prevailed, almost!!!

Surprise! Surprise! Apparently, the procedure had changed in the month since the prior classes of Black pilots were shipped over. The next morning our Liberty Ship and others were back in the Mediterranean Sea. Three days later the mini-convoy docked at a harbor in Marseille, France. It was the 23rd of December, 1944 two days before Christmas.

All pilots and aircrew members were taken to a separate staging area on the outskirts of the city across the *"CHATEAU D'IF"* prison island. We could actually see the prison buildings from the shore. The first evening, all "newly-arrived" personnel, the 15 of us along with the Whites, were assembled for an important briefing by the Commander of the Staging Area. We were told to stay close to the area and to check-in daily. We would be at this site no longer than three days and we would ship out to our assigned units singly, in pairs, or no more than three to the same place, for our permanent overseas duty assignments.

The Black pilots knew that there was only one place for all of the 15 of us could go. We knew we were destined for an army airfield in Italy, on the Adriatic Sea side in the Foggia area. We were 15 Black American single engine replacement combat fighter pilots, eager to join the 332nd Fighter Group and test our metal against the enemy.

At this staging site, we experienced equal treatment, the same as the Caucasian officers. The exception was that we did not ship out individually, or in twos, or in threes to various sites as was the case with the White officer counterparts. It took thirteen days for the Transportation Corps to re-arrange shipping instructions and orders to start us toward our home airfield in the United States of America.

This is another instance of the price America paid during the war because of discrimination and segregation. We will never be able to calculate how many lives of American young men were lost due to discrimination and "restricting protection" for military personnel who first happened to be White.

During this waiting period, the Black pilots were able to go to Marseille almost daily, wandering around, taking in the sights, and marveling over being in Marseille, France. Hitching rides into the city was no problem because G.I. trucks were constantly rolling, coming and going on the highway. We usually traveled in two's and three's.

Some of us made contacts with a few Black PFCs (Privates First Class) and corporals who were port battalion GIs. They unloaded ships and loaded and drove G.I. trucks delivering government supplies and equipment to various campsites needing re-supply. We found later that some of the supplies never reached their intended military destinations. They were intentionally diverted into the Black market. In some instances the 6x6, GI trucks, were sold along with their cargos.

These GIs, literally, had pockets-full of French francs they could not dispose of in the proper manner. They had French francs to spend, and spend it they did! Military enlisted personnel were only permitted to send home the equivalent of their base pay, plus 10% more. No more! I realize the term "they" is generalization or stereotype work and should be used with caution. However, these GIs could not go to the Post Exchange to make purchases of socks, undershirts, and/or shorts, or any other sanitary or toilet articles. They could and would enter a bar or tavern and buy drinks for all Americans, including White officers, in the place.

Some had managed to get French girlfriends who traveled with them at night. The girls carried "wads" of the GIs money in their purses so the GIs would not have the francs on their persons. Many bought buildings and French businesses in their friends' families names.

Only a few of the port battalion soldiers had ever seen Black officers and none had ever seen Black pilots. They were delighted to "sponsor" and serve us in the taverns. They elevated us to a very high status. I don't think I saw one port battalion soldier with a rank higher than corporal.

French taxi drivers, with their charcoal burning autos, would form a queue at the main gate just before retreat each evening. They waited for "their" daily permanent fares to complete their duty day and be ready to ramble from 1700 hours until 2300 hours, which was curfew time. The GIs paid the equivalent of $100 a day for their "personal taxi" to chauffeur them everywhere and anywhere they desired. After the soldiers were delivered to their front door (the main gate), the drivers were told to drive us, the Black pilots, to our staging area. This was possibly 20 kilometers (8 miles) away.

The drivers began to complain and added an additional amount to their charges each day, because of the extra driving to the outskirts of the city. The GIs didn't complain. While we were in Marseille, France, we experienced our first German night raid. Sirens wailed, ack-ack guns fired, searchlights pierced the dark sky. Civilians cried and screamed and yelled while running madly in all directions. Some ran past the shelters in their excitement. They carried anything they could get their hands on; pets, mattresses, baskets of food, you name it. That was a real ordeal!

Through some very pleasant quirk of fate, I encountered two high school acquaintances from Cleveland, Ohio, as we walked in the city. In addition, my French speaking ability was almost a problem for me. Some of the French people thought I was Tunisian. At times, I had to produce my U.S. Air Corps Identification Card to convince them as to my real identity.

Among the strange things that happened during this time was that one day F/O Samuel Washington wondered somewhere, away from the rest of us because he was not having his fun and was "out-of-it!" He slept for three days and only wanted to drink water. We surmised and worried he may have wondered into Kasbahs. We were happy that he was back with us.

It took 10 days, from 24 December 1944 until 3 January 1945, for new shipping instructions and orders to arrive, which would get the 15 of us from Marseilles, France, to our area base site in Italy. A beautiful part of this occurrence was our sailing from Marseille, France, to the Italian port city of Taranto, around the toe and into the arch of the "boot." We were quartered aboard the French Luxury Liner, the "VILLE D'ORAN."

The American officers were first class passengers for the three days we were aboard. The allied officers were a few beside the 15 of us were second-class passengers, enlisted personnel were third class, and there were many "repatriated" male and female civilians in steerage. There were no American enlisted men on the ship. We were on the top deck and the class delineation was down. Steerage was in the lowest deck.

We ate in "first-class style," at tables with plates and flatware; in steerage, the repatriates were fed from large metal containers. A bad thing was, to get to the dining room; one had to pass the entrances to the steerage dormitory where personnel slept in hammocks in tiers of three or four. They swayed with the ship's motion. Some "up-chucked" their "cookies" and the stench could be smelled, along with the odor of their unwashed bodies, in the corridors as one passed the open bulkheads going up to the dining room.

In Taranto, we were shuttled, again into 6x6 trucks, to a waiting freight train, which had the famous 40 and 8 boxcars. (Qurante hommes ou huite chaveaux: forty men or eight horses.) It took approximately three days for the train to go approximately 150 kilometers (approximately 92 miles) over hills and steep terrain.

Again, we were loaded into trucks and carted off to our camp location at

Ramitelli, Italy. The trucks, containing pilots and baggage, rumbled through the narrow Italian streets to the site, on the Adriatic Sea side. We arrived about 0200 hours. The entire camp component turned out to rejoice and greet us. The whole 332nd Fighter Group was relieved and happy when we finally arrived. They were sorely in need of replacement pilots.

It had been a long time since our departure from the United States or since no one; "back home" had heard anything about us. Not a word from 1 December 44 until 6 January 45. Rumor had spread that out Liberty Ship had been torpedoed and all aboard had been lost. We underwent physical examinations immediately in order to get us into combat. Flight Officer Robert J. Murdic could not take the pressure. The anxiety and excitement of combat was too much for him. The Flight Surgeons considered him a risk in combat and ordered him returned to the United States, at once, because his blood pressure would not go down to an acceptable level. He never flew a combat mission.

MY FIRST AIR RAID

One evening during our unscheduled stay in Marseille, some of us had gone into the big city from the staging area. Everyone heard the drone of airplanes in the sky. Every person soon realized it was a flyover the city by some unidentified, unknown, aircraft. As I recall it, there was no moon, just a pitch-Black sky. I think there were clouds.

Immediately, the sirens began their wail and the searchlights began to penetrate the black sky with piercing thread from the beams of the searchlights. They were probing the sky for the night invader. Trying to locate the intruder on the tranquility that had prevailed earlier. Soon the "ack-ack" guns began to punctuate unfolding saga with the piercing staccato sounds of firing artillery.

My classmates and I had never been in a real air raid before and we stood mesmerized by the sight and sound of what was going on. The French, however, had experienced many such flyovers accompanied with bombings. They were panic-stricken. Some ran carrying pets, dogs, cats, and birds in cages, while others ran carrying food. Others ran carrying bed clothing and small mattresses. All running, seeking shelter from the unknown.

They ran for the sake of running. Some ran toward the air raid shelter while others, in panic, ran past shelters and/or in the opposite direction. Some Good Samaritan was upset with our (my classmates) fascination in what was happening and insisted we should go into a nearby shelter. Inside the shelter, people were praying, crying, screaming, hollering, kissing, and babbling incoherently. Some were so frightened they lost continence and were relieving themselves on themselves. I don't remember approximately how many hours we remained in the shelter until the all clear was sounded, but it was a relief to get away from the frightened French people. As far as I know, no bombs were dropped that night.

MY FIRST COMBAT STRAFING MISSION

I joined the group as a replacement pilot as Germany was losing its power prominence in the European Theater. The majority of the combat missions assigned to the 15th Air Force's four fighter groups in Italy were bomber escorts. The morning of 17 January 1945, I flew my first, of several, combat-strafing missions. The pilots assembled in the Briefing Room at the appointed hour. The pilots with more combat experience emitted verbal expletives! Anxiety permeated the air.

There was only one line on the briefing-wall-map to a target area for the day's mission. This meant strafing or dive bombing. If there had been two lines (a red and a green), meeting over the coast of Czechoslovak for a rendezvous area, it would have been an escort mission of some sort. At the briefing, the air was impregnated with a pre-mission anxiety and tension. We were given the days code-names and allocated a search and destroy area in Gloggnitz, Germany. (This data came from my personal log.) Before I climbed into the cockpit of my plane, "*Boss Lady*," I put two sticks of chewing gum in my mouth to quell my nervousness and excitement.

We flew to our target area as a group. A target was cited and we separated into flights. We jettisoned our external tanks, maneuvered into echelon, peeled off, and rolled-out on a moving German troop train. I was flying the number two position, the flight leader's wingman. We went into our dive, in trail. I "fire-walled" my throttle, took aim on a boxcar. I squeezed the trigger. My adrenaline cut-in as I felt the plane shutter when my six guns fired at the targeted boxcar. I would see silver streaks from my tracer bullets converging in a pattern in front of me.

Suddenly I noticed tracers going past me on both sides. I thought I was flying faster than my bullets. Then it occurred to me. Those Germans were shooting at me! This possibility had never been mentioned or discussed in flight training or ground school. Nor had I ever experienced a situation like this before in my life.

Suffice it to say, my next thought was to get the hell out of there! We hit several targets, joined-up, and returned to our home field. I landed, parked my plane, and stepped out on the wing. Then I noticed I had a mouthful of BB's. I had literally chewed the gum so forcefully that all of the cohesion in the gum was gone. After the post mission inspection performed by my crew chief, he informed me that there was one bullet in the tail of my/his plane.

HOW P-51 NO 26-THE FIRST "BOSS LADY" WAS LOST:

The first P-51 Mustang I was assigned was No. 26. I decided to name the plane "Boss Lady"(planes, boats, cars, etc. are always referred to as female). Once a pilot has a plane assigned to him, he inherits the crew chief and armored/radio man along with the plane. Although the plane was referred to as mine, it belonged to the Group (all American citizens). I had the privilege to fly it daily. It is strange that a closeness developed between my crew chiefs and me, I do not remember either of their names or where they were from. However, I do remember my last radio man's name was Bill Peaks from Toledo, Ohio.

When a plane needed repairing that would take some time, the pilot to whom it was assigned flew another of the Group's planes. If the pilot knew whose plane he was going to fly, it was courtesy, custom for him to ask permission. (I don't know of an instance in which one was refused, or if it could be done.)

When pilots were assigned to a squadron, their names were placed at the bottom of the roster for rest and recuperation (R & R) at our Rest Camp for one week. One week, then it was my turn to go out to Rest Camp in Naples, Italy for one week. Our campsite was on the Adriatic Sea (east) side of Italy and our Rest Camp was on the Mediterranean side of Italy, about 150 miles across the mountainous terrain. My friend, Arnett Starks' plane required repair for some reason. My plane was assigned to Arnett while I would be away. He mentioned the assignment to me at breakfast the day we were leaving for Rest Camp. At the end of each week, the Rest Camp exchange in residents took place. A 6x6 from the 332nd site would bring the new "recuperates" to the Rest Camp and pick up the "rested" members for transfer back to the campsite.

On 23 March 1945, the truck arrived from the base campsite with the new "batch" of 332nd personnel, as scheduled. After lunch and a brief rest, the driver loaded-up, the returning "batch" and started back to our campsite on the other side of Italy. The sun set while we were en route and the cold mountain air was severe in the bed of the truck. After dark as we were rolling toward our home base, more than halfway there, the truck developed some sort of engine trouble. Cappodichino Army Air Field was the closest Military Installation to where we were. We "limped in" and repairs were made as quickly as possible. We then proceeded to our base and arrived after 0200 hours, cold, hungry, and tired.

Luckily, Capt Maloney, a Flight Surgeon, was one of the passengers on the truck. He made a declaration that not one pilot on that truck would fly combat that morning of 24 March, 1945. The daily flight schedule had been posted in the mess hall the evening before, as customary. I was slotted in the "purple heart" Charlie position. The Purple Heart Charlie position was Yellow Four. That's the fourth man in the fourth flight (number last), the position that is the easiest to attack from the rear. There is no one behind him to cover his rear.

At breakfast, my name had been scratched out and Arnett's name was hand written in my place, flying plane No. 26. Arnett came to me at breakfast and said he noticed he was flying my plane in my place and asked if it was OK? One doesn't exactly say "No" in a case like that! The mission took off "sans moi." The target area was Berlin. The group engaged in enemy air action that mission. In the encounter, Arnett was shot down and the plane was lost. His remains were never found. The age-old adage, "There, but for the grace of God, (and the truck problem) that might have been me!!"

MONITORING EAGLES - "MY WORST THREE DAYS IN MILITARY"

Briefings were always held early in the morning, prior to takeoff time. At briefings we were told the type of missions we would fly that day, the mission target area, our group's "Call Sign" name for that day, the call sign of group to be escorted bomber, supply dropping, photo reconnaissance, or ground support escort. The lead squadron for that mission was disclosed, the effort for that day (maximum or limited), etc. These significant facts were given during the briefing.

Maximum effort for the 332nd Fighter Group, "The Red Tails," consisted of four flights of four planes each (red, White, blue, and yellow flights) plus two spares per squadron or a total of 72, P-51 (Mustangs) for a "maximum effort" mission. Limited effort numbers varied. We were the only Fighter Group in the Fifteenth Air Force with four-fighter squadron. When the Group leader was a member of headquarters element, the lead flight for the Group always referred to as "Percy."

Trim tab colors identified the squadron (squadrons) within the Fighter

Group to which a Red Tail P-51 was assigned. The 99th Pursuit Squadron's call name was "Subsoil," its planes had "Blue" trim tabs; the 100ths call name was "Counter" with "Black" trim tabs, the 301st's call name was "Bubbles" with White trim tabs, and the 302nd's call name was "Doorknob" and its planes had "Yellow" trim tabs.

On 20 February 1945, the pilots, planes, and flight maintenance personnel of 302nd Fighter Squadron were redistributed among the other three Squadrons. On 05 March 1945, the balance of the official functions of the 302nd Fighter Group was deactivated and all remaining personnel and material were re-assigned and distributed among the remaining three squadron. The Group's lead squadron was always designated by that (PERCY) call name, e.g.: "Counter Red Leader." The group's lead squadron commander is designated as "Counter Red One." The group's lead squadron leader's wingman, Counter Red Two, (number 2 man) was always assigned as the individual responsible for monitoring the eagles (bombers) on the radio. His primary duty was to maintain liaison with the specific group for which the Fighter Group was designated to fly escort and maintain cover for that mission. Call sign names for each fighter group and its designated bomber group's call sign were given at the morning briefing.

Counter Red One and Two taxis onto the runway and assume takeoff positions waiting for the green flare from the control tower. This specifies its takeoff time. At the flare, they hold their brakes and slowly ease into full throttle. They released their brakes and accelerate down the runway to takeoff. When the last plane, the 18th, of the lead squadron has broken ground, the lead plane of the second squadron (at the same end of the runway, opposite side of the landing strip) begins its takeoff roll. As the last plane of the second squadron (the 18th) cleared the far end of the runway, the control tower would fire a second green flare. The lead plane of the third squadron begins its takeoff run in the opposite direction. This continues until the 72nd plane has broken ground. If an accident or emergency occurred on the runway, the control tower fired a red flare to temporarily cease take-offs. The Group Leader must possess and demonstrate tremendous skills and flying knowledge in order to lead a Fighter Group of 72 airplanes (maximum effort), which included two spare airplanes for each squadron and a total of eight spares.

The Group Leader's takeoff procedure after becoming airborne is to throttle back to a safe slow flying speed and climb straight ahead, a well-anticipated distance, before he begins his 180 degree turn to the left. Each pilot following slides into position, four planes to a flight, four flights to the squadron plus two spares.

The leader of the second squadron assumes his position to the right of the Counter Red Leader. His pilots glide into position as the two flights fly over the home airfield. The third squadron should be taking off at this time and the leader rapidly climbs to position himself to the left of Counter Red Leader. His pilots get into position, as do the pilots of the fourth squadron.

If necessary, Counter Red Leader will steer the group over the home field again to pick up his compass heading to the target area for the day. Climbing all the while to get to the assigned altitude. Our course, the flight was generally always to the north, 360 degrees plus or minus 15 degrees. A prominent place for rendezvous was over the Northern coast of the Adriatic Sea. Our assigned altitude was usually about 25,000 feet. Bombers usually flew about 20,000 feet. We wanted to be at our altitude before we reached the coast. We flew about 5,000 feet above the bombers and supply dropping planes we escorted. We flew at the same altitude the reconnaissance planes flew. When we escorted photoreconnaissance planes, the reconnaissance pilot's decided targets and altitudes to fly. We flew off their wings with three planes on each side in a "V" formation.

As this specific bomber escort mission approached the coast, I would begin my broadcast to try to raise (hear from) our "eagles" (bombers). Continuous repetition of both call names, like "Hello Cupcake, hello Cupcake, this is Butterfly, over" I was waiting for a reply of, "Hello Butterfly, hello Butterfly, this is Cupcake, our position is approximately 'X' minutes to rendezvous point, over."

On this mission, I was the number two man in the lead flight. I was the group leader's wingman. It was my responsibility to establish and maintain radio contact with our eagles.

The spares had been released before the Group reached the Czech coast, to return to home base. The rest of the mission's planes reached altitude before the rendezvous point. All the time I was transmitting our call names, hoping for the anxiously awaited reply.

Finally, I received a faint response. "Hello Butterfly, hello Butterfly, this is Cupcake, this is Cupcake, we have "sack-time" (aborted, scrubbed the mission and returned to home base). I requested the transmitter to "say again" his message. He did. I switched to our group's radio channel; channel "B" to inform Counter Red Leader our eagles had "sack timed." Counter Red acknowledged my transmission and decided the group's rendezvous point. We made two orbits in our rendezvous area before we also would enjoy sack -time.

When the mission returned to our home field, the lead squadron was the first to land. Before the planes were in the revetments, Colonel Davis, the Group Commanding Officer, had his driver rush him in his jeep to the mission leader's plane. Colonel Davis wanted to know why all of the planes from the group on the mission had returned so soon. The Red Leader told him we had received a transmission from our eagles announcing they had aborted. The Colonel wanted to know who had monitored the eagles. He was told "Mann" had.

Colonel Davis immediately came to me and gave me the "third degree" about the transmission between the eagles and me. I repeated what I had heard and what had happened. I was greatly relieved when Lt. Henry Peoples, one of my squadron members spoke up. Lt. Peoples said he had switched to "C" Channel and overheard the transmissions between us.

Needless to say, during the critique (post mission review of what happened during the mission) I was very worried. The concern and anguish lasted for the next three days. I kept waiting. I was afraid I would hear the Germans had tricked an entire group of American fighter planes away from their eagles, had gone in, and had a "field day" shooting down American bombers like "fish in a barrel."

I never found the reason, but the transmission from "Cupcake" had been authentic. Everything had been in order. The eagles had aborted their mission and returned safely to their home base. Whew!

NO MISSION TODAY - DO NOT GET INTO TROUBLE

The day began with pilots scheduled to fly the mission on February 1945, reporting for briefing at the designated time. We sat anxiously listening to the Group Executive tell us areas where enemy fire, both air and ground, was anticipated to be the heaviest. As soon as the mission briefing ended, the Group Adjutant announced that the mission had been "Stood Down." "Stand Down" was pilot jargon for the mission today is "scrubbed" (not going to happen!)

All personnel who could be spared from duty made plans to go into Foggia, Italy to imbibe and do what military personnel can find to do to amuse themselves on a non-flying day. My buddies and I made our plans, also. Lt. Roland Moody was not in the mood to go into town. He admonished us that we would go into town, get drunk and rowdy and get into trouble. (This was not necessarily the way things went, but this was his admonition.)

Lt. Roland Moody decided to take the path of no resistance, no tempta-
tion, and go into his tent to relax. While alone in his tent, he went to sleep.
A "freaky" thing happened!! As Lt. Moody slept, a P-38, "Lightning," fighter
plane flew past near our airfield and went out over the Adriatic Sea. The pilot
made a tight turn and attempted to jettison his external gas tanks. As fate
would have it – only one tank came off out over the Sea, as expected. The
tanks did not release simultaneously. The other tank did not release. When the
tank did release, through some mishap of fortune, it spiraled down. The turn
was over the tent-housing area of the 332nd Fighter Group, and with empty
tents all around, men away enjoying what they wanted to do on a non-duty
day, were there waiting. The tank of gasoline spiraled down and hit the one
tent with a person in it.

We heated our tents with natural airplane gasoline, piped under the floor-
boards to homemade heaters burning the fumes of the gasoline. That did it.
There was an explosion. The tent went up in flames. Lt. Moody woke up at
the explosion. He rushed out of his tent. He inhaled so much heat his lungs
scorched. He died soon after they got him to the hospital. So much for staying
in camp to relax and not going into town to drink

A TYPICAL DAY IN THE LIFE OF A WORLD WAR II COMBAT FIGHTER PILOT

The combat-day actually began at the evening meal the day before. The Squadron's Flying Schedule was posted on the mess hall bulletin board. It listed, by name, who would fly and the position each pilot would fly in for the next day's mission. It also showed the Group's Briefing Time.

It was each pilot's responsibility to check the bulletin board each evening. When Class 44-F arrived at the overseas airfield site, the 332nd Fighter Group had moved to Ramitelli, Italy. The Group was still composed of four Squadrons; the 99th, 100th, 301st, and the 302nd. In the military, as in other organizations of the U.S. federal services, the last activated is the first to be deactivated. The 302nd Fighter Squadron was deactivated 20 February 1945 in order for the 332nd Fighter Squadron Group to be in conformance with the Table of Organization of the other three Fighter Groups of the Fifteenth Air Force: the 31st, 52nd, and the 325th.

In addition to the designation of each position in a squadron's flight of 18 planes, each squadron had a permanent call-code designation: Headquarters was "Percy;" the 99th was "Subsoil;" the 100th was "Counter;" the 301st was "Bubbles;" and the 302nd was "Doorknob." The spares were the Squadron's spare one and spare two.

For typically maximum effort missions each squadron in the Group would put-up four flights of four planes each, plus two spares. The flights were always designated as Red, White, Blue and Yellow flights. The positions in each flight were one, two, three, and four. The squadron lead-flight was Red One. The pilot flying in that position was the Squadron leader for that mission. Red two was his wingman, who flew on/to his right and slightly behind him. Red three was an element leader and flew on/to Red One's left and a litter further behind. Red Four flew on/to Red Three's left and a little behind red three. The configuration of each of the other three flights of the squadron was the same.

The position a pilot was to fly-in may indicate how he would rest that night. Yellow four was "lovingly" referred to as, "Purple Heart Charlie." (He was the last man in the squadron's combat formation.) The two spares went along for the ride on a typical mission. They were there in case a plane of one of the flights developed a problem en-route to rendezvous and had to return to home base, in which case a spare took his place and the other spare escorted the cripple plane home. If there was no problem, the two spares returned home as the missions reached the rendezvous point.

I don't recall a bugler blowing reveille or taps overseas at our airfield. (I know there was not one at rest camp.) One woke by whatever means he required. He did his toileting as best he could try not to wake his tent-mates, in case they were not scheduled to fly and wanted to sleep (if they could). One walked to the mess hall and "did the chow line." The Air Corp's Mess Sergeants were an ingenious lot. They came up with "goodies" like fresh eggs and meat, which was not usually found among the "ground troops" mess halls.

Six by six trucks bussed the pilots to the Group's Briefing tent. The Briefing Officer, Col. Davis, his executive officer, or his Adjutant (the Executive Staff) would have received a coded message during the night, deciphered it, and prepared a briefing and the Briefing Chart. The huge area-map on the far wall opposite the entrance showed the circumference of the entire European-area the Group could have covered.

As the pilots entered the briefing area, their eyes would go immediately to the Briefing Map and they would wonder about the up-coming missions. If the map had a red string from our camp location and a green string from another airfield, coming together just about the coastline in Czechoslovakia, it would be an escort mission which would be minimum danger for fighters.

If there was only one red string ending in an area held by the enemy, it would be strafing mission. Strafing mission usually brought expletives from the fighter pilots because they exposed the planes and their pilots to direct fire from the ground troops.

"Attention!" was shouted when the Briefing Officer entered the room. Everyone would hop up and stand at attention. He would shout back, "At ease!" and everyone would be seated. Getting down to business at hand, the briefing officer would tell the pilots: the type of mission; the mission target area; what Intelligence had reported could be expected about the target area – pertaining to anticipated ground fire and aerial attacks.

Headquarters, XVth Air Force, had provided the Group with the "Eagles" Group and the Group's Coded-Call-Name. We called American and allied bombers "Eagles" and "Friendly's". If it were a bomber escort mission, the rendezvous area was provided.

This information was basically the same for a supply dropping, reconnaissance, or convoy escort mission, except the number of escort planes varied. The pilots were told to synchronize their watches at a time determined by the Briefing Officer. They were told the start-engine time, the time the mission would take-off, and the start on course time. The mission route and compass heading direction. The estimated rendezvous time and place. In addition, the estimated total mission time. Pilots were told what to expect the "friendly" partisans would be wearing.

At the end of the briefing, the Squadron's trucks drove the pilots to their planes in their revetments. Each crew chief was there to greet his pilot as he completed the pre-flight of his plane. The crew chief would have done all of this before the pilot arrived, of course. The pilot would climb on the plane's left wing in full combat flying gear, except his parachute, which was in the bucket seat in the airplane. His crew chief would help him get into his plane's cockpit and buckle-up. Idle, nervous conversation endured until start engine time.

In turn, according to position to be flown, each pilot began taxiing to the end of the runway. We had only one runway, from which all four Squadrons would take-off. Two Squadrons would take-off from each end of the runway. After the magneto check, the planes would set idling until take-off time. The lead plane would have taxied on to the runway waiting for the tower to fire a green flare into the air exactly at take-off time.

When the flare was fired, the Group leader would hold his brakes and advance his throttle. He would get off his brakes and his plane would start its roll down the runway, accelerating in speed. Number two would have been in place and follow as Number one lifted off the strip. Number three would have maneuvered into place so he could follow. This procedure continued until the second spare of the lead squadron lifted off, at which time the lead plane from the second squadron would be in place and start its take-off roll on the run-way. One or more of the squadrons always had a head-wind, a tail-wind, or a cross-wind.

The Group Leader was competent enough to estimate how far to fly in his take-off, before he would begin his gradual turn to the left to permit all 18 planes from his squadron to be air borne and in formation. The planes from the other squadron at his end of the runway would be airborne and forming into position on the right side of the Group leader.

As those two squadrons are forming up in position, the planes should pass over the home airfield. A second green flare is fired from the control tower and the lead plane from the third squadron, at the other end of the runway, would be taking-off. The last two squadrons should join the first two squadrons in time for all four squadrons to fly over the field and start on the compass heading to the rendezvous point.

This would have continued as the third and fourth squadrons got into position to the left of the Group leader. The fourth squadron of 18 planes (72 airplanes total) should, ideally, pass over the airfield at the on-course time for the Group Leader to get the on-course heading for the rendezvous.

The Group's lead squadron was always designated by that squadron's call name, e.g.: "Red Leader." The group's lead squadron commander is designated as "Red One." The group's lead squadron leader's wingman, Counter Red Two, (number 2 man) is always assigned as the individual responsible for monitoring the eagles (bombers) on the radio.

The average flying time for a bomber escort combat mission from take off 'til landing, toward the end of the WWII, was approximately 4:30. Some much longer and some much shorter. When all the returning airplanes were parked in their revetments and the pilots were collected and driven to the administration building, critique of the mission was held.

The pilots verified what had occurred during the mission. What they had observed confirming or contrary to what they have been told at the morning briefing, e.g. amount of ground fire, enemy aircraft in the vicinity, or anything unusual or unexpected.

Six-by-six trucks from each squadron drove the pilots back to their respective areas and then to dinner and to observe the next day's mission flying schedule. The daily cycle starts over again!

AVERAGE DAY ON A COMBAT CAMP SITE

There are many personnel on a military installation, like the bugler, cooks, motor pool workers, crew chiefs, and many others, who have been up for hours before the official workday starts. Eventually, we were summoned to get up and be ready for the day's activities.

The impersonal, "You," is used to help the reader understand the writer's position (view or standpoint). If this is a duty day for you, you grudgingly get out of the sack, which is your cozy cot, and start your toileting. If it's winter season, this chore is amplified. An empty, 55 gal drum, modified into a furnace to burn the fumes from a brick inside the tank, was our heating source. The fuel reservoir was braced outside the tent. Fuel was piped into the tent, under the wooden floor, so that it came up in the center, then into the furnace. A shut-off valve regulated the drip of fuel onto a brick. Fumes rising from the brick were ignited for our fire heat. Some tents burned using this heat-source.

After the necessities were taken care of, you head for the squadron's mess tent for breakfast. Army Air Corps personnel ate well. Our cooks were very resourceful. We frequently had fresh meat, eggs, and milk. Pilots scheduled to fly that day were driven to the briefing tent then to their planes in 6 x 6 trucks. Other pilots were at liberty to do as they pleased, unless they were scheduled for something else. When we were stationed at Ramitelli, Foggia was the closest city. It was about six-miles away. American soldiers, officers and enlisted men, could/would start walking to "town" and they were usually picked up by an American or allied trucks would pass on the frequently traveled road and were happy to give you a ride to town or back to the camp.

Camp maintenance and other menial, non-classified, chores included: erecting buildings, assembling non-classified military things, moving equipment, and clean up, were performed by Italian men and boys from the area. Their pay in Lira was handled by someone unknown.

Miracles were accomplished by a 5 cents pack of cigarettes or a 6 oz bottle of Coca Cola. Our laundry was done by the wives of the men who did labor work at the campsite. One or two weeks of soiled clothes would be laundered for one pack of cigarettes. It amused us to see the husbands who delivered the clean clothes accept the cigarettes as payment for the service then open the cigarettes and begin smoking them, after the wives had done the work of washing and ironing the clothes.

One sunny afternoon, either after a mission or a stand-down-day, three of us, Leon Spears, Wyrain Schell, and I decided to go to town. Schell had said he wanted some real Italian spaghetti. A camp worker (I don't remember his name) told us, using his broken English, and we, using our broken-Americanized Italian, to go to town and meet him at the tavern. He said we could go to his home and his wife would fix spaghetti for us.

What American wife and/or mother would ever allow her husband to bring total strangers into her home and change the simple dinner she had planned for her family? The three of us Americans hitched a ride and arrived at the tavern in town well before our "Italian host." American and allied drivers would not, or were prohibited, from giving the Italian workers a ride in their vehicles. We went to his hole-in-the-wall "home" with this worker, where his wife waited with his children, two I think, and his dinner ready. When we entered, and after amenities, the worker told his wife to fix spaghetti for us.

The wife did not get excited, as Italian women are purported to do. She calmly set her prepared meal aside, opened the table, removed pasta flour from the bin under the table, and proceeded from scratch, to make spaghetti. This including mixing the water, kneading the dough, rolling-out the dough, using the spaghetti cutter to make the strips; then boiling water to finish making spaghetti. I don't know how long this preparation took, but the family meal was postponed until our spaghetti was ready. I think we had fried fish and wine.

We left several Liras more than the cost to cover our meals. The three of us hitchhiked back to camp after a meal of real Italian spaghetti. This does not fit into the average day at camp, but it is how we were regarded by the Italian workers we were associated with around camp. As long as we were not scheduled to fly combat or whatever, we were on our own and could do as we wished. Of course, there were limits that we were expected to remain within. A few of our men managed to obtain motorcycles from the British stationed nearby. The method of barter for acquisition, not mentioned! In addition, scotch whiskey could be obtained on rare occasions.

They would get petrol (gasoline) from military petrol points for free. To get military issued gasoline, vehicles had to have serial numbers on them. The men stenciled random numbers on the fenders of their bikes and obtained free gasoline.

Two of our pilots, Lt. Clarence Oliphant and another, decided to ride their motorcycle from our campsite at Ramitelli on the Adriatic side of Italy to our Rest Camp in Naples, on the Mediterranean side of Italy, one evening. A distance of about 150 miles over mountainous, turning roads. As the driver and passenger were returning to camp, zooming around the curves in the mountains, they hit a sandy area in the road and the bike slid out of control.

They were both banged up pretty badly. Lt. Oliphant's leg was broken. I don't remember the other person's injuries. Colonel Davis, our Commanding Officer, issued a Command Order, "there will be no unauthorized motorcycles on this field!"

BARI FLYOVER – 15ᵀᴴ AIR FORCE HAS FLYOVER BARI, ITALY

On the 6ᵗʰ of May 1945, the entire 15ᵗʰ Air Force participated in an Aerial Flying Review over Bari, Italy. As we made a wide sweep around Naples, circling to get into position for the big formation, my location was such that I flew directly over the big opening in the crater of Mount Vesuvius. I looked directly into that eye. This was another "I'll never forget situation!"

"YOU BOMBED MY HOUSE!"

When I joined the 332ⁿᵈ Fighter Group, our home field was near the small village of Ramitelli, Italy, which is on the Northern shore of the Adriatic Sea side of the peninsula. We were the only four Fighter Squadron Combat Group in the Fifteenth Air Force of the United States Army Air Corps. Our landing strip was constructed of steel matting. It ran roughly southwest to northeast or vice versa northeast to southwest, depending upon which way one was landing. The eastern end was about one half mile from the shore.

The 100th Squadrons were opposite each other at one end of the 301ˢᵗ and 302ⁿᵈ squadrons on opposite sides at the other end. Group Headquarters was about in the middle of the area. Mission headings were on a northerly route in the vicinity of zero degrees. The Northern shore of the Adriatic Sea was usually our rendezvous point.

Ramitelli is slightly northwest of Foggia, which juts out into the sea. Neither the Fifteenth Air Force "high brass" nor anyone else knew the war in Europe would be officially terminated on 8 May, 1945. However, we flew our last combat mission from Ramitelli on 26 April, 1945. The Americans and our allies were advancing north so rapidly the "smudge pots" (smoke pots) could not be moved forward as fast as the troops advanced. The smudge pots marked the areas behind which our planes were not to perform any combat activities, like bombing, strafing, or firing on targets of opportunity. One day we inadvertently bombed a barn and damaged a house nearby.

Our group moved north from Ramitelli to Cattolica on the third of May 5, 1945. This move was to put us in better striking range of, and shorter distance to, targets in Germany. This was, of course, a few weeks after northern Italy had been liberated. Cattolica is on the Adriatic Sea side also. It is southeast of Ancona.

Pilots of the 332ⁿᵈ Fighter Group with 50 or more missions, certain support personnel, and P-51 Mustang airplanes with less than 100 flying hours on them, were returned to the United States shortly after VE Day. Those individuals were returned to Tuskegee Army Air Field. The material was made ready for shipment to the Pacific War Theater. The pilots were to return from the Pacific Theater Aerial Warfare.

The balance of the Group's personnel and equipment remained at the campsite in Italy to be returned home later. Since I had only 48 missions, I was in this category. This Group did not ship out until 1 October, 1945. There was no place to send all the Black personnel except back to the segregated Air Base at Tuskegee, Alabama.

In the meantime, the pilots flew to maintain their flying proficiency. I don't know how the ground support personnel occupied their time. I do know there was liberal leave granting of time at the various rest camps on a space available basis.

LOCKED IN, HOW DO I GET OUT?

I have written earlier that pilots with 50 missions or more were returned to the states relatively soon after our war ended on 08 May 1945. Those of us with less than 50 missions were left in Italy with the Group. We did not return until October. There was leave policy. We could travel to various R&R (Rest and Recuperation) sites, if we could get a space available slot. I&I (Intoxication and intercourse) were not on the menu!

I was able to get to Rome, Pompeii, Venice, Milan, Pisa, and other places. I do not remember the dates or whom I traveled with. I regret I did not go to Switzerland the one chance I had. I thought the opportunity would occur again.

William "Porky" Rice, another pilot buddy, and I went to Rome on one of those Rest and Recuperation weeks when we were permitted to "visit" areas with permission. We went to the La Scalla and the Baths Opera houses, and just killed time with no particular plan in order.

One evening, Porky and I went separate ways. I was up alone in an exclusive area of Rome with large apartment buildings that had not been devastated by the bombings and war. I wandered into one of the buildings with a large palatial-style foyer and a magnificent stairway. I was in awe at the sight. While nosing around inside, it got dark. I started out and I could hear the voices of a small group of Italian men outside. They stood near the door jabbering away. It had gotten dark outside and the Blackout rules did not permit hall lights after dark. In this foyer near the door, the brick walls had indentations, about two feet wide, as decorations.

Porky had bought a large switchblade knife, about a six -inch blade, which he had loaned me that evening for my protection. I pressed myself into one of the recessed areas with Porky's knife open and ready, just in case.

I do not know how long, how many minutes; I stayed there just waiting for the men to disburse, and just go away. When the group finally broke up, a couple came into the foyer and the others left. Those who came in locked the door behind themselves.

There I was, in this strange building, waiting for time to pass in order for me to try to unfasten or unlock this foreign door lock. I was in the dark. I did not want to get caught by men who would have thought I intended to harm them and their families. I was fumbling and sweating, nervous as all get out (euphemism)! Imagine this quandary. Try to escape unknown danger in an alien predicament. Try to unlock a door, in a dark confinement, without lightening a lighter or a match.

Finally, I was successful and unfastened the lock. You had better believe I got out of the area and back to the hotel in a hurry!!

ANOTHER FRIGHTENING P-47 VS. P-51 EXPERIENCE

The war in Europe officially ended 8 May 1945. All fighter pilots with 50 missions or more, and P-51 Mustang Fighter Aircraft with less than 100 flying hours, were returned to the states. Pilots with less than 50 missions, and P-51s with more than 100 flying hours (mostly "P-51C" models), were left at our air base site in Italy until October '45. After the end of the war, we flew to "improve our proficiency." Flying around Italy performing local area, cross-country, and whatever flying maneuvers came to mind.

There was a Brazilian Fighter Group, flying P-47 Thunderbolt aircraft, north of our 332nd Fighter Group site in Catollica. We were all on the Adriatic side of Italy. The P-51 had a Rolls Royce, 1500 horsepower, North American engine; and the P-47 had a Pratt Whitney engine, with a 2,300 horsepower, Republic engine; the power plant rating of an average liberty ship was 2500 horses, only 200 horses more than the P-47.

A fully combat-loaded P-51 weighed three tons; a fully combat-loaded P-47 weighed about seven tons, the average weight of a loaded big-city bus was about the same. Occasionally, to break the monotony, pilots from the Brazilian group would fly south and "buzz" our field as an invitation to "come out and play." Our pilots who wanted to "play" would rush out, jump in their P-51s, take off and simulate "dog fighting" between the groups.

On 12 June, 1945 (I will never forget that day), some of us decided to fly north and "bounce" the Brazilian field. After a few very fast, low, fly-overs, or buzzes, some of the Brazilian pilots rushed to their planes and took off. I was high in an excellent 90 degree position to observe a P-47-D start its take-off roll down the runway. I did a wing over and went into a dive toward the plane as it was about to "break ground."

The P-47s were sluggish. They were heavy according to fighter plane standards at that time. I had to "lower gear and flaps" on my P-51C in order to stay behind my target as he climbed. I had him in my gun sight. I was "shooting him down!" He was my "kill." My plane climbed slowly. When the pilot reached the altitude he wanted, he executed a wingover and went into a dive.

I stuck with him. This was great fun!

He pulled up into what amounted to a half loop. At the top, he executed a beautiful emmelman. I stuck with him through the half loop; however, my emmelman was sloppy. I went up, and up, and up, until I lost my flying speed. I could not complete my emmelman. My plane did a whipstall. It snapped back and went into a spin toward the earth.

AT THIS POINT I DID THE UNPARDONABLE!

I was stuck with the plane. In ground school, we had been instructed that if we ever got a tactical airplane in a spin, bail out. My plane spun to the left. When I attempted to correct the spin, it would spin to the right. Then left, and then right, all the time the altimeter was indicating that I was losing the altitude rapidly. I managed to pull out of the spin just over the treetops.

My Rolls Royce engine had thrown oil all over the front of my windshield. In as much I was completely disoriented and did not know where I was, I called my home field for a heading to get me home. I had to request two of my fellow pilots to fly me in for the landing; one of on left and one on my right. I could not see in front of me.

I did not realize the danger I had been in, nor did I get weak, until I stepped onto the wing of my plane. At that time, my knees buckled as if they were made of rubber. Think about the reports/forms I would have had to write/complete, if I had bailed-out of the government airplane. Think about the reports/forms the Investigating Officer would have had to write/complete, if I had "cork-screwed" the government airplane into the ground!!!

HOMECOMING, THE REMAINDER OF THE 332ND FIGHTER GROUP RETURNS

Immediately after World War II ended, America's military personnel were returned home from all over the world. Our war in Europe ended 08 May 1945; Armistice in the Pacific was signed 25 August 1945. In late June 1945, the personnel of the 332nd Fighter Group began receiving orders to return to the States. Enlisted personnel were returned according to a point system. Pilots with 50 missions or more were returned relatively soon following the end of our war and planes with less than 100 hours were prepared and returned to the states to be made ready to be sent to the Pacific Theater of Operations.

All pilots with less than 50 missions and planes with more 100 hours were kept overseas awaiting further orders. The big problem with the living bodies was "where to send them?" This did not become apparent to us until much later.

Pilot Training Classes were still in the pipeline at all the Flying Training Schools, Tuskegee Army Air Field included. The big difference was that White pilots from the other schools, upon graduation, received their commissions and gold bars, along with their silver pilot wings, could be deployed anywhere to any airfield in the states. The Black pilots, upon graduation, had no place to be assigned, but to remain at Tuskegee Army Air Field with a military operation specialty of Pilot (Single Engine or Twin Engine). Tuskegee Army Air Field was literally bulging at the seams.

Segregation, still being the nation's problem, made the mixing Negro officers with White enlisted personnel impossible. It left the War Department with a huge dilemma, the Tuskegee Army Field was the only solution for what to do with remaining members of the 332nd Fighter Group. Our newly acquired airfield at Catollica, Italy, to which we were moved in anticipation of flying missions to be closer to the enemy, was an answer. The Group completed the move from Ramitelli to Catollica on May 5, 1945.

At the Catollica Air Field, the pilots had no additional duties to perform. Occasionally, one may be selected to fill-in for something, but their only specialty was Combat Fighter Pilot with no combat going on. We used the P-51 to perform proficiency flying. Liberal leave was granted, but we had to find and apply to go to a rest camp in a luxury hotel, which had been taken over by the government. The cost was usually $1.00 a day, with amenities galore. Sightseeing was arranged by the individual himself.

I was able to get to Milano, Rome, Pompeii, (It's not clear now whether or not I also got to Florence and Pisa). I had an opportunity to go to Switzerland and postponed the trip. I regret it now because I never got the chance again.

POST WORLD WAR II AND THE 332ND FIGHTER GROUP'S HOMECOMING

Finally, the word "came down" in late September of 1945; those of us who had been left in Italy were "**Going Home!**" We packed our personal belongings and prepared our campsite in Catollica for our evacuation. Somehow, the word had gotten out to the Italians in the area. The day of the big move to the staging area arrived.

Scavengers with horse and ox drawn two-and four-wheel carts lined the road outside our camp, waiting for anything not taken away. We were told to make huge piles of unwanted articles in open space areas. Gasoline was poured on the piles and they were set afire. The Italians begged to be permitted to get to the piles, but were refused access to them. All the personnel at the site were hustled aboard army 6 x 6 trucks and trucked off to a staging area outside Naples. In less than a week, our Liberty Ship, the S.S. Levi Woodbury, arrived to take us home. On 01 October 1945, our convoy sailed for American shores.

Aboard the ship, the individualities began to come out. In Italy, the camaraderie was there, the togetherness spirit was strong. It was not unusual for one man to toss his wallet to a buddy and say, "Hang on to my wallet, I'm going to fly." Aboard ship, gambling losses and debts not paid were remembered. We were not dependent upon each other anymore.

Seventeen days later, our convoy pulled into the harbor of New York. A ferryboat with a huge banner saying, "**Welcome Home**" was hanging on each side. There were young Black divas on the ferry, cheering and waving. Scat Man serenaded us as the ship docked. We imagined there would be some sort of welcome celebration to honor us. Surprise, surprise, surprise! We were hustled off the ship and in to the coaches of the train waiting on the track beside the pier. As soon as all troops had come down the gangplank and boarded the train, it left the pier. A short time later, it stopped in Ft. Dix New Jersey. No divas, no celebration, no anything special, to welcome us home.

THE 332ND FIGHTER GROUP RETURNS HOME

The 332nd Fighter Group flew its last combat mission 26 April 1945. The U.S. and Allied ground troops were advancing so rapidly enemy targets and troops could not be properly identified from the air. The war in Europe ended 08 May 1945.

The Black pilots of the 332nd Fighter Group with 50 or more missions, and the P-51 Mustang airplanes with less than 100 flying hours on them, were returned to the States to prepare to go to the Pacific and assist in the war there. I don't know the criterion used to determine which enlisted personnel would return with those going home early.

The war in the Pacific ended 25 August 1945. Neither the Fighter Pilots nor the P-51s got to the Pacific Theater. The Black B-25 Pilots had been told they would be sent to the Pacific Theater, but that never materialized. The remaining members of the 332nd FG were released from assignment to the XV Air Force, APO 520, to the Zone of the Interior, on 20 September 1945 to depart Italian shores, by Liberty Ship, on 1 October 1945.

We went by motor vehicle, 6x6 again, our usual more of group ground travel, to a "Repple Depple" staging area outside Naples, Italy. Volleyball and various sports occupied our time. The 332nd Fighter Group had been moved north to Cattolica, Italy, at the end of April, in order to be closer to the enemy. Our airfield at Cattolica had been dismantled and all surplus supplies, equipment, material, etc., had been burned before the eyes of the poor Italian civilians who waited on the road, with carts and various other types of vehicles, to scavenge anything left behind.

We boarded the "S.S.LEVI WOODBURY" Liberty Ship, segregated again, and sailed for the States. We sailed past the "LADY" into the New York Harbor and docked on 17 October 1945, 16 days after leaving Italy. Special Services had arranged for the "Scat Man" and contingent of Black New York Divas, aboard a ferryboat, to meet and greet the S.S. Levi Woodbury with its returning Black heroes.

ARMY SERVICE FORCES

TRANSPORTATION CORPS

ARMY OF THE UNITED STATES

NEW YORK PORT OF EMBARKATION

1st Lt. Hiram E. Mann,
100th Fighter Squadron
332nd Fighter Group

returned to the UNITED STATES on the
ship_____S. S. Levi Woodbury_____
which sailed from_____Naples, Italy_____
on_____1 October 1945_____

Sig. _____
Title _Lst Lt. TSC_

We were hastened down the gangplank and onto the coaches of a waiting train. When all the ship's passengers had disembarked, the train moved-out to Ft. Dix, New Jersey. There were no handshakes, hug, or kisses from the Americans waving welcome home banners.

BILLETING OFFICE CASH SHORTAGE

When the bulk of the personnel left at Tuskegee Army Air Field (TAAF) were finally transferred to Lockbourne Army Air Field (LAAF) outside Columbus, Ohio, in May of 1946, we were assigned additional Army Duty Specialties. I was designated the Assistant Billeting Officer and the Officers' Club Officer, under the administrative supervision of an old pre-World War II, "Spit and Polish," army serviceman, Major Percy L. Jones.

Among my duties was the daily bank run. This included collecting the "bank cash bags" from each activity on the base which collected money for any reason whatsoever: such as; the Billeting Office, Officers Club, NCO Club, Base theater, Post Exchange, etc. Each activity had a bank account at the Washington Courthouse Bank in Canal Winchester, Ohio.

Each duty day, a driver with a staff car would come to the Billeting Office to pick me up for the trip to the bank. I would strap on my trusty .45, remove our cash bag from the safe, and be driven to each place on the field, which collected cash during its daily operations, to get its cash-bag with deposit slips and denominations of cash to be returned to the unit. This was done without verifying the money count. Each component's bag was marked on the outside. We would then drive some 20 miles southeast to the bank. I would go into the bank with about nine bags of cash, wait for a teller to become available, and place all the bags in front of the teller. The teller would open his grid, pull the bags into his work ledge, lower his shade, and proceed to comply with the instruction in each bag without making a verification of the exchange count. When I was finished, the teller would raise his shade and push the bags to the edge of his window ledge. I would gather the bags and return to the waiting staff car for the trip back to Lockbourne Army Air Field (LAAF).

At the Air Field, I would distribute the bags to each element as marked and return to the Billeting Office with our cash bag and place the bag in the office safe. Someone in the office would check the count and verify that all was as it should be. One day, Mrs. Spears, our office assistant bookkeeper, had caught up with her workload and asked me if I could like for her to checkout our cash bag. I gave her permission to proceed.

Very soon after, she came into my office wringing her hands and quite upset. She said, "Lieutenant Mann, I've checked and re-checked the bank run bag and it is $400.00 short." She was visibly quite shaken, which, of course, upset me. This was in 1946 and $400.00 was an enormous amount of money. It was more than a month's base pay, plus flying pay, plus living allowances, for me. The only handling of the bag before Mrs. Spears started the validation was when I took the bag from the safe, turned it over to the teller at the bank, received it from the teller, and placed it back into the safe.

I was bewildered and confused and did not know how to handle this emergency situation. I immediately called my supervisor, Major Jones, whose main office space was in the Recruiting Office at another location on the base. He rushed to the Billeting Office. He did not call for a staff car to transport him from his office to mine. He did not have a privately owned vehicle. (Automobiles were just getting back into production after the manufacturing freeze during the war, so he walked.)

As soon as he entered the Billeting Office, he went to the desk he used in the office, pulled open a drawer where he kept his shoe-polish rag and "dusted" off his spit-polished, well-shined shoes. Then he wanted a recounting of just what had happened. I related the scenario to him step by step. He thought it over a short while, picked up the telephone and asked the base operator to connect him with the bank in Washington Courthouse Bank in Canal Winchester, Ohio.

Someone at the bank answered the ring. Major Jones identified himself and told the person on the other end of the line that we were having a "little problem" in our office. It seemed we were $400.00 short in our bank-run cash for that day. The man on the other end was very relieved to hear that. He said they were having a problem at the bank. They were $400.00 over and no one could account for it. The Major offered to have someone drive over to get the money. The man at the bank told him one of their employees passed the base on his way home and he would drop it off at our office. This news brought relief to me and to both sides of the shaky situation.

BUDGET OFFICER COURSE, LOWERY AIR FORCE BASE, CO

Reservists were required to perform two-weeks of active duty each year in addition to attending monthly reserve meetings at their home meeting site. In 1954, I applied for and was approved to serve my two-week tour attending the Budget Officer course at Lowery Air Force Base near Denver, Colorado. I left home and family in Cleveland, Ohio, on a balmy Easter Sunday afternoon. I considered myself prepared for the weather in Denver. I arrived at the civilian airport (Love Field) that evening and called the Base for transportation. In the Bachelor Officers' Quarters (BOQ), I was billeted in a room with twin beds, which shared bathroom facilities with the adjoining room. While settling in, I heard a female voice in the bathroom. I called the office and was assigned another room with twin beds. This was my first base assignment since the military had been integrated. I began to wonder what my roommate would be like and what his attitude would be. I prepared for bed and went to sleep without a roommate. When my clock alarmed the next morning, I awoke to find that during the night, a man had slipped in quietly, prepared for, and had gone to bed, without disturbing me. We spent a very nice two weeks together.

The big surprise was that also during the night; four inches of snow had fallen and the entire place was a mess. The residents of Denver were accustomed to large accumulations of snow in short periods of time. Out of area, people were astonished. The United States Air Force Academy (USAFA), near Colorado Springs, was not completed and the first classes of USAFA Cadets were billeted and attended classes at Lowery. There were several specialty schools of various courses being taught at Lowery simultaneously, in addition to the routine classes for the Cadets. The specialty schools operated on an eighteen-hour schedule of three shifts of six hours each (0600-1200, 1200-1800, and 1800-2400 hours respectively).

My Budget Officer Course was the first shift, 0600-1200, Monday-Friday. The Cadets were not officers but they were a different breed of enlisted personnel, the same as we were as Aviation Cadets. They also used the Officers' Mess Hall for meals. The Cadets marched to the mess hall in formation for each meal. When they arrived at the front door, the formation would halt and single file into the building. If the officers did not beat the Cadet formation into the mess hall, they would have to wait until the last Cadet entered and was at the mess line. Late arriving officers would have to follow the Cadets through the "chow line." I don't remember how many classes were there at that time, nor do I know how many Cadets were in classes there, but there were a lot!

The Officers' Mess was a large open building with three- or four-section folding windbreakers, to deflect the blowing wind, just inside the large double doors. The first Monday I was there, I had to "feel" my way around to get the procedure. I did manage to get to the mess hall ahead of the Cadet formation. I came away from the serving line, carrying my breakfast-tray, and walked in front of the windbreaker trying to make up my mind which way to turn. I heard a voice from somewhere in the middle of the mess hall yelling, Hiram Mann! I walked far enough to try to distinguish where it came from and who was shouting my name. I saw a form standing at a table waving his hands.

It was a former 44-F Classmate, Edward Woodward. "Woodie" had been eliminated from Cadet-flying training at TAAF, but he had managed to get into, and had graduated from, Bombardier/Navigator Training. How he managed to see or recognize me through the opening of one of the sections of the folding windbreaker, I'll never know. I was glad he had. We could have spent my two-weeks there and never have run into each other.

I was a Major in the reserves, attending the Budget Officer Course at Lowery. Woodie was an Active Duty Captain at Lower training with a B-29 crew, preparing for whatever was anticipated during that period of the Cold War in 1954. His class schedule was the 1200-1800 hour tour. After the evening meals, we would be together each day, until the end of my tour.

SUNDAY AFTER THANKSGIVING'S DAY EMERGENCY LANDINGS "TWICE IN ONE DAY"

I was recalled to active duty in the Air Force in 1956. I was ordered to attend the Command and Staff College at the Air University at Montgomery, Alabama. My class was of 57, which began 04 September 1956. There were 990 plus male officers in the class. There were 54 officers from 24 allied countries. There were only four Black American officers: Lt. Col. Daniel "Chappie" James, Jr., (deceased); Major Lee Archer; Major Dudley Watson (deceased); and me, Major Hiram Mann.

Among the countries, the allied officers were from: The Philippines, China, Japan, Turkey, Spain, Korea, Germany, and Pakistan. (I have a complete list of these officers and their countries.) The Air University had several colleges on the campus site with rated flying officers attending each college. There were various types of aircraft on the flying line (B-25s, C-45, F-80s, etc.).

Because of my eyesight and non-participation in flying while in the Reserves, I had been grounded prior to going to the University. My orders read that I was a pilot, "not on flying status, not to participate in flying activities as a crewmember."

We were assigned permanent seats in the auditorium for daily morning assembly. We were assigned to seminars for afternoon class work and study. I was in seminar number 29 including 21 American Caucasian officers, and one Filipino officer. We had great rapport!

Although the military had been integrated (de jure) since 1948, my attendance at the University provided another disgusting segregated experience: The Montgomery City Bus Boycott began in December of 1955 when Rosa Parks, going home after a hard day's work at her assistant tailor's job, boarded a local bus. She was tired; she sat in a vacant seat in the front of the bus. She refused to give up her seat to a White man and go stand in the back of the crowded bus as the southern laws and custom required at that time. She defied the City Ordinance of segregated seating.

My tour at the Air University began eight months after the beginning of the 381-day boycott, which led to the Supreme Court order outlawing discriminatory practices on Montgomery buses.

In 1956, the American Government was still using Italian and German prisoners of war in the United States to perform menial labor at military installations. (I first saw this in 1944 at Walterboro Army Air Field, South Carolina. I know it was done at other installations because General Davis and other Tuskegee Airmen have reported similar situations.)

The Montgomery Chamber of Commerce and local chapters of national fraternal organizations, such as the Lions, Kiwanis, Odd Fellows, D.A.R., etc., would sponsor the prisoners on weekends at local White USO dances and gatherings and they would take them to movies. However, for the four Black military officers, they were not allowed to attend the same dances with the White officers. Segregation was rampant at that time in the community and among these service clubs and entertainment places such as movie houses.

Being Black and an officer in the military did not prevent the White population from discriminating against us.

The four-day long Thanksgiving weekend of 1956 was a popular time for the pilots to perform extended flying for their proficiency and to accumulate flying hours. One of my classmates, who was already a senior pilot, was about 30 flying hours short of the requirement to qualify for his command pilot's wings. He let it be known that he would sacrifice his holiday with his family to fly a taxi service. He would shuttle class members to various destinations and return to the Air University. He drew a C-45, Expediter, for his taxi service. I managed to get on his manifest for a flight to Cleveland, Ohio. My wife was teaching there. She didn't want to resign her job or to enroll our son in school in the racial climate that existed in Montgomery at that time.

Take-off time from Tuskegee was Wednesday, after duty hours, about 1700 hours (5:00 p.m.). Our first stop was at Wright-Patterson Force Air Base outside Dayton, Ohio. It was a night landing and it was snowing. Cleveland was snowed in. I took a bus and got home Thanksgiving morning.

The pilot and I had agreed that I would be the first person to be picked up Sunday morning after Thanksgiving Day for the return flight to Tuskegee. The pilot called my home Saturday night from a downtown hotel in Cleveland to confirm our departure. He had arrived from Chicago. We made arrangements for my family to take him to Cleveland Hopkins Air Terminal.

The pilot and I performed the IFP for our pre-flight check procedures and he filed an Instrument Flight Plan (IFP). I was the co-pilot, illegally. Extremely severe weather was coming in from the west. At the plane, the pilot reviewed the log and noticed the plane had not been fueled in Cleveland as he had requested. Calculations indicated that we would have sufficient fuel to get us to our first stop for the day, Wilkes-Barre, Penn.

We were in and out of clouds and heavy rain almost all the way. When we landed at the civilian airfield in Wilkes-Barre, the two officer-passengers returning to the Air University were waiting.

CLASS OF '57, COMMAND AND STAFF COLLEGE

I was recalled to active duty in August to attend the Air Command and Staff College Course, which began 03 September 1956. In a class of 990 plus, there were only four African-Americans: Lt. Col. Daniel "Chappie" James, Jr., Majors Lee Archer, Dudley Watson, and Hiram E. Mann. General James died in 1978, one month after he retired from active duty. I don't know when Watson was killed in an airplane crash.

There were 54 Allied Officers from 24 Allied Countries. In my class, there were officers from Brazil, Chile, China, Colombia, Denmark, Ecuador, Germany, Greece, Iraq, Iran, Italy, Japan, Mexico, the Netherlands, Nicaragua, Norway, Pakistan, Peru, Philippines, ROKAF, Spain, Thailand, Turkey, and Venezuela. Please notice, there were Allied Officers from countries with who our country had recently been at war. Their country had been in mortal combat, killing our military personnel. There were also Allied Officers from ethnically diverse countries.

COMMAND & STAFF COLLEGE, 1956
MEMBER COUNTRY LOCATION
CLASS COMPOSITION OF ALLIED OFFICERS
CLASS 57
(54 STUDENTS FROM 24 "ALLIED" COUNTRIES)
BRAZIL, CHILE, CHINA, COLOMBIA, DENMARK, ECUADOR, GERMANY, GREECE, IRAN, ITALY, JAPAN, MEXICO, NETHERLANDS, NICARAGUA, NIGERIA, NORWAY, PAKISTAN, PERU, PHILIPPINES, REPUBLIC OFKOREA, SPAIN, THAILAND, TURKEY, VENEZUELA.

<u>ALLIED STUDENTS' COUNTRIES</u>

BRAZIL	Lt. Col. VASCONCELLEA, J.S.
CHILE	Lt. Col. ORTEGA, Ricardo
CHINA	Lt. Col LEO, Chang-Yuan
	Maj. KU, Chan-Chang
COLOMBIA	Maj. GIRALDO, Alfonso
	Capt. MORENO, GuiHermo
	Capt. NIETO, Hernando
DENMARK	Maj. HOVGARD, Anton
ECUADOR	Maj. HIDALGO, Luis
GERMANY	Lt. Col. BERTRAM, Heilmut
	Lt. Col. CRAMER, Hems
	Lt. Col. KROLL, Walter

GREECE	Lt. Col. KOUNANIS, Dimitrious
IRAN	Lt. Col. RAFAT, Ali
	Col. ZARRABI, Abmad
ITALY	Lt. Col. VODRET, Piero
	Lt. Col. BELLENZIER, Aldo
JAPAN	Lt. Col. UCHIRO, Mitka
	Lt. Col. YAMAMOTO, Shigeo
MEXICO	Lt. Col. SUAREZ, Fernando
NETHERLANDS	Lt. Col. KELDER, August F.
NICARAGUA	Maj. GUITERREZ, Santiago
NIGERIA	Maj. GUTIERREZ, Julio
NORWAY	Maj. SKRAUTVOL, Torbjorn
	Maj. SOLEM, Par
PAKISTAN	Maj. SHAH, Manscor A.
	Lt. Col. MARSTON, Vivian
PERU	Maj. CARRION, Alfonso
PHILIPPINES	Lt. Col. MENDIGO, Cirilo A.
	Lt. Col. ISBERTO, Leandro
	Maj. PESTANO, Felix A.
REPUBLIC OF KOREA	Maj. YOEN, Pug Yui
	Maj. HONG, Yoon Bum
	Maj. JOE, Young Back
	Maj. OH, Jurn Sek
	Maj. PARK, Hi Dong
SPAIN	Lt. Col. F'RENCO, Carlos
	Lt. Col. RODRIGUEZ, Jose
	Maj. ALONZO, Manuel
THAILAND	Col. KUNJARA, Kongtip
	Col INDRATNA, Krasae
	Col. CHUTIWONGSE, Chusakdi
TURKEY	Col. GOKDEL, Kemal
	Col. MUSCABUTE, Feachi
	Col. PAYKAL, Vedat
	Maj. TABU, Turgut
VENEZUELA	Col. MORENO, Felix R.

This graduation from Command and Staff College Air University, located in Alabama was indeed an important accomplishment for me to be involved in Command and Staff College with so many racially and ethnically diverse individuals from all over the world. Despite this high level of officer training, I was deeply hurt by the pervasive discrimination that existed even after the end of World War II. I believed that 10 years after World War II and the integration of the military, I expected to be treated with dignity and respect as an equal citizen of the United States of America. Yet, Jim Crow was still active and alive in the South, including Alabama.

FLYING TO CLEVELAND AS A B-25 CO-PILOT

The United States Air University at Maxwell Air Force Base (MAFB) in Alabama had many, many various makes, models, and styles of airplanes on the flying line. These planes were for the students with pilots' ratings, on flying status, who were attending the various colleges of the university. They were to use the planes to fly in order to maintain their flying proficiency.

World War II officially ended in August of 1945, Class 1957 began in September of 1956. The war had been over for 11 years. Please notice, there were "allied" officers from other countries who our country had recently been at war. Our countries had been in a mortal combat, killing our military personnel. There were also "allied" officers from dark skinned countries.

My recall orders read: "Pilot, not on flying status, not to participate in flying activities as a crewmember." I had been grounded earlier in 1956 as a reservist for lack of participation in flying activities. (My reserve unit in Cleveland, Ohio, did not have airplanes for the reservists to fly.) I managed to keep my rating as a pilot for the rest of my life.

The procedure at the Air University was that American pilots, on flying status, could formally/officially request any airplane they had been checked out in, for weekend flying in order to maintain their proficiency while attending school. Destinations were not limited and reasons were not questioned, as long as the flying could be accomplished during the specific off-duty time. It was not unusual to request a plane to attend a football game, to attend a wedding, to spend time with relatives, or any legitimate reason imaginable was acceptable to get a plane. Once a request was approved, the pilot had to post his name, rank, permanent seat assignment in the auditorium, his destination, and the estimated time of departure and return to the University on the bulletin board. Whenever I saw a plane going to Cleveland, Ohio, I tried to get on the manifest in order to visit my wife and son. I also went to Los Angeles and Miami on two weekends when there was not a flight to Cleveland, Ohio.

One particular weekend there was a B-25 approved to go to Cleveland, Ohio. I contacted the pilot by his seat number and asked him if I could be a passenger on this flight. I don't remember his name, now. He told me, "Yes," and that I should report to the base operations room that Friday, about 1600 hours from takeoff. I showed up as scheduled as the pilot was coming from the operations room. I was the only passenger. The pilot had arrived early, obtained the routing, and checked the weather and completed the necessary forms.

He informed me I was flying co-pilot. I told him I could not participate in flying as a crewmember. He told me again, I was flying co-pilot. Again, I told him I was not to participate in flying as a crewmember. The pilot was a Lieutenant Colonel and I was a Major. What was I to say? In addition, I wanted to get to Cleveland, so when he told me I was flying co-pilot I did not comment anymore. He informed me that the officer who was to have been his co-pilot had hurt himself that afternoon at physical training and was in the base hospital.

We were transported to the assigned plane, performed the per-flight check, assured the plane was gassed, requested and received taxiing instructions, then took off. Just the two of us, headed for Cleveland. All things went well on the trip north. We landed at Cleveland Hopkins Airport about four hours later that Friday night. We taxied to the military parking space and agreed upon a time for takeoff the next Sunday morning to make the return trip to MAFB. Kathadaza, my wife and Eugene, my son came to get me at the airport. That Sunday she got me to the airport at the arranged time. I went with the pilot to make the necessary clearance and checked the plane. We took off for MAFB. Again, things went well until we approached MAFB. The pilot called for landing instructions. The Control Tower cleared us to land. Soon after we received, landing instructions there was a transmission from the tower that the field was closing. Bad weather was setting in. All planes in the area should proceed to an auxiliary field. The pilot did not respond. He reached down, unplugged the radio, and commented to me that we did not hear that transmission.

We continued our flight plan and made a safe landing. Although my companion was a senior pilot, we were flying under Visual Flight Rules (VFR). He had not filed our flight plan under Instrument Flight Regulations (IFR). Had we gone to another airfield we would have had to remain overnight and obtain another clearance the next day, which would have been trouble since I was not supposed to be flying as co-pilot?

AN ACT OF OMISSION OR COMMISSION?

Shortly after I was transferred to Lockbourne Army Air Field (LAAF), Ohio, in 1946, Kathadaza, my wife "bumped into" an old schoolmate, either Eloise or Nathaniel Noble, while shopping in town. We had known the Nobles since we were all at Philander Smith College in Little Rock, Arkansas, in 1939. That was before either couple married.

After that chance meeting, the two couples spent many pleasant days and evenings together while I was stationed at Lockbourne. I was in charge of the Officer's Club. I was the Officers' Club Officer.

There are other "Epistles" associated with my Active Duty period at Lockbourne Army Air Field (LAAF) near Columbus, Ohio. This specific incident happened after my retirement.

In August of 1982, Kathadaza and I went to Cleveland, Ohio, to a Dinner for the Defense Contract Administration Services Region (DCASR) Federal Civil Service Retirees. After spending a few days in Cleveland, we went to Columbus, Ohio, to spend some time with the Nobles.

Whenever we were in the Columbus area, we would go to dinner at the Officers' Club at Lockbourne Air Force Base (LAFB). On 17 August, we invited the Nobles to be our guests for dinner in the Officers' Club at the Rickenbacker Air National Guard Base, Ohio. This was the re-designated name of the former Lockbourne Air Force Base.

Following the Fourteenth Annual National Tuskegee Airmen Convention in Dayton, Ohio, 05 through 11 August 1985, Kathadaza and I went to Columbus to spend a few days with the Nobles, again. Before we went to the Base, that particular evening. We spent time reminiscing at their home. In the Officers' Club dining room we had, another drink and our waiter gave us menus. The menus had a "History of the Base" printed on the reverse side. After we decided what we wanted to eat, we read the Base History, which my group had been a part of. I had to read and re-read and re-read again the History. I couldn't believe it! I read the Base History, from the first tenant through the current occupant, over and over. The era of the Black Pilot's Group (the 332nd Fighter Group through the 477th Composite Wing) was not included among the various base tenants.

My liquid intake had reached a level that my indignation directed me to have a talk with someone. I went seeking the Officers' Club Officer or his assistant. Neither was available. I asked for the Base Commander's name and mailing address. When Kathadaza and I returned home, I immediately searched for documentation to prove the Group (and I) had been assigned to that Base. I had pages from Charles Francis' book, "The Tuskegee Airmen," and copies of Special Orders assigning me to units on Lockbourne Army Air

Field in 1946, reproduced.

I made a package and mailed it to the attention of the Base Commander. A couple of weeks later I received a letter from the Base Commander stating that the records of the Base had been researched and the 332nd Fighter Group and the 477th Composite Wing had, indeed, been assigned to the Base. It further stated that when the Menu was reprinted, that which had been omitted would be included therein.

I documented this incident and mailed it to the Headquarters of the Tuskegee Airmen National Organization and to the Eastern Region President. The National Body did nothing and it was dropped there.

P.S. REPLY FROM HARRY STEWART COMMENTS FROM THOSE WHO WERE THERE

Subj: **Rickenbacker ANG Base**
Base: 2/11/02 11:57:07 AM Pacific Standard Time
From: *taswell@mediaone.net*
To: Livglegend@aol.com, MANNHE@aol.com
Sent from the Internet

I visited Rickenbacker ANG Base (formerly Lockbourne AFB) in 1995 to attend an ESGR meeting. While at the headquarters building, I observed a large display posting the history of the base including all of the units that had been stationed there. That's Right...No 332nd Fighter Group!

HOW DO I GET TO THE WAAF SITE?

It began with an inquiry and ended with a rededicated Memorial Park and a Monument to the Tuskegee Airman (TA). In addition, the charter for the HIRAM E. MANN Chapter, a new chapter of the Tuskegee Airman, Inc., was a residual. The saga begins: It was in the fall of 1991. My wife and I were returning to our home in Titusville, Florida, from a trip we had made.

Driving south on Interstate 95, in the state of South Carolina, I noticed the gasoline gauge was getting near the one-quarter remaining indicator. It was time to "fill-her-up." A highway sign read Walterboro "X" miles ahead. I pulled off the Interstate at exit 57, found a gas station, and filled the tank. When I paid the attendant, I asked for direction to the old Walterboro Army Air Field (WAAF) site. The young man didn't have any idea what I was asking of him. I decided it was not that important. We continued our drive home.

In March of 1992, my wife and I had a timeshare exchange on Hilton Head Island. For "something-to-do," we decided to spend a day in Charleston, South Carolina. The route I took to get to Charleston from Hilton Head was west to I-95, north to exit 53, which is Walterboro, then east to Charleston, S.C. This time I was determined to find the site of the former Army Air Field. I started asking "locals" how to get to the site. I knew it had been there because I was stationed there from August till November of 1944.

The younger people had no idea what I wanted. The older people directed me to the Walterboro Airport. I told them I did not want the Airport, I wanted the site of the former Walterboro Army Air Field. Finally, I conceded and said, "OK, how do I get to the site of the Walterboro Airport?"

Following directions, I arrived at a new, modern, one-story building. Across from the front was "Walterboro/collection county airport." I got out of the car and walked around looking in amazement at what I saw. A short, thin, elderly man with grey hair in a pony-tail, casually wearing jeans, and a jacket came out the front door, approached me and asked, "Kin I he'p ya?"

I told him I was looking for the site of the WAAF. He told me, "This is it!" I gave him my calling card and told him I had been stationed there in 1944. Our pilots (the Black pilots) were sent there for overseas replacement combat training in the P-47, Thunderbolt, also referred to as the "JUG." We were replacement pilots for the 332nd Fighter Group, in the XV Air Force, in Italy. I wanted to see the field again. The man told me his name was Lloyd Vickers, the airport caretaker. He said they called him "Airport Daddy." He was a retired Navy Pilot. He invited Kathadaza and me into his office in the Airport Lobby.

In his office, he told me he had been looking at blue prints of the airfield recently and saw there had been a White Officers' Club and Colored Officers' Club. I told him that was correct; the field was segregated at that time. He called a younger pilot into his office and told him to, "Take the Colonel up for a local orientation ride and see what he recognizes or can remember." We went up in a Cessena 172. When airborne the pilot told me to take the yoke. I managed to keep the nose on the horizon while we flew around about 15 minutes then returned to the field.

Lloyd asked what I recognized. I told him the water tower at the end of the runways was the only thing I remembered. We spent a pleasant afternoon, talking about first one thing and then another. Needless to say, Kathadaza and I did not go to Charleston that day. A little over a year later I received a letter from a Mr. Jonnie Thompson, Mayor Pro-Tem of the city of Walterboro, dated 24 September 1993. I was invited to serve as Grand Marshall for the 1994 Martin Luther King Birthday Celebration Parade on 16 January 1994. The parade was sponsored by the Shiners Arabian Temple #139. I was, of course, elated. This was the highest single honor I had received, to that date.

Mr. Thompson, Chairman of the Black Leadership Community, had gotten my name from Lloyd Vickers. Some of the citizens of Walterboro, White as well as Black, cared and did not want tainted thoughts of their community to remain with those who were maltreated while stationed there. They took constructive actions to erase ugly thoughts and replace them with pleasant ones.

They sought and received approval from their Black and White Washington representatives, down through the Governor, through the other local state, county, and city representatives, including the Mayor and other responsible elected and appointed individuals, including the local airport authority. All were sought to memorialize a permanent site for the former WAAF, a Monument to the TUSKEGEE AIRMEN.

BLACKS IN AVIATION: PAST, PRESENT, AND FUTURE

Before the Tuskegee Airmen were thought of as a group of pilots or had a chance to demonstrate their skills to fly, there was Negro or Colored aviators, or whatever society chose to call them at that time, piloting airplanes.

Among the more notable pioneers was Eugene Jacque Bullard. He was born in Columbus, GA, in 1894. His exploits began as early as World War One. He was an infantryman with the French Foreign Legion. In 1917, he flew as an observer for the artillery. In 1922, Bessie Coleman became the first female licensed Black pilot in the United States. It should be noted that Coleman was licensed long before Emelia Earhart, the white pilot counterpart. Coleman went to France to get her license because the United States would not issue a license to her. After her flight training and licensing in France, she returned to America to follow her career as a barnstormer. She died in 1926 in an aircraft accident at the age of 33. Her brief career inspired other young Blacks to enter the field of aviation.

Dr. A. Porter Davis, as shown in the picture in Chapter III of this book, received his pilot license in 1928 and became the fourth African American to receive his pilot license. He owned his own plane called "Porter Field: Model Number NG-16451." He was considered a ranking aviator between the periods of 1929-1939, the start of the Tuskegee Institute Flying School program to

ANOTHER FEW WORDS

We, Kathadaza and I, went to Columbus, OH, after the 1982 TAI Convention in St. Louis, MO. We took our friends, the Nobels, to dinner at the Rickenbacher Air National Guard Base Officers' Club, which was formerly the Lockbourne Air Force Base. The menu had the installation history, from it's beginning through the present, printed on the reverse side. After I selected what I wanted for dinner, I read the base history. After reading and re-reading and re-reading the history several times it became apparent to me that there was an omission of any mention of the period of the 332nd Fighter Group and/ or the 477th Composite Group (Wing) occupied or were tenants on the base.

As mentioned above, I brought this to the attention of the chapter at our next meeting. I was told to send it to National through the Regional President, R. R. Richards, which I did. It was bounced back to me and I attempted to take the initiative to have something positive done about it. A letter from Base Commander is among my records.

IT COULD NOT BE THAT LONG AGO

It couldn't be that long ago. Sometimes it seems like yesterday, and then I get up out of my chair and hear all the joints creak and complain and I'm forced to accept the facts.

Happy Anniversary Guys. Do you remember this?

> *We're the rising wings of a brand new world*
> *In addition, we are bound to win a victory*
> *We will carry on for those who've gone*
> *Blazing tails in skies far away*
> *And if Thou will it*
> *God, we'll do it*
> *Upward, Onward*
> *The fight is not yet won*
> *Upward, Onward*
> *The battle's just begun*
> *Wings*
> *Give us wings*
> *Contact!*

I may not have all the words right but this is pretty close. This was one of our (44 F's) class songs, written by either George Catlin or John B. Turner when we were in lower preflight.

JUNE 27TH – EMAILS

June 27, 2002

Wow! I remember June 27, 1945. It was our first anniversary. I think that we were still at Ramitelli. We had a real blow that night. Oceans of water have gone under the bridge since that day. Time for roll call. How many of us are left Harry?

I do not know how many of the twin-engine guys are left. It's been several years since I talked with John B. Turner.

I also talked with "Rip" Johnson a couple of years ago. Retired from active duty with some 30 years of service, he was not too interested in reestablishing the contact with the guys. Maybe we can get caught up a bit more at the convention.

Lew Lynch

ADDRESS OF LT. COL. HIRAM MANN TO VALIANT AIR COMMAND, TITUSVILLE, FLORIDA

Good evening fellow members and friends of the Valiant Air Command. I regret that my copilot of 55 years had another commitment. However, as usual, it is always a pleasure when I can fellowship with you.

This evening I have the honor of representing another distinguished flying organization of which I am a member, the P-51 Mustang Pilots Association. The P-51 MPA is a group of male and female pilots and associates who are dedicated to the perpetuation of the memory of a great fighter aircraft, the revered North American P-51 and our comrades who flew them. These long-range, versatile, also known as the "Cadillac's" of reciprocating-engine fighters, and their pilots, contributed significantly to the US victory in World War II and Korea. It was probably the most effective piston-engine fighter the US has ever had.

The P-51 MPS members wish to ensure that this great aircraft will not be forgotten with the passage of time. When I learned that these beautiful bronze plaques were available and donated to qualifying organizations, I volunteered to establish that our VAC was worthy to attain one. I assured the MPA that our Valiant Air Command was eligible. The necessary steps were taken by our officers. Alice Icazzuco had a bit part in it.

The plaque arrived yesterday; the truck broke down, right in front of my house, after he delivered it. We, the VAC were the lucky #13 to receive a plaque, there are 12 others including the USAF Academy in Colorado Springs, Naval Museum in Oregon, the Greensboro Memorial Museum in NC, the Champlin Fighter Museum in Mesa AZ and the Commerative Air Force in Midland, TX.

Kevin, on behalf of the P-51- MPA, it gives me great pleasure to transfer ownership of this commemorative plaque from the P-51 Mustang Pilots Association to our Valiant Air Command Museum in Titusville, FL. I am certain that it will be mounted in a prominent place so that all who come to our museum will be able to appreciate it.

'Till we fly together again, let's "get the wheels in the wells' and head for blue skies with a good tail wind."
Editor's note: Lt. Col. Mann flew with the 332nd Fighter Group in Italy.

HIRAM

Hiram-
You are right about the "Fighters" and the 50-mission crush, but do you remember that we had to wear those very <u>unflashy</u> "Luxemburg" for graduation parade? I think I only wore that big ugly monstrosity twice after we graduated. It disappeared someplace between Tuskegee and Walterboro and I never missed it
Do you remember Hugh and his White wedding uniform? I do not think he got to wear that too many times either.
Ah, the good ole days.

Lewis John

FINAL THOUGHTS ON THE EPISTLES
The words and phrases expressed by Lt. Col. Hiram Mann come directly from his first hand recollection of his experiences as a Tuskegee Airman who experienced combat as a pilot against the Germans during World War II. It is evident throughout these first hand experiences that he was pained by the dualism of fighting overseas in Europe for the freedom of others in the world, as an officer in the United States Army Air Force, yet, he served in segregated military flying units.

Upon returning home to the United States of America he and the other

African American servicemen and women never received any ticker parade in the downtown where they lived. There was no public recognition ceremony for The Tuskegee Airmen and other African American enlisted personnel. In fact the only public welcome was the proliferation of the Jim Crow signs such as "White Only drinking fountains," "White Only military officers quarters" and "White Only housing and restaurants" to name a few of the visible symbols of the system of racial segregation that was so rampant in the United States of America.. Indeed, he was refused service in restaurants; access to movie theaters frequented by Whites and forced to live in predominantly segregated African American communities.

This monument inscription is a fitting tribute to the Tuskegee Airmen who distinguished themselves as pilots during World War II. It should be noted that communities like Titusville, Florida and others have dedicated monuments to the Tuskegee Airmen.

Monument Inscription
(On The Walterboro TAI Monument)

THE TUSKEGEE AIRMEN OF WORLD WAR II

In honor of the Tuskegee Airmen, their instructors and ground support personnel who participated in preparing for combat training at the Walterboro Army Airfield during the Second World War

Because of their heroic action in combat, they were called Schwartz Vogelsmenshen (Black Bird Men) by the Germans who both feared and respected them. White American bomber crews, in reverence, referred to them as the "Red Tail Angels," because of the identifying red paint on their tail assemblies and because of their reputation for not losing any aircraft, they protected (escorted) to enemy fighters as they provided fighter coverage for missions over strategic targets in Europe.

> *"History, despite its wrenching pain, cannot be unlived, and if faced with courage, need not be lived again."*
>
> *(Maya Angelou)*

CHAPTER X

The Reaction and Recognition

THE MAJOR CONCERN that most of the Tuskegee Airmen and African Americans who served in World War I and II has expressed was the limited recognition they received. In fact, many felt that the "White public and the media did not honor us for the contributions that we made in defense of the American flag and the freedom of many in Europe." Many of these servicemen said that the first recognition came in 1979 with documentary "Blacks in White America" and the 1990 in the showing of the HBO movie on the Tuskegee Airmen. Thus, after 68 or more years, for the first time there is better evidence that the public is becoming fully aware of the contributions of the Tuskegee Airmen and other African American enlisted military personnel during World War II.

During several discussions with a retired officer in the Navy, a history and social studies teacher, following his retirement from the United States military, who said, "I heard something about the African American fliers in World War II, but this was not really amplified in military history." As his mentor teacher in social studies, I was impressed with this teacher's zeal and willingness to share not only the HBO movie on the Tuskegee Airmen but engage his students in a protracted discussion about the roles and contributions of African Americans to the military in the United States of America. Lt. Col. Hiram Mann, a retired Tuskegee Airman and Pilot said, "Yes, I remembered there was a movie starring Ronald Reagan while he was an actor in Hollywood. This film showed the contributions, but it was not very descriptive as the HBO movie with respect to the flying and training experiences of the enlisted personnel."

In a 1979 documentary film on "Blacks and Whites in America," an ABC Special narrated by the late President Reagan prior to his assuming the office of the Presidency of the United States of America showed Lt. Colonel Benjamin O. Davis, Jr. who we regarded as the top pilot at Tuskegee Airmen Pilot Training Program during World War II. In fact, "We all called him Commander because he had significant impact on all of us who were striving to become pilots in the military." This film also showed Colin Powell, a four Star General and a Commander of the Armed Forces of the United States of America. He became the first African American to rise to this top military position in the United States of America. However, it should be noted that General Daniel "Chappie" James, Jr. became the first African American to be promoted to the top military position as a four star general prior to the similar appointment of General Colin Powell.

Lt. Col. Hiram Mann further stated that, "The public heard about the Tuskegee pilots, but not many of them were aware of the Tuskegee Airmen Experience that started in 1941. Col. Mann said "I spoke to many of my neighbors over the years since I left the military, and I was surprised to find that less then ten percent of them were aware of the details of the Tuskegee Airmen Pilot Experience." What was even more shocking was the fact that the history books do not discuss in any details the Tuskegee Airmen Flying Experience, which began in 1941. These first recruits in the Tuskegee Flying School Program in Tuskegee, Alabama became a part of the United States history, World War II history and the history and contributions of African American Service personnel. The information, which follows, provides an estimate of the achievements of the Tuskegee Airmen Experience of the 1940s in which the African American pilots and servicemen and women demonstrated intellectual and aeronautical sophistication and confidence. The data proved that they were indeed competent to be fighter pilots in the United States Military Service. The following information in the next paragraph shows some of the accomplishments of the Tuskegee Airmen and pilots of World War II.

ACCOMPLISHMENTS FITTING FOR HEROES

The summary of the data indicate that according to Charles E. Francis (1988), The Tuskegee Airmen showed that the Tuskegee pilots were awarded a total of 150 Distinguished Flying Crosses. It was also estimated by "Black Americans in Defense of Our Nation" that additional awards and honors received by the Tuskegee Airmen included, Legion Merit I, Soldier Medal 2, Purple Heart 8, Bronze Star 14, Air Medals and Clusters 744 and Distinguished Flying Crosses 95. This later figure is in sharp contrast to Charles F. Francis (1988) book that documented 150 Distinguished Flying Crosses earned by the Tuskegee Airmen. They flew over 1,578 missions, destroyed and damaged over 136 enemy aircraft, 40 barges and boats, 619 boxcars and other rolling stock. The total estimated number of pilots that graduated from the Tuskegee Pilot Experience was approximately 992 pilots. Among these pilot graduates, about 450 of these pilots went overseas. This report does not include any of the Tuskegee Airmen Ground Support Team, which is well documented by the 50th Anniversary of World War II Commemoration Committee, HQDA, SACC Pentagon, and Washington, D.C., that "although the primary mission and reason for the Tuskegee Airmen Experience was for flying, not all of the enlisted personnel were trained to be pilots. Many were trained for other responsibilities. Among the initial personnel to be trained at Tuskegee Air Facility were 210 enlisted and 33 officers were assigned as part of the 99th Pursuit Squadron. About 160 enlisted men and 10 officers were assigned to the base group unit, 20 enlisted and two officers were assigned to service duties (Carter, 1995 p. 1-16; Black Americans in Defense of Our Nation, 1979). It should be noted that Ret. Lt. Col. Hiram E. Mann was a part of the Tuskegee Pilot Training Class of 1944 who were Cadets assigned to pilot training duties as part of the Tuskegee Airmen Experience. "It should be pointed out that the ground support personnel were very important to the success of the pilots. One can estimate that it took about ten ground crew support personnel to get the aircraft flying and in good maintenance." The record clearly indicated that there is increasing interest in recognizing the contributions of the ground support personnel who played an important role in supporting the Tuskegee fighter pilots. It was heartening to hear every Tuskegee pilot expressing open support for the ground support personnel. The comment that was often echoed by the Tuskegee Airmen was," My success and efficiency as a pilot was directly related to the high quality work of the 'ground crew who maintained the aircrafts in tip top condition, assuring that our radios worked well, our guns and other weapons were loaded and in good working condition, fueled the planes, and assisted in reconnaissance runs by taking the aerial photographs." Each Tuskegee Airman and pilot was and still is indebted to the dedicated ground crew and other support personnel who played key roles in their success as pilots.

BLACK MEDIA COVERAGE OF THE TUSKEGEE AIRMEN EXPERIENCE

The African American news media including radio stations and newspapers were very crucial in distributing information to the community and public about the success and progress of the Tuskegee Airmen pilots who were being trained at the Tuskegee Air Field Field, Tuskegee, Alabama and other airfields in the United States of America. As many Tuskegee Pilots often said, "the Black media was the central media links in the predominantly Black communities and cities." Col. Mann said that "There was one African American in the media that special tribute must be specially paid to and that was, Tony Brown, Commentator/Host of the "Tony Brown Journal." This 1970s television show hosted by Tony Brown, reached the Black and White community by having Tuskegee Airmen pilots on the show. I mean real life pilots who were part of the "Original Tuskegee Pilot Training Program." Many still argue that the Tony Brown show was among the first and early media proponents who began the journey of uncovering and demonstrating the positive contributions of the Tuskegee Airmen and pilots who were African American pilots in World War II. These Tuskegee Airmen pilots were acclaimed as the pilots who "never lost a single bomber that they escorted during World War II."

A further validation of the success of the "Red Tails" also known for the red markings on the planes flown by the Tuskegee Pilots was an event that I witnessed on February 10, 1997, at a Community Reception at the Public Library in the City of West Palm Beach, Palm Beach County, Florida. This gathering was public, and a cross section of the residents of Palm Beach and West Palm Beach were in attendance. I noticed an elderly man was very nervous and focused his complete attention on the Tuskegee Airmen who were present and enjoying their interaction with the guests who were present. Then, I decided to approach the elderly man, a White man, and he said, "Sir, I am a retired World War II bomber pilot. During the war, there were "Red Tails" who escorted our bombers; we all believed that with their escort, we were sure to get back to our base. I am not here to talk about the "Red Tails" heroic military records as fighter pilots. Rather, I am here to thank the Tuskegee Airmen for saving my life. Sir let me tell you what it is. During World War II, we were returning from a bombing run. My plane developed some problems and was losing speed. I was hit. The other fighter planes in the formation took off, and I flew slowly back to base, I suddenly encountered a fleet of "Red Tails" aircrafts. The "Red Tails" escorted me slowly back to my base, and as I prepared to land, the "Red Tails" peeled off, and all I saw were the 'Red Tails' on their fighter planes. I am here tonight to thank the "Red Tails". So, as soon as I saw the newspaper announcement of this reception for the Tuskegee Airmen, I decided to come and thank them personally."

Thus, I said to the elderly man, "Let me introduce you to the Tuskegee Airmen." I took him over to Capt. Charles Hill and Capt. Mary Hill, Lt. Walter J. Palmer and Major Roland Brown. After the introductions, the elderly man said with tears and his face flushed. " I never knew who you were when you escorted me back to the base when my bomber ran into problems. I am in-

SPREADING THE WORD

The final thought about the HBO movie is that the storyline failed to capture the significance of the broader achievements of the Tuskegee Airmen. Despite going through their training as fighter pilots in a segregated military and knowing that, everyone was betting on their experience to fail. The fact that these men were able to succeed was probably one of the most significant achievements by African Americans enlisted military personnel to date. These "Original Tuskegee Airmen" were directly responsible for forging the integration of the Armed Forces by President Truman in 1948.

Ret. Lt. Col. Hiram Mann said that "The best therapy for all of us who went through the experience is to be vigilant in telling our side of the Tuskegee Airmen story and the rich experiences that so many African American enlisted personnel and their families shared in military services. Their primary objective was to earn the respect and acceptance as equal human beings in the sight of all who lived in the United States of America and the World." Mann and others always argued that "The Civil Rights movement went through a real test during our experiences in the military. Our success in integrating the military in 1948 was indeed a real positive and uplifting event for the entire African American population. One more triumph in ensuring our liberty and pursuit of happiness was not taken for granted as we defended the flag of the United States of America, in Europe and the rest of the world."

One way to continue the legacy of the Tuskegee Airmen and the fighting pilots whose heroic acts as pilots remain as a special military record in which the "Red Tails," the Tuskegee Pilots, did not lose a single bomber that they escorted during World War II. However, this legacy can be preserved by joining the Tuskegee Airmen Incorporated (TAI) with chapters all over the United States.

JOINING THE NATIONAL MEMBERSHIP OF THE TUSKEGEE AIRMEN

"The challenge for each Tuskegee Airman is to keep the dream alive and share this positive history that shaped the civil and human rights of African Americans living in the United States of America."(Coggins 2001)

Joining the National Tuskegee Airmen Incorporated and/or a local chapter will be a positive step in assisting in telling the positive story of the Tuskegee Airmen Experience of 1940's. Thus, I encourage each citizen, young and adult, to guarantee that the Tuskegee Airmen legacy will continue in perpetuity by joining the National Tuskegee Airmen Incorporated. The annual dues vary .Most individuals reported the membership this fee entitles the member to newsletters, participation in national and local conferences, and other events. It should be noted that the local dues vary based on the policies of the local chapters. A tentative list of local chapters of the Tuskegee Airmen Incorporated is provided in the appendix of this text. The National Membership of the Tuskegee Airmen is a further reminder about the need to celebrate the achievements of the Tuskegee Experience. Each generation can preserve this history by becoming a member of the Tuskegee Airmen Incorporated, an organization that hosts an annual conference and vigorously advocates for the preservation of the history of the Tuskegee Airmen.

In the final analysis, all of us as citizens of the United States of America and the world will have to recognize that the Tuskegee Airmen are also veterans who should be included in the celebration of Memorial Day and other days recognizing the gallant services rendered by the veterans. We should continue to recognize the contributions of all of those men and women who sacrificed their lives for the freedom, which we all enjoy in the United States of America and the Free World. The Tuskegee Airmen were heroic fighter pilots during World War II who fought for the freedom of the United States, other European and North African countries. Indeed, their efforts helped in freeing oppressed individuals who suffered under Hitler and the Nazi Regime during the 1930's and 1940's who were bent on military and political control and genocide of Jews and other groups in Europe at that time.

Americans had to go through before they were granted civil rights. However, to hear what this man actually encountered, even after he stepped up to serve our country, was tremendous. Lt. Col. Mann's story was very emotionally uplifting and I consider myself very lucky to have met him and hear about his journey. After all that he went through, the amount of pride he continues to have for the United States is amazing."(Student A)

"One thing that really stood out for me in this presentation was how Lt. Col. Mann and all his friends were treated, even after they had gone through proper training and had served the United States to the capacity of White men. They were still shunned from restaurants and stores, having people turn them away simply because they were Black. One would think that a storeowner or waitress would be thankful for the men, especially the pilots, who were putting their lives on the line. All of the men took such pride in what they were doing, and I believe that they deserved the same respect as everyone else."(Student B)

"I know that the Tuskegee Institute was begun as a place for African Americans to have the opportunity to gain a higher education and the ability to become pilots. However, from hearing this story I know that it was also a place where African Americans and Whites worked together towards one common goal. They were trying to better the military and American society by gaining education and skills that would last them a lifetime. The Tuskegee Institute serves as a wonderful model of an institution that truly worked to improve African American and the American society."(Student C)

WHAT IS THE MESSAGE TO THE CITIZENS OF THE UNITED STATES AND WORLD?

As Lt. Col. Hiram Mann, USAF, Ret. puts it, "the basic message to our citizens is not to focus primarily on the success of the combat record of the Tuskegee Airmen that included 996 silver wings, shot down over 409 German aircraft, destroyed over 950 Units of Ground Transportation, completed over 200 bomber escorts not losing a single one, sank a destroyer using only machine guns, completed over 15,000 flying missions, was recognized and honored with 150 distinguished flying crosses, purple hearts, 14 Bronze stars, 744 Air medals, three distinguished unit citations. Rather, each citizen must make a commitment to work hard to ensure that segregation and discrimination based on race, gender, nationality or other characteristics is fully eradicated from our institutions and community life. Of course, on November 6, 1998, President Clinton helped establish the Tuskegee National Historic site at Moton Field in Tuskegee, Alabama through the passage of Public Law 105-355. Most recently, on March 29, 2007, President George W. Bush and the

Congress of the United States awarded the "Congressional Gold Medal" to the Tuskegee Airmen who were Pilots during World War II. "

While all these achievements are worthy and should be celebrated, "I would like to see our youth graduate from high school and go on to college. However, they should not stop their pursuit of a career." The demands of joining the various branches of the military today require that one must study Sciences, Math, and Language Arts, and other subjects such as Technology, History and the Arts. I encourage the youth to join the military and learn all about the high technical fields and computers since the present and future of the world; will depend on these essential skills.

"However, most importantly, the youth of today and tomorrow must have sound values in order to be successful. These values should include honor, pride, determination, self responsibility, caring, and most of all an unconditional love of God, self, parents, and family."[47]

THE LEGACY STANDS

A final note on the legacy of the Tuskegee Airmen that even the HBO special film missed was the fact that the African American men and women who participated in the Tuskegee Airmen experience came from all educational, occupational backgrounds and geographical corners of the United States of America. Some were from the Northern States, Southern States, and the States in the West Coast, Central and Eastern States of the United States of America. The three examples of the legacy that follow show the brief achievements of the Original Tuskegee Airmen that came from, Cleveland, Ohio, Punta Gorda, Florida and Brazil, Indiana. The common experiences that all three of the "Original Tuskegee Airmen and pilots" share include 1) The fact that they were each trained at the Tuskegee Institute in Tuskegee, Alabama, 2) They were each Tuskegee pilots that were combat pilots during World War II. 3) They all had a sense of urgency and a deep determination to succeed against all odds. However, what was even more remarkable, was the fact that even though they came from different parts of the country they still were able to focus on a common goal of becoming a pilot and fighting in the World War II. This sense of common vision and mission was instilled in them even though they were from different graduation clases.

"Lt. Col. Hiram E. Mann, a graduate of the Tuskegee Airmen Pilot Program, Class of 1944. He was as one of the pilots who headed for Africa on the "Nathan Hale" ship. A native of Cleveland, Ohio, he enlisted in United States Army Air Force (USAAF) after attending Philadelphia Smith College, Little Rock, Arkansas. He received the following citations: 3 OCL to Air Medal, Distinguished Unit Citation, Certificate of Valor, EAME Ribbon, ATO Ribbon, and WWII Victory Ribbon."

"Lt. Col. Charles P. Bailey, a graduate in the Class of 1943 at the Tuskegee Airmen Pilot Program, was one of the pilots headed for Casablanca, Morocco, aboard USS Mariposa. He is a native of Punta Gorda, Florida. He had enlisted in the U.S. Army Air Forces (USAAF) after attending Bethune Cookman College in Daytona Beach, Florida." He received the Distinguish Flying Cross on May 12, 1995.

"Lt Charles B. Hall, a graduate of the Class of 1942, the first Tuskegee pilot to score a confirmed kill when he fired a long burst into a German Focke FW-190 fighter plane. He was a native of Brazil, Indiana." His achievement was crucial in changing the perception of the military about the capabilities of the Tuskegee pilots.

The unselfish nature of the Tuskegee Airmen, coupled with their mutual respect for each other, constituted the glue that enabled them to individually, and collectively create a distinguished flying record as military fighter pilots during World War II. The success of these and the hundreds of Tuskegee pilots was exemplified by fact that Lt. Col. Hiram E. Mann returned to the

U.S. and held such high ranking positions as the USAF Liaison Officer, U.S. Air Force Academy. Lt. Col. Charles Bailey went on to be a flying instructor at the Tuskegee Institute, Flying School Tuskegee, Alabama. Like Lt. Col. Hiram E. Mann, who settled in Titusville, Florida, Lt. Col. Charles Bailey settled in Deland, Florida until his passing in 2004. The record will show that each of the Tuskegee Airmen, upon leaving the military went on to pursue successful careers in all fields and occupations.

CHAPTER XII
Final Thoughts for the Future

Reflections on the Legacy

THE FINAL THOUGHTS for the reader is to reflect on these spirited African American men who were educated, determined and hopeful that they would overcome the trials and tribulations fostered by a segregated Armed Forces and society that did not value the contributions that they could make as pilots in the military. Yet, for these brave men, there was a keen sense of purpose, confidence and determination as expressed in the "fight song" of the first African American Fighter Squadron, the 99th Pursuit Squadron (Homan, 2001, p.41).[48] The song reads:

> **"Fight! Fight! Fight! Fight!**
> Fight! Fight!
> The fighting Ninety-Ninth
> We are the heroes of the Night
> To hell with Axis Might
> Rat-tat ! Rat-tat-tat !
> Round in the planes we go
> When we fly, Ninety-Ninth
> This is how we go!"
> (Homan, 2001, p. 21)[49]

While it was not possible to find the lyrics to this fighting song of determination, the words once read, echoes both the struggle and the sense of defiant pride that the 99th Pursuit Squadron was able to garner up among the fellow pilots art the Tuskegee Army Air Field and of course while they served their country fighting in the European theater during World War II. As McKissack (1995)[50] said," The Tuskegee Airmen not only won their battle over the enemies on the battle fields in Europe, they also succeeded in opening the way for the career success for such persons as General Colin Powell, and several astronauts such as Guion Bluford, Ronald McNair, Frederick Gregory and Charles Bolden. The Tuskegee Airmen served as an inspiration for other enlisted African Americans and many other war veterans from the Korean, Vietnam, Persian Gulf Wars and other military conflicts."

Thus, it is within this context of extraordinary achievement that this book argues for keeping the legacy of the Tuskegee Airmen and the pilots of World War II not only as part of African American history, but, more so, as an integral part of the history of the United States of America. The information in this and other books should convince readers that these men, the Tuskegee airmen should be considered as heroes, not only for what they accomplished in the air as pilots, but, for what they accomplished for all humanity in the Americas and the world. Let us not forget that these are the same men who climbed into the cockpits of the planes every day, not only facing the enemy and possible death, but, they also faced the added pressure of proving to the world their legitimacy as pilots and as human beings (Homan, 2001).[51] Yet, upon their return home, these African American servicemen were not embraced equally as their White counterparts and servicemen who were greeted with an open sense of appreciation for protecting the freedom of the Europeans and others of the civilian population. Ironically, another setback was the fact that most of the Black fighter squadrons that were formed during the war were deactivated immediately at the end of the war in 1946 (McKissack, 1995).[52] These Tuskegee pilots were good enough to defend the liberty of the world, yet, they would still have to suffer the reality of racial discrimination and segregation in their hometowns, communities and states (Homan, 2001, p.46).

Lt. Col. Hiram Mann said, ", 'Chief,' as we called him, took the challenge into his hands. Realizing that this was a 'make or brake' moment, as was depicted in the HBO movie. Mrs. Eleanor Roosevelt, wife of the President Franklin D. Roosevelt, visited the pilots at Tuskegee Army Air Field, Tuskegee, Alabama. When she challenged the Tuskegee Pilots to take her up for a fly, took that challenge and successfully flew Mrs. Eleanor Roosevelt." This success with the President's Roosevelt's wife provided the crucial evidence that African American pilots were capable and ready to fly military airplanes for the protection and freedom of peoples in the world. The Tuskegee Airmen understood that their achievement was just a small part of a bigger set of achievements, which hundreds of other African American men and women accomplished with similar or even higher ranks in the Armed Services of the military of the United States of America.

One of the enlisted personnel who fought the war on the ground was Sgt. Elton Williams. He entered the military on April 20, 1944 as a SS Rifle paratrooper just out of high school and because of his leadership and marksmanship skills; he achieved several medals of honor and was promoted to sergeant. Like others, Sgt. Elton Williams, Major Roland Brown, and Ret. Lt. Col. Hiram Mann were not alone in singling-out one person who had a real positive influence on every African enlisted personnel. Four Star General Benjamin O. Davis Jr., who always said "We must strive to be our best even against all the odds and obstacles that were in our way." This self-determination has continued among the Tuskegee Airmen in their civilian life. Ret. Lt. Col. Hiram E. Mann, Lt. Walter J. Palmer, Major Roland Brown, Capt. Mary Hill, Capt. Charles Hill and others have all devoted their lives to hours of lectures that tell the Tuskegee Pilot story to students in schools and to adults in the community. These Tuskegee Airmen and World War II veterans have all pursued very successful civilian careers in the fields of industry, education, government and other specialties.

As the reader moves to the final chapter of this book, the critical lessons that I wanted to share with the reader was the story of the Tuskegee Airmen Experience. I also wanted the focus on the veterans of World War II and members of the 99th Pursuit Squadron and the 332nd Fighter Group who were an integral part of the Tuskegee Airmen Experience at the Tuskegee Airfield in Tuskegee, Alabama and in the European Theater of WWII.

Lt. Col. Hiram Mann has made it clear in his definition of the Tuskegee Airmen "It is a retrospective term that was not used until almost 30 years after World War II ended. Thus, an original Tuskegee Airmen is anyone, male and female, Black and White, military or civilian, who served/worked at least one day at the Tuskegee Army Air Field (TAAF)." Like other Tuskegee Airmen, Lt. Col. Mann feels strongly that the story of the Tuskegee Airmen must be one that transcends the pilots to focus on the sacrifices of so many of the military and non-military personnel as well as the ground support team personnel who were dedicated to ensuring that the pilots succeeded and that the planes were mechanically safe and the airfields were well maintained.

The youth of today and tomorrow must feel the joy and the pain that were integral parts of the previous generations of African Americans. The past generations modeled how to strive for one's goals and succeed despite the obstacles of segregation, racism, and discrimination that they faced each day and in every situation at home, in the community and while serving in the military at home and overseas.

SPECIAL MESSAGE TO OUR YOUNG PEOPLE IN SCHOOLS AND COLLEGES

In speaking with several Tuskegee Airmen, I asked them how they would like to complete their final message to our youth. "We want all of the youth in American and the world to understand the struggle for equal rights, justice, and freedom were the central part of our daily lives during the 'Jim Crow' era, where there was essentially blatant segregation and discrimination, we mean open segregation with signs that said, "This bathroom is for Whites Only," and the signs at the officer clubs on bases which read "Whites Only," or being called the 'N-word.' Yes, it hurts, but we were determined to fight for our rights as human beings and as men and women that were fighting to preserve the flag of the United States of America and the preservation of world peace. It is important that our youth understand the rights that they enjoy today were not available in the 1940's when we were young men and young adults in the Tuskegee Airmen Experience at the Tuskegee Institute, Tuskegee Army Air Field, Tuskegee, Alabama."

As the reader peruses the final chapter of this book, it is necessary to refocus on the critical lesson in this book about all veterans of World War II and in particular the African American veterans who were part of the Tuskegee Airmen Experience while serving in the 99th Pursuit Squadron and the 332nd Fighter Group and other fighter units. The Tuskegee pilots were clear about the fact that the Tuskegee pilots were successful because of the numerous support personnel who were attached to Tuskegee's Army Air Field. These members of the ground crew were critical to our success."

As the late Major Roland Brown stated, "While I went through some of the basic training as other enlisted men completed at the time, I was a navigator for the bombers and I was part of the bombing squadron that never saw any real combat overseas even though we were ready to fight. It is not because I was afraid of flying, as my friends often kidded; rather, it was because I was interested in navigational sciences and the inner workings of the airplane. I often wondered about what I would have done if I had to do it all over again. My answer is that as a member of the navigational crew, I would serve my country proudly. I have always felt that the pilot of an airplane feels much safer in flying when there is confidence in the navigational systems, the support that the pilot receives from the co-pilot, the navigator, the gunners, and the ground crew that kept the plane flying."

The security of the pilot was enhanced with the belief that the ground crew did their jobs well. The ground crew was involved in carrying out various jobs. These responsibilities required that the guns and the ammunition to be loaded and secured properly. The fuel must also be sufficient for the mission and the electrical and electronics features and navigational systems of the plane are functioning efficiently. The maintenance of the runway must be perfect as well as the tires on the plane must be maintained to the required standards. There should be efficient air traffic controllers when guiding the landing and take-off of the planes. One pilot in support of the claims stated that "the story of the ground crew is as important as that of the pilots."

Lt. Walter J. Palmer, past president of the Tuskegee Airmen Chapter in Indiana, and an Original Tuskegee Airman, said, "All enlisted personnel who served as ground crews have legitimate concerns and the organization has been trying to improve the image of the non-pilots." However, "Whenever someone from the Tuskegee Airmen Chapter is asked to speak, it's always a "pilot" that is requested." Thus, it is necessary that we continue to broaden the perception and the definition of who is a "Tuskegee Airman" and be sure to include the ground crews as well as the pilots in any definition.

PRESERVING THE LEGACY OF THE TUSKEGEE AIRMEN

The preservation of the important legacy and history of the Tuskegee Airmen will rest in the hands of historians and military historians in particular and every educator who has the responsibility for educating each generation about the history of the United States of America, World War II and African American history. This awesome study of the history of World War II can be enriched by correcting our text books that make little or no reference to the outstanding contributions of these African American pilots who fought to protect the freedom of Europeans while they themselves lived in a segregated country of the United States of America.

As one person asked Lt. Col. Hiram Mann during a 2005 lecture at Stetson University. "Sir, explain to me how you were able to go overseas and fight for the United States of America when you were being segregated back in your own home town and in the towns where the United States have its military bases and installations." The room of over 75 persons stood still momentarily as each person pondered the answer to this question. Col. Hiram Mann responded with a smile, "This is my country, the United States of America. This is the only country that I know. I believe that I struggled for equality each day that I lived in the United States and the struggle for freedom. My freedom and the freedom of African Americans has been a long and continuous struggle for equal treatment as guaranteed by the Constitution of the United States. I and all of the Tuskegee Airmen knew in our hearts that by proving to the world that we can fly would make a difference in the amount of freedom and the extent to which institutions like the military was integrated." We saw the integration of the military in our lifetime and of course other institutions in the United States are for the most part fully integrated."

A good model for preserving the legacy of the Tuskegee Airmen is illustrated in this 1999 celebration of the contributions of the Tuskegee Airmen. This was a community event that was sponsored by the local city government in Florida. In addition to the city celebration, it should be noted that local churches and elected officials honored these Tuskegee Airmen with a variety of appearances and celebrations. It was indeed especially heart warming to see the mayor and governmental officials give the Tuskegee Airmen the keys to the city of West Palm Beach, Florida. The fascinating fact that resulted from the Tuskegee Airmen's visit to Palm Beach County, was the open expression from most people who attended the lectures. They stated that they had learned little or nothing about the Tuskegee pilots in their history classes or in the books that they read on World War II. Furthermore, many people indicated that they were keenly aware of the other infamous Tuskegee Experiment, called the Tuskegee Syphilis Experiment which was conducted at the same Tuskegee Institute, Tuskegee, Alabama. One person even admitted that he came to the reception and lecture thinking that he would hear from some of the survivors of the Tuskegee Syphilis Experiment. At the end of the evening he stated that," I am delighted to open my eyes and witness the heroes of an important period of African American history and the struggle for equality in the military, overcoming "Jim Crow" in the South while dealing with discrimination in the United States of America in general."

RECEPTION HONORING

The Famous Tuskegee Airmen

In Celebration Of African American History Month

Saturday, February 27, 1999

4:00 PM

Riviera Beach City Complex
600 West Blue Heron Blvd - Riviera Beach, FL

Free And Open To The General Public

COME AND BRING YOUR FAMILY AND FRIENDS

It should be noted that celebration was attended by hundreds of residents from Rivera Beach, West Palm Beach and other areas in Southern Florida. I observed children, and adults of all races who eagerly waited for an autograph or who listened attentively to every word that was expressed by the Tuskegee Airmen.

The next day the Tuskegee Airmen were guests at the special celebration hosted by Trinity United Methodist Church at West Palm Beach, Florida. Again, it was clearly observed that for many residents, guests and youth who attended the special presentation at the church, this experience and interaction with the Tuskegee Airmen was inspiring and informative.

You're Invited!!!
Trinity United Methodist Church
will be honoring our Unsung Heroes

BLACK ELECTED OFFICIALS OF PALM BEACH COUNTY
THE ORIGINAL TUSKEGEE AIRMEN AND AIRWOMEN AND
UNSUNG HEROES II OF THE PALM BEACH POST.

For The Annual African American History Month Worship Service
Sunday, February 28, 1999, 11:00 a.m.
.Come and fellowship with our honored guests.

Trinity United Methodist Church
1401 Ninth Street
West Palm Beach, FL 33401

For more information contact Chairpersons:

Marie Richardson	Otelia Dubose	Donna Ross
659-1493	686-7039	848-6796

The Tuskegee Airmen were guest speakers in the Palm Beach County School District, local churches. City governments and the local Veterans hospital where they were honored by other veterans and the hospital's staff.

Since on occasion I had to introduce them, I emphasized to the children and adults that there were many roles played by the Tuskegee Airmen and other ground support personnel. The children and adults readily embraced both the pilots and the members of the ground crew. The audiences in Palm Beach County received their message with great enthusiasm and amazement at this new information, which was never taught to them in their American history classes. The Tuskegee Airmen, who were the presenters, modeled the unity between the pilots and the ground support personnel. Col. John D. Silvera, National Public Information Officer for the Tuskegee Airmen Organization stated, "If we ever get to the point where we do a motion picture on the Tuskegee Airmen or a documentary, I would hope there would be considerable evidence of the importance of ground support, but the words and desires of Lt. Palmer and Col. Silvera fell on deaf ears with the launching of the 1999 HBO special on the Tuskegee Airmen."

The 1995 HBO special on the Tuskegee Airmen enlightened the nation and the world about the fine accomplishments of the Tuskegee Airmen. The general consensus from most of the Tuskegee Airmen that were interviewed with respect to their perceptions of the HBO special said that the "HBO special romanticizes the role of the pilot. This movie did not set the record straight that planes fly with the pilots and the critical assistance of the ground support team, who ensures that the plane is properly maintained. According to every Tuskegee Airman I encountered the general thought was that "it took at least 10 ground support personnel to keep one pilot flying".

Lt. Col. Hiram Mann further stated with deep emotions that "To get into the military today is very competitive and each applicant must complete high school. If you join the military, follow the examples of the Tuskegee Airmen and learn all about the high tech fields and computers for the present and future of the world will depend on these highly technical skills. The future world will evolve around the high tech fields, computers and electronics that will be the centerpiece of knowledge and career success. But most importantly, the youth of today and tomorrow must have sound values in order to be successful." The legacy of the Tuskegee Airmen can be sustained best by focusing on central themes and values that were a part of the Tuskegee Airmen experience.

VALUES BUILD STRONG FAMILIES AND COMMUNITIES

Therefore, what does this mean to have values and how can they learn about these values? It is the responsibility of parents, adults, and teachers to teach these values. The Tuskegee Airmen including Lt. Col. Mann said quite convincingly that, "The responsibility for teaching and ensuring sound values in our youth is the shared responsibility of the parents, teachers, and the community at large." One easy way to teach this history is to link the history of the Tuskegee Airmen and African American veterans of World War II with the seven Kwanzaa principles. The story of the Tuskegee Airmen, World War II, and African American veterans describes the experiences about African American men and women who were an integral part of the military and the excursions in World War II. These veterans were applying principles of Unity, Self-Determination, Faith in Self and Others, clear Purpose, Creativity in flying and fighting, sustained Cooperation and Collaboration long before Dr. Karenga in 1966 codified the seven principles of "Nguzo Saba." The seven principles of "Nguzo Saba" include Umoja-Unity, Kujichagulia-Self-Determination, Ujima-Collective Work and Responsibility, Ujaama-Cooperative Economics, Nia-Purpose, Kuumba-Creativity, and Imani-Faith (Karenega, 1966).

The Tuskegee Airmen Pilot Experience was intended to "prove that African American men could not fly an airplanes," according to many of the Tuskegee Airmen and African American World War II veterans, "Each of us were determined to make sure that many of us were successful as pilots and air support personnel."

1. **Umoja - Unity.** As many of the survivors of the Tuskegee Airmen Experience and anyone associated with the Tuskegee Airmen Experience often cited "That the real success of the Tuskegee Airmen was due in part to the support that each person provided for the other. We knew that we were under the microscope and therefore, we could not afford to fail. Failure was not an option and it never crossed our minds during the entire time we were there in flying school. If we found someone was having any kind of problem, we were able to reach out and provide whatever help that was needed." Another example of unity was stated in a very clear statement that, "One of the greatest demonstrations of unity was when 101 Black officers, were arrested because they tried to integrate the 'White Only' Officers Club on the base. They were assigned to the United States Military and even though the government used threats and intimidation, they tried to break the spirit of the protest. They all stood together, and as a result, the potential harm, and exacting of punitive actions by the military brass was prevented. "What we, the Tuskegee Airmen learned in the 1940s is not any different today." In order to secure the rights that are guaranteed by the Constitution of the United States of America, each of us must be united and ensure that each person, despite their race, ethnic group, gender, cultural or national background will enjoy and feel secure in achieving their rlights guaranteed by the Constitution of the United States of America. These fundamental constitutional rights include a safe life, liberty, happiness, an education and occupation that will all be realized in an atmosphere of equality and respect for the human dignity that we all share in this planet Earth.

2. **Kujichagulia - Self Determination.** This principle and value of self-determination was at the heart of the success of each of the Tuskegee Airmen Officers and other Tuskegee Personnel. As shown in the HBO movie and confirmed in interviews with several Tuskegee Airmen can be best expressed as, "Each of the pilots was determined to complete the program and we set individual and group goals, which were only realized by each person's concerted efforts. We were called all kinds of racial slurs and names. We were told that we were not smart enough to fly a plane, yet deep down inside of each of us, we knew that the only thing that could have stopped us was ourselves and if we succumbed to the negative and wavering thoughts that could have eroded our self-confidence in our abilities." The record of Ret.Lt. Col. Hiram Mann, who joined the military as a flight trainee enlistee, left as a Lieutenant Colonel, is one example of the enlisted individual's determination to succeed against all

odds. "We all left the military with a sense of high achievement of our goals that many said were impossible, yet we overcame the odds that we could not fly. For many, the day of vindication was when Mrs. Eleanor Roosevelt visited the Tuskegee Army Air Field and said, 'If these men are trained pilots, and then let them fly me." Lt. Col. Mann reflected, "That the measure of a great man and woman is not what he plans to do, but rather, it is what he or she endures and successfully completes to the end." These feelings of self-determination and self-responsibility defined the Tuskegee Airmen's self-determination values that should guide and anchor our youth as they pursue the future challenges in their community, the United States of America and the World.

3. **Ujima -Collective Work and Responsibility.** The attainment of most of our goals will usually involve the assistance of other individuals. "We have always been a team and had to work together to ensure that all of us passed the flying tests and become pilots." Another example was a ground crew member Lt. Pompey Hawkins explained his role in the military. "As a ground crew member we had to work very carefully and cooperatively, while one person was checking the tires, the other was fueling the plane and yet another was checking the electrical systems to ensure that the airplane was fully serviced and ready to be flown."

Embedded in these comments is the essential value and drive of the Tuskegee Airmen who always said that "there were no excuses and complaints when we each had to step up to the plate and pass all of the flying tests." In responses to the question of where did they learn these values. They responded that "one of the first things that the officers taught them was to be willing to help another soldier because one never knew when one might be in need of help from others."

Our youth must develop the spirit of collaboration and working in harmony for a common goal. As one Airmen concluded, "If you look at any symphony or orchestra; the results are positive only if everyone does their part and contribute to the positive sounds that are created by the group." Thus, Collective Work is essential to the success of the extremely responsible "Red Tails."

4. **Ujaama - Cooperative Economics**. Lt. Col. Hiram E. Mann said, "We learned this lesson well when we were part of the Tuskegee Airmen Experience. We had to rely on each other for all help and any financial assistance. If we were broke, we could rely on calling home for financial assistance. Many times the financial help came from the good heart of strangers, who lived in the Black community. They knew we were away from home and they helped us. "I remembered one time while based in Mississippi; two of the Black officers did not have any money for rent.

Therefore, we got together and used our resources to help them until they were able to get their own money." Yes, they paid us back and we were happy. We also learned a valuable lesson about cooperative economics and how the Black businesses relied heavily on us buying from them." "They knew that no White person would leave their side of town and come to shop and support the Black stores." Segregation was deep-seated and carefully enforced by the White power structure. "My message to our young people is to pool their money and work cooperatively to develop businesses that will provide services for all people who live in and out of their community." It is necessary that we encourage all of our youth to learn a trade or develop essential career skills, get an education that can assist them in their own economic ventures and businesses. There are unlimited opportunities that are out there for young people who are equipped and ready to take on the challenge of cooperative economic opportunities.

5. **Nia - Purpose.** "A goalless person is an aimless person." Set goals and work hard to achieve them. Lt. Col. Mann was very clear in connecting this value of "purpose" to his own life. He stated "As I reflect on my parent's life, they always encouraged me. I remember their goal in life was to make sure that Black people were treated fairly regardless of the color of their skin. They always believed, "That we as African Americans have made many contributions to the United States and the world. As proud African descent people, we must strive to make sure that everyone is treated equitably and fairly. "On a personal note, my main goal was to become a Colonel, but I achieved Lt. Colonel. I worked hard to move from a Lieutenant to a Lieutenant Colonel when I retired from the military. I want to say to everyone that the more difficult the task ahead appears, is the more I found it essential to set clear goals to pursue them with all of my energy." This sense of purpose was crucial for the outstanding achievement of the Tuskegee Airmen who successfully completed the flight school training and became fighter pilots during World War II.

As General Colin Powell said" Success is the result of perfection, hard work, learning from failure, loyalty and persistence." Thus, it is necessary to have a perspective rooted in a deep understanding of the importance of goal setting, coupled with a strong commitment to pursue one's goals with hard work, is the message and road map for our youth to follow as they strive for a bright future.

6. **Kuumba - Creativity.** In response to the question how did he use his creativity while in the military? Mann's answer was "I knew that I had

an aptitude to fly an airplane and become a Tuskegee pilot since I was a young kid. I was able to compete and do well on all of the examinations especially those exams in the Tuskegee Flying School. As a military officer, I was discriminated against and witnessed that all of the Black officers were not allowed to stay on the base or live in the officer's quarters. The Tuskegee Airmen and the ultimate success of the 'Red Tails' who flew cover for the bombers was due in part to the creativity and efficiency of the highly skilled pilots as well as the extraordinary support these pilots received from a capable ground crew who maintained the airplanes. Today's youth must apply their talents in ways that are both productive and linked to achievable objectives so that with strong faith, persistent and creative energy the desired results will be attained."

7. **Imani - Faith**. The frequent comments of the Tuskegee Airmen was that "their journey before, during and after they left the military required them to have both faith in God and in their own abilities." Like many other men and women involved in the Tuskegee Airmen Experience, they believed that with hard work and determination, they would be able to succeed. Yes, there were numerous days that "many of us did not believe that we would succeed in flying the airplanes and conquering the doubts of White society and in some cases a small part of the Black community." The faith exhibited by the Tuskegee Airmen can be best characterized by the Rae Noel's stating that, "Whenever the human adventure reaches great and complete expression, we can be sure that it is because someone has dared to be his/her unwavering self." It is clear that the achievements of the Tuskegee Airmen were outstanding given their ultimate track record especially the one often discussed i.e. "They never lost a bomber that they were assigned to protect."

The faith in their ability was expressed by one of the Bomber pilots...the 'Red Tails' as being exceptional. "Many of the White bomber pilots including myself had so much faith in the ability of the 'Red Tails' pilots for they had gained the reputation of not losing any of the bombers that they escorted". That level of faith held constant throughout the World War II. This faith was the foundation for the vindication of the Tuskegee Airmen then and today. Lurking in the process of success was the deep sense of commitment and the knowledge that there was unwavering support of their communities, I mean the Black communities and parts of the White were ready and willing to support us. There was always the feeling that they had faith in us and that one-day we will succeed and compete as viable fighter pilots in the military of the United States of America.

The Tuskegee Airmen Experience of the 1940's was a triumphant success, which proved that African Americans could fly any airplane. Our young people today must understand that their imagination drives their faith. "They can either focus on distress or failure or they can picture beauty, success, and the desired positive results." This faith in ones' self will create a future that is both positive satisfying and meaningful for self, for family and for the community.

A FINAL THOUGHT ABOUT THE TUSKEGEE AIRMEN

"Life is like a tiger,
You either lie down or let it lay
Its pay on your head—or you can
Sit on its back and ride it"
(Dan Zadra)

The Tuskegee Airmen refused to lie down and be defeated by prejudice, segregation and discrimination in the military, in their communities and everywhere in the United States of America and in Europe. Rather, the Tuskegee Airmen flew over and through discrimination and segregation and rode the waves of determination and achievement that served as a means of excelling as fighter pilots during World War II. All the men and women who served our military during World War II believed deeply that they were Americans who earned the fundamental right that Thomas Jefferson often argued and it was also reiterated in our Constitution: *"We hold these truths to be self evident: that all men are created equal; that they are endowed by their creator with certain unalienable rights; that among these are life, liberty, and the pursuit of happiness..."*

The Tuskegee Airmen believed that the God, who gave us life, gave us liberty at the same time. This innate feeling of liberty and freedom to achieve and excel was the glue that cemented the extraordinary achievements of each Tuskegee Airman and pilot such as Ret. Lt. Col. Hiram E. Mann and all of the pilots and other personnel who participated in the Tuskegee Airmen Experience in Tuskegee, Alabama.

The hope in writing this book is that as Rev. Dr. Martin Luther King said, "I have a dream that one day, this nation will rise up and live out the true meaning of justice and understand that 'injustice anywhere is a threat to justice everywhere." It is essential that legacy of the Tuskegee Airmen which includes their successes as fighter pilots, be celebrated as an integral part of military and American history.

We hope in our lifetime we will never again have to live in a segregated society where ethnic and racial minorities, including African Americans, live in defacto or dejure segregation. It is hoped that our society and nation will never reinvent a military where access, deployment, promotion, and recognition are based on race, ethnicity, gender or any other limiting characteristics. Therefore, the legacy of the Tuskegee Airmen can best be preserved through our discussion of these extraordinary men who understood that failure was not an option and who said each day that their success was due in part to the belief that they can achieve any insurmountable goal by having faith in self and in others. The Tuskegee Airmen and pilots made the first step in securing their distinguished achievements; the next step is up to you, me and our communities to ensure that their pains, their struggles and most importantly, their legacy of determination, excellence despite ever present obstacles and an unwavering belief in their knowledge, skills and abilities as pilots will never be forgotten in our history books and any discussion of African American heritage and contributions to the United Sates of America and to the world during World War II.

APPENDICES

Tuskegee Airmen Incorporated Chapters Adopted From TAI, 2004)

ALFONZA W. DAVIS CHAPTER
Omaha, NE
(402)292-9842
mcglownb@stratcom.mil

ALVA TEMPLE CHAPTER
Columbus, MS
(662)329-1298
(662)329-1298 fax
brodhe@cableone.net

ATLANTA CHAPTER
Atlanta, GA
(770)389-6650
(770)389-5112 fax
Valarcher1@yahoo.com

CENTRAL COAST/VANDENBERB AFB CHAPTER
Lompoc, CA
(805)733-3319
(805)733-3319 fax
anhatlpc@aol.com

CHARLES B. HALL CHAPTER
Inactive
Oklahoma City, OK

CHARLES E. McGee CHAPTER
Hanscom AFB, MA
(603)891-3295
winstoncampbell@hanscom.af.mil

CHICAGO "DODO" CHAPTER
Chicago, IL
(773)721-6777
(773)978-7734 fax
bevdunjill@juno.com

CM. SGT. FRED ARCHER CHAPTER
Inactive
Tuscan, AZ

SAM BRUCE CHAPTER
Seattle, WA
(425)827-4862
Boo2com@verizon.net

SAN ANTONIO CHAPTER
San Antonio, TX
(210)679-7237
Sarah-williams@sbcglobal.net

SPANN WATSON CHAPTER
Columbia, SC
(803)788-4940

THOMAS L. WASHINGTON CHAPTER
Lansing, MI
(517)485-2760
jennietai@aol.com

TIDEWATER CHAPTER
Norfolk, VA
(757)484-1988
imblezed@verizon.net

TUSKEGEE CHAPTER
Tuskegee, AL
(334)727-3381

WILLIAM "BILL" CAMPBELL CHAPTER
San Francisco, CA
(510)653-7145
donna@Blackaviation.com

WILSON V. EAGLESON CHAPTER
Goldsboro, NC
(919)736-7202

Rejection Letter

99TH PURSUIT SQUADRON
CHANUTE FIELD   RANTOUL, ILL.

June 19, 1941.

Mr. Hiram E. Mann
2484 E. 84th Street
Cleveland, Ohio

Dear Sir:

Your letter of June 18, 1941, making application
for enlistment in the 99th Pursuit Squadron has been
received.

We are sorry to advise that the quota has been
filled for sometime. However, we will keep your
letter of application on file, and in the event any
opening occurs at a future date, we will advise you
accordingly.

Yours very truly,

W. L. KLUM,
1st Lt., A. C.,
Personnel Officer.

WLK/wot

Holway, J. (1997). <u>Red Tails Black Wings</u>. New Mexico: Yucca Tree Press.

Homan, Lynn and Reilly, Thomas. Black Knights: The Story of The Tuskegee Airmen (Gretna, LA: Pelican Press, 2001.)

Jakeman, Robert J. (1992) "The Divided Skies" p416. University of Alabama Press, Tuscaloosa.

Johnson, Theopolis. "How many Tuskegee Airmen?" Tuskegee Airmen National Newsletter. Jan, 2000.

Jones, Paul R. (1941) "Eleanor Roosevelt with 'Chief' Charles Alfred Anderson," Paul R. Jones Collection, Atlanta, Ga. 3

http://www.museums.udel.edu/art/past/polk/gif/eleanor.html

Date Accessed: April 1, 2002

McGee, Charlene, (2000) "TUSKEGEE AIRMAN: The Biography of Charles E. McGee," Smith, Brandon Publishing Co.

McKissack, Patricia and Frederick McKissack. (1995) <u>Re-Tail Angels: The Story of the Tuskegee Airmen of World War II</u>. Walker Pub. Co., New York, NY.

McNeely, Gina. "Legacy of Flight," July 1997, Aviation History Vol. 7 Issue 6, p. 82.

McRae, Bennie J. Jr., National Airmen Association of America. Website, "Before the Tuskegee Airmen" http://www.coax.net/people/lwf/NAAA_CHG.HTM Date Accessed: December 23, 2007

Murphy, Carl. "In Defense of Democracy: The 99th Squadron Goes to War." http://www.afroam.org/history/OurWar/murphy.html

Myers, Walter Dean (1996). "Toussaint L'Overture: The Flight for Haiti's Freedom," Simon & Schuster Books, New York, NY.

Norrell, Robert J., <u>Reaping the Whirlwind</u>. Alfred A. Knopf Publishing, NY, 1985.

ON CLIPPED WINGS; The Story of Jim Crow in the Army Air Corps. New York, NAACP, 1943.

Osur, Alan. *Black in the Army Air Forces during WWII: The Problem of Race Relations*. Washington D.C.: Office of Air Force History: U.S. Government Print Office, 1977; Arno Press, 1980.

Pacific Northwest Tuskegee Airmen, Inc. (2005)
http://sun.kent.wednet.edu/staff/rnakatsu/TuskegeeAirmen/Tuskegee_Oraniz.html

The Penn Current, Tuskegee
http://www.upenn.edu/pennnews/current/2001/032201/feature5.html
            Date Accessed: December 23, 2007

Percy, William. "Jim Crow, Uncle Sam and the Formation of the Tuskegee Flying Unites." <u>Social Education</u>. Jan/Feb 1999, vol. 63 Issue 1, p14-21.

The Road That Led to the Sky. (1990) http://www.afro.com/tusk/creation.html Date Accessed: December 23, 2007

Rose, Robert A., Lonely Eagles: The Story of America's Black Air Force in World War II. Tuskegee Airmen, Inc., 1976.

Sandler, Stanley. (1997) Segregated Skies: All-Black Combat Squadrons of WWII. Smithsonian Press.

Salute to Veterans. Presented by the Memorial Day Weekend Corporation. The Tuskegee Airmen.
http://www.salute.org

Schultz, S. (1987). The Maverick War: Chennault and the Flying Tigers. New York: St. Marin's Press. Images of America: The TUSKEGEE AIRMEN, by Homan, Lynn and Reilly, Thomas, Designs, Arcadia Publishing

Sherrer, John, "Alfred C. Anderson: The Most Famous Black Aviator in America." http://www.coax.net/people/lwf/CHIEF.HTM
Date Accessed: December 23, 2007

Silvera, John D., <u>The American Negro: His History and Literature</u>. Arco Press Inc. 1969.

Sitkoff, Harvard. <u>A new deal for Blacks: The emergence of civil rights as a national issue.</u> New York: Oxford University Press, 1978.

Smith, Gene. "Colonel Parrish's Orders: He was to turn a segregated little army into the world's first Black pursuit squadron." <u>American Heritage</u>. May/June 1995, Vol. 46 Issue 3, p110.

Smith, V. E., (1995). Segregated Sky. *Newsweek*, 126, 9. 54.

Tuskegee Airmen. http://www.geocities.com/Pentagon/Quarters/135

Tuskegee Airmen http://www.neptune.k12.nj.us/nhs/history/AfricanAmerican/Tuskegee%20pages/index.html

Tuskegee Airmen. http://xroads.virginia.edu/~gu02/NewYorker/Race.html

Tuskegee Airmen. http://www.va.ucf.edu/features/BlackPatriots/Early%2020th20century/TuskegeeAirmen

Tuskegee Airmen. Online Bookstore. http://www.jodavidsmeyer.com/combat/bookstore/BlacksinWWII.htm

Tuskegee Airmen of World War II. http://history.acusd.edu/gen/WW2Timeline/Tuskegee.html

Tuskegee Airmen: Lonely Eagles to Red Tail Angels. http://sun.kent.wednet.edu/staff/rnakatsu/TuskegeeAirmen/Tuskegee_Aircraft.html

Tuskegee Airmen Timeline. (1997) http://web.bryant.edu/~history/h364proj/sprg_00/air1/history.htm

Tuskegee Airmen in Action. http//www.ritesofpassage.org/mil_air.html

Tuskegee Airmen Inc. National Headquarters. Who Were the Tuskegee Airmen of World War II? http://tuskegeeairmen.org/airmen/who.html

Tuskegee Airmen—Red Tail. http://www.waterholes.com/~dennette/models/ww-ii/redtail.htm

Tuskegee Airmen: The Black Red tail Angels, Heroes of WWII and Freeman Field, http://www.world-wide.net.com/tuskegeeairmen/

The TUSKEGEE AIRMEN: BLACK HEROES of WORLD WAR II, by Harris, Jacqueline L., Dillon Press 1996

The TUSKEGEE AIRMEN: THE MEN, WHO CHANGED A NATION, By Francis, Charles E.., Braden Pub Co (Now 4 Edition)

The Tuskegee Airmen by HBO Pictures, 1990

"Tuskegee Airmen Fact Sheet," Dr. Coggins. 2003, Multicultural Institute, DeLand, FL

An Unofficial Tuskegee Airmen Home Page c1998 v1.05.
http://sun.kent.wednet.edu/staff/rnaktsu/TuskegeeAirmen/Tuskegee_Homepage.html

USAF Museum History. "Pre-WW II History." http://www.wpafb.af.mil/museum/history/prewwii/ta/ht

Walbert, Kathryn L. *Teaching the History of all Americans, All Year Round.* http://www.learnnc.org/index.nsf/doc/history0404-1?OpenDocument

War Department Citation of 332nd Fighter group: United States Fifteen Air Force, U.S. Army: Washington D.C., 9 August, 1945.

Warren, Lt. Col. James. "The Tuskegee Airmen Mutiny at Freeman Field." http://www.tuskegee.com

Washington, Booker T. "The Awakening of the Negro." http://eserver.org/race/awakening.txt

Waters, Enoch P. (2000) "Tuskegee Airmen," Chicago Defender.

Webster's Classic Reference Library Dictionary. (1999). Ashland: Landoll's.

Weil, Martin, (2002) "Benjamin O. Davis Jr.: First Black General In Air Force" Washington Post, July 6, p.B7.

White, Mindy. "Tuskegee Airman Charles P. Bailey kept watch over his flock of B-24s on their way to Targets in Germany." Jan. 1998. Aviation History, Vol. 8 Issue 3, p66.

VIDEO The TUSKEGEE AIRMEN - Available at BLOCKBUSTER Video Rentals and others

INDEX

Afterword

This riveting book on Lt. Col. Mann's life provides a clear sense of personal achievements and the military battles that he and fellow pilots experienced during World War II. The epistles are a source of hope for overcoming prejudice and discrimination. He believes that the "race of life is not won by the swift but by the one who endures to the end.

Dr. Barry E. Daly
Licensed Clinical Psychotherapist
Gotha, FL

The book reaffirmed my belief that the story of the contributions of the Tuskegee Airmen must become a part of American and world history since these brave and talented pilots fought gallantly during WW II. They defended the freedom of many in Europe despite the fact that they knew that they would return home to a segregated United States. This is a must read for anyone who is interested in the struggle for civil rights and freedom of all people.

Dr. Christine Taylor
Assistant Area Superintendent
St. Lucie County School District, FL

This book is a griping story of the life of Tuskegee African American pilots who demonstrated that by setting high expectations coupled with diligent work can lead to success. These fighter pilots succeeded in a climate of discriminatory barriers and segregation. The timelines provide a systematic history of the Tuskegee Airmen experience. This is a book that is hard to put down once you are started reading it.

Mr. Kevin Perry
Alpha Phi Alpha Fraternity, Inc.

I was moved to read a book that provides the roadmap for achieving one's career and life's goals. Lt. Col. Mann demonstrates that being focused, securing an education and working hard will produce positive results. The diary enabled me to empathize with pains and joys that Tuskegee Pilots endured during World War II.

Dr. David Washington, Public School Principal
Ft. Pierce, FL

Endnotes

1 Coggins, Patrick C. (2001) "The Tuskegee Airmen: Flying from the Ground Up" Unpublished manuscript, Deland, Florida: Multicultural Education Institute, Stetson University, pg.128.

2 Carter, Herbert. E. "The Legacy of the Tuskegee Airmen." National Forum. Fall 95.vol.75, issue 4: p10, 6p, 3bw.

3 Academy of Achievement, 2000. http://www.achievement.org

4 Jacqueline Harris, The Tuskegee Airmen. "Black Heroes of World War II." Dillon Press, January 1996.

5 Civan, MB., A. Morisett-Metellus, and F. Vilsaint. The Haitians, their History and Culture: Washington: The Refugee Service Center, Center for Applied Linguistics (1994)

6 Walter Dean Myers. Toussaint L'Overture: The Fight for Haiti's Freedom. Simon & Schuster Books, New York, NY. (1996)

7 Anderson, Peggy (1992) Great Quotes from Great leaders, Lombard, IL: The success collection, Celebrating excellence, Inc.p.ld17

8 Bailey, R. (1981). Prisoners of War. New York: Life Time Books.

9 Holway, J. (1997). Red Tails Black Wings. New Mexico: Yucca Tree Press.

10 Hershey, J. (1989). Into the Valley: A Skirmish of the Marines. New York: Schocken Books.

11 George, C. (2001). Tuskegee Airmen. New York: Children's Press.

12 Coggins, Patrick C. (2001) "The Tuskegee Airmen: Flying from the Ground Up" Unpublished manuscript, Deland, Florida: Multicultural Education Institute, Stetson University.

13 www.AllensCreations.com.Bafsol.html

14 Blacks in Aviation, p. 17.

15 Blacks in Aviation, p. 19.

16 Metro-Dade Aviation Department, 1996; Blacks in Aviation, Miami, FL.

17 Blacks in Aviation, 1996, p. 4.

18 Enoch P. Waters. Tuskegee Airmen. Chicago Defender (2000)

19 Blacks in Aviation, 1996, p. 12.

20 Blacks in Aviation, 1996, p. 17.

21 Holway, 1997.

22 *Tuskegee Airmen in Action.* http//www.ritesofpassage.org/mil_air.html

23 *The Road That Led to the Sky.* http://www.afroam.org/history/tusk/creation.html

24 George, 2001.

25 Holway, 1997.

26 Holway, 1997.

27 George. 2001.

28 Schultz, S. (1987). *The Maverick War: Chennault and the Flying Tigers.* New York: St. Marin's Press.

29 George, 2001.

30 Holway, 1997.

31 American War Library. (2000). *Weapons of World War II.* CA: Lucent Books.

32 Holway, 1997.

33 George, 2001.

34 George, 2001.

35 George, p.41

36 Charles E. Francis, The Tuskegee Airmen, (1988)

37 Homan and Reilly, Black Knights, (1997)

38 Francis, (1988)

39 A. Russell Buchanon, (1977) p.13

40 Martin Weil, "Benjamin O. Davis Jr.: The First Black General in Air Force." The Washington Post. July 6 (2002) p. 87.

41 Weil, (2002)

42 Charles E. Francis, "Tuskegee Airmen", (1985) pp 28-31

43 Herbert Carter, "The Legacy of the Tuskegee Airmen," (1995)

44 Carter, 1995

45 Robert Jakeman, "The Divided Skies," (1992) p.146

46 Carter, 1995

47 Stanley Sandler, "Segregated Skills: All Black Combat Squadron (1992)

48 Patrick Coggins, "The Tuskegee Airmen: Flying From the Ground Up."

(2001) p. 128.

49 Lynn Homan and Thomas Reilly, "Black Knights: The Story of the Tuskegee Airmen," (2001)

50 Homan (2001) p.21

51 Patricia McKissack and Frederick McKissack, "Red Tails Angels," (1995) p.121

52 Homan, 2001

53 McKissack (1995) p.121

LaVergne, TN USA
18 August 2009
155187LV00004B/39/P